ORIGINS OF THE CULT OF THE VIRGIN MARY

Also available from Continuum:

Mary: The Complete Resource, edited by Sarah Jane Boss

Mary: Grace and Hope in Christ, The ARCIC Statement

Studying Mary: The Virgin Mary and Anglican and Roman Catholic Theology and Devotion, edited by Adelbert Denaux and Nicholas Sagovsky

ORIGINS OF THE CULT
OF THE
VIRGIN MARY

EDITED BY

CHRIS MAUNDER

burns & oates

Burns and Oates, a Continuum Imprint

The Tower Building, 11 York Road, London SE1 7NX

80 Maiden Lane, Suite 704, New York NY 10038

www.continuumbooks.com

First published 2008

British Library Cataloguing-in-Publication Data

A catalogue record for this book is available from the British Library.

ISBN 978-0860-12456-6 (paperback)

Typeset by Kenneth Burnley, Wirral, Cheshire

Printed and bound by Cromwell Press, Trowbridge, Wiltshire.

CONTENTS

CONTENTS

Notes on Contributors

Dr Antonia Atanassova, Boston College, Massachusetts

Margaret Barker, Former President of the Society for Old Testament Study

Prof. J. K. Elliott, Professor of New Testament Textual Criticism, University of Leeds

Dr Alistair MacGregor, Librarian, Ushaw College, Durham, until his death in September 2007

Dr Chris Maunder, Senior Lecturer, Theology and Religious Studies, York St John University

Rev. Prof. John A. McGuckin, The Nielsen Professor of Early Christian and Byzantine Ecclesiastical History, Union Theological Seminary, New York; Professor of Byzantine Christian Studies, Columbia University, New York

Geri Parlby, Roehampton, Exeter and Plymouth Universities

Dr Richard M. Price, Senior Lecturer in the History of Christianity, Heythrop College, University of London

Eileen Rubery, Senior Research Fellow, Girton College, Cambridge

Dr Stephen J. Shoemaker, Associate Professor, Department of Religious Studies, University of Oregon

Editorial

Chris Maunder

The Centre for Marian Studies was established in 1996, due to Sarah Boss's vision in founding an institute to provide a dynamic focus for research, education, resources and networks in the study of all aspects of the cult of Mary. The founder members wanted this to be governed by the academic disciplines, and not by a particular Christian denomination. Sarah was already organizing conferences and research seminars in the subject at that time, and since the founding of the Centre this work has been enhanced and expanded. A periodical, *Maria: a Journal of Marian Studies*, was launched.[1] Some important new publications appeared, written by members: Sarah's own *Empress and Handmaid: On Nature and Gender in the Cult of the Virgin Mary* and *Mary*; Tina Beattie's *God's Mother, Eve's Advocate: a Marian Narrative of Women's Salvation*.[2] Most recently, Sarah has edited a new work for the purposes of providing a scholarly textbook for Marian Studies, *Mary: the Complete Resource*.[3] The strength of this publication lies in the range and high standard of scholarship represented in it, a testimony to the success of the Centre in bringing together a group of academic writers with expertise in the subject area.

In July 2006 a conference on the 'Origins of the Cult of the Virgin Mary' was held by the Centre at York St John University. It was organized by Sarah and myself, although I would like to acknowledge Sarah's role in ensuring a really good and competent programme of speakers. The conference followed the work of Sarah, Tina and other Marian researchers in reopening familiar issues, while – and this is the important point – challenging familiar but sometimes weak assumptions about the data. Just as Sarah and Tina have re-examined patristic and medieval writers to consider anew exactly what they said about Mary, so the conference speakers looked again at the early centuries and asked: just when and how did what we know as the 'cult of the Virgin Mary' emerge? Those speakers' papers have been reworked after the conference and are included in this book. There are also some contributions from scholars who could not attend on the day, but whose work was valuable in this area. The contributors constitute a range of people from British and American universities.

Marian Studies brings the researcher into contact with strong feelings, ideological positions and passionate writing. The feminist view that the symbolism of Mary was irretrievably linked to an outdated patriarchal culture was given much impetus by Marina Warner's *Alone of All Her Sex: the Myth and Cult of the Virgin*

Mary.[4] Yet many Catholic feminists wanted to retrieve something of the Marian tradition from this devastating critique. In doing so, they have sought to diminish the distance between the great virgin mother and ordinary women. Elisabeth Johnson, in her book *Truly Our Sister: a Theology of Mary in the Communion of Saints*, attempted to rediscover the very human Mary (Miriam) of history in a 'Mariology from below'.[5] However, Charlene Spretnak, a liberal Catholic, resisted this trend amongst liberals and feminists in her *Missing Mary: the Queen of Heaven and her Re-Emergence in the Modern Church*.[6] She prefers to celebrate the extravagance of the Marian cult: 'Mary's partial "goddess nature" – her larger cosmological dimension – cannot be severed from the whole of her, from who she is and what she does in the fullness of her own integrity.'[7] She argues that Catholicism should be comfortable with its pagan heritage: '*of course*, all the powerful streams of ancient religions flowed into and found a Christianized place in the "greater glory" of the new religious era. All (neolithic Goddess) roads lead to Mary!'[8] Clearly, precise historical analyses of the relationship between Mary and classical goddess cults will be of considerable importance in illuminating these questions.

The attempt to get back to a 'Mary of history' before all the presumed theological excesses and pagan incursions of the 'Queen of Heaven of faith' has its precursor in the 'quest' for the historical Jesus. In relation to that enterprise, Jonathan Z. Smith pointed out that there was a Protestant bias in denying all Hellenistic influence on Christianity before Constantine, in the belief that 'pagan' elements of Christianity arrived with the later growth of Roman Catholicism and could be excised in a return to the source.[9] This was in part a reaction to the James Frazer thesis, very popular despite the weakness of some of its historical arguments, that Jesus was one of a number of dying and rising gods, such as Attis or Osiris.[10] In Smith's view, the Jewish heritage had been overplayed by scholars in order to deny the Greco-Roman, and therefore pagan, associations.[11]

Clearly, with Mary too, the question as to how far 'paganism' and goddess worship penetrated Christian ideas and imagery after Constantine can become an ideological issue. The fact that there is scant evidence of a cult of Mary before the late fourth century lends weight to the idea that the main Marian streams in Catholicism and Orthodoxy were heavily influenced by the state-enforced conversion of the devotees of the cults of, for example, Isis, Cybele, Demeter/Ceres and Artemis/Diana. It is commonly believed that the Council of Ephesus (431), in which a theological debate about Mary's status was necessary in the clarification of Christology, provided the favourable context necessary for this process to occur.[12] However, there is also a viewpoint that the origin of the Marian cult should be placed well before the fifth century which cites, for example, the third-century image in the Catacomb of Priscilla that appears to be a Madonna and Child.[13] There is also the question of the high Mariology of the *Protevangelium* or *Infancy Gospel of James*, which has been dated to the second century.[14]

The *Protevangelium* is a key text in the understanding of early Christian reflections on Mary as they developed after the New Testament period. The influence of this document on later Marian devotion is irrefutable. Despite its exclusion from the canon by Pope Gelasius (492–496),[15] the narrative introduces several concepts that became enshrined in Catholicism: the holiness of Mary from the beginning of her life (although the details of the 'Immaculate Conception' were, of course, hotly debated for centuries); the idea that the birth of Jesus did not effect any physiological change in Mary's hymen;[16] the fact that Mary's marriage to Joseph was not consummated, and other children in the family were not Mary's, i.e. the 'Ever-Virginity' of Mary. The difficulty is that there is no evidence for a second- or even third-century cultic context for the ideas in the *Protevangelium*. Stephen Benko is going beyond the evidence when he states, 'Apparently, the author's aim was to elevate Mary to the level of the great virgin-mother goddesses of the Greco-Roman world.'[17]

An important question that emerges is: where do we draw the line as to what constitutes 'cult'? Three things delineate a cult in religious terms: first, its focus is on a relationship with a spiritual being (which may or may not be a human person, living or dead); second, it includes devotional attitudes to and beliefs about that being which have effects on behaviour; third, it involves the gathering of like-minded people in religious practices.[18] From the fifth century onwards, it is clear that we do have a 'cult of the Virgin Mary', in images, prayers, feast days, processions, claims of the miraculous. There is some evidence of it in the fourth century, and a couple of hints that it may be there in embryonic form in the third. In the first and second centuries, there are simply texts (the New Testament; the *Protevangelium*; brief mentions in the *Odes of Solomon* and *Ascension of Isaiah*) and the writings of some theologians (Ignatius of Antioch; Justin Martyr; Irenaeus; Tertullian).[19] The existence of these writings, and the prominent role Mary plays in some of them, does suggest that an element of devotion to Mary existed in very early Christianity. But is devotion necessarily the same thing as 'cult'? Stephen Shoemaker remarks, 'To be sure, Mary was an important focus of Christian theology and even devotion already in the second century, as Irenaeus of Lyons and the *Protevangelium of James* attest, but it is not until the later fourth century that we first encounter unambiguous evidence of cult and prayer offered to the Virgin herself.'[20]

This book attempts to provide a scholarly underpinning to a historical understanding of the growth of the Mary cult by examining well-worn assumptions and subjecting them to a closer analysis. Given the prominence of these issues in the overall debate, this volume includes chapters on the catacombs, the *Protevangelium*, the Council of Ephesus (431) and the *Theotokos* title, and the influence of the goddess cults. In addition to these, there is a new exploration of Mary in the New Testament, the link between Mary and the figure of Wisdom, and the development of Marian art. None of the contributors wants to rest content with easy answers. Between them, they provide a richness of scholarship and analysis that will inspire the reader to take the issues further and to explore the interesting links between the various articles. At the root of the discussion is the problem stated above of the relationship of early Christianity to its multicultural milieu. How far does the understanding of Mary remain faithful to its Jewish inheritance, in the use of Hebrew scriptural concepts such as Wisdom and the covenant, and to what extent does it borrow from classical literature and imagery, utilizing poetic and mythological ideas which include references to the ancient Mediterranean goddesses?

As these questions are so central, the volume begins with John McGuckin's chapter, 'The Early Cult of Mary and Inter-Religious Contexts in the Fifth-Century Church'. John's scholarship in patristics, especially in research on Cyril of Alexandria and Gregory of Nazianzus, is well known.[21] His work is well placed as the book's opening chapter, as he gives a really excellent overview of the issues involved in making sense of the data that might inform us about the cult of Mary in the first five centuries of Christianity. He asks that very important question without which the rest of the collection would lack its foundations: What kind of evidence is required for us to establish an early cult of Mary? John gives examples showing how easy it is to make assumptions about the dearth of a phenomenon from silence about it, yet developments in archaeology show how poor the conclusions from such an approach can be. We must not say, from limited evidence, that there *cannot* have been a cult of Mary in the very first centuries of the Church, only that we do not know that there was, and what form such a cult might have taken.

John also has much to say to those who assume the cult of Mary to have been a straightforward transfer of goddess cults into Christianity. While he does not doubt the associations between the two, he warns against believing that they were the same thing and finds reasons to suggest that they were quite distinct. At the same time, he gives us a clear example of how the missionary activity of the Church presented the devotees of goddess cults with radical new ways of belief and practice, a far cry from simply allowing them to continue their former adherence with a goddess named Mary instead of Isis or Cybele.

After this setting of the scene, the chapters proceed in chronological order. My chapter, 'Origins of the Cult of the Virgin Mary in the New Testament', takes the cue from John's chapter in suggesting that the existence of texts that extol a particular figure may tell us *something* about the meaning of that person for Christians in the same era. Although it can be accepted (drawing on the work of our art historians, Geri Parlby and Eileen Rubery) that evidence for images of the Virgin is near to being non-existent in the pre-Constantinian Church, nevertheless John has reminded us of the dangers of making bald statements about early devotional attitudes. In order to ask about first-century Christian attitudes to Mary, we must interrogate the texts for the major themes that emerge from them. However, we cannot do this without acknowledging that literary devices were employed in classical writing which idealize feminine figures and separate them from actual women living in that time. To what extent the Mary of the New Testament is herself a 'myth' is the problem here. Nevertheless, present in the Passion and Easter accounts there are some clues to the relevance of the historical Mary for early Christian communities.

Geri Parlby tackles the question of the Madonna figure in the catacombs in 'The Origins of Marian Art in the Catacombs and the Problems of Identification'. Her scholarship uncovers some disturbing facts. First of all, the image of mother and child that is cited as an example of third-century piety is neither prominent, nor even upright. It is in a corner of one of the tableaux. She suggests to us more well-founded and plausible explanations for the identity of the figure, and then turns to other examples of Mary depicted in the catacomb drawings. In doing so,

Geri engages us in a deeper understanding of the origins of Christian art and its probable meaning.

The *Protevangelium* and other apocryphal works are so central to the developing story of Marian devotion that we have invited Keith (J. K.) Elliott, well known for his recent updating of M. R. James's *Apocryphal New Testament*,[22] to contribute a chapter on 'Mary in the Apocryphal New Testament'. His work informs the reader as to the main themes in the most important documents, and the versions which are available. He also brings us up to date with scholarly opinions on the texts. His work helps to cast light on our main theme. To give one example: '. . . Ronald Hock, probably correctly, defines the *Protevangelium* as an encomium, that is an extended homily to Mary, praising her, describing her origins and character and extolling her virtues and accomplishments.' This does capture the essence of the *Protevangelium* as being more than a story that fills in the gaps, a second-century 'prequel'. It arises from a context of devotion.

Stephen Shoemaker's chapter, 'The Cult of the Virgin in the Fourth Century: a Fresh Look at Some Old and New Sources', comes logically after Keith Elliott's in the sequence. This is because Stephen has become an authority on traditions about Mary's Assumption or Dormition, which appear in apocryphal texts by the end of the fifth century.[23] Yet Stephen wants us to look a century or more earlier, into the fourth, where we might find the origins of such traditions. The implications of his work are that we do not fully know when such ideas first circulated, and we should beware of being too sceptical about the possibility that they are relatively early. Thanks to Stephen's research, we can be more confident that some form of the Marian cult pre-dates Ephesus by a considerable margin. He also considers hints from the third century, the prayer *Sub tuum praesidium* and the apparition to Gregory Thaumaturgus, recorded by Gregory of Nyssa.

Stephen's work on the famous complaint by Epiphanius, about certain women who had 'replaced God with Mary', is closely argued and very interesting. Stephen suggests that we cannot be certain that these so-called 'Kollyridians' were goddess-worshippers who had corrupted the Christian message; rather, they may have been examples of a fourth-century Marian cult, which again brings evidence for it earlier than conceived of in previous scholarship.

Richard M. Price's 'The *Theotokos* and the Council of Ephesus' draws upon his own rich scholarship of the conciliar period which is well attested in published material.[24] His work critiques another of the common assumptions made about Ephesus: that the Council and the Nestorian controversy that triggered it were crucial to the growth of Marian devotion. Christology was the focus for these proceedings. Richard points out that the term *Theotokos* was not defined at the Council, but had been in use for a long period before Ephesus. He therefore suggests a more gradual evolution of the cult of Mary, although generally his view is that the evidence suggests the Marian cult, as a standard element in Christian devotion, to have been a late development, in contrast to – for example – the cult of the saints and their relics.[25]

The chapter by Antonia Atanassova complements that by Richard Price because, while he wishes to play down the link between Nestorius, Cyril, Ephesus and Mariology, Antonia, in 'Did Cyril of Alexandria Invent Mariology?', wants to tease out the full import of Cyril's writings on Mary, and suggests that he does stand at an important point in the history of theological work on Mary. Antonia is concerned with Cyril's *corpus* as a whole, before and after Ephesus. How could he be understood as the 'inventor' of Mariology? Antonia answers that his work is a key development in arguing that a Mariology is fundamental to proper Christology; a detailed theological exposition on Mary is necessary for a full appreciation of Christ's incarnation, mediation and divine-human personhood.

The book continues with coverage of Marian devotion that can be dated well after Ephesus, in the sixth or seventh centuries, but where the origins of the practices may date from an earlier time, which gives us clues as to some of the processes by which the cult of Mary emerged.

Margaret Barker's 'The Life-Bearing Spring' looks at the New Church in Jerusalem, the *Nea*, built in 543 by Justinian and dedicated to the 'Holy Mother of God, the Ever-Virgin Mary'. The placing and design of the church, and the coinciding of its dedication day with the Feast of the Presentation (entry of Mary into the Temple), show that its designers regarded it as a rebuilding of Solomon's Temple, the post-exilic reconstruction of which, according to the *Protevangelium*, was the childhood home of Mary. Margaret shows how closely the description of Mary's childhood in that document parallels the Hebrew concept of Wisdom, and from this we may be confident that it was intended that Mary was identified as the personification of Wisdom by the builders of the *Nea*. Margaret goes on to show that the link between the mother of Christ and Wisdom has its roots in the book of Revelation and represents an old Jewish tradition in which the feminine aspects of the Temple cult were preserved despite suppression. The chapter gives us an insight into the vision and scholarship that characterize Margaret's books on this and other biblically related subjects.[26]

Certainly by the end of the seventh century, the cult of Mary was fully developed, and two of our contributors begin with Roman feasts or artwork that can be dated to that period and attempt to trace their origins back earlier in time. Alistair MacGregor's work, 'Candlemas: a Festival of Roman Origin', has already been published as an article, but in publications with limited readership; it deserves wider attention and so it is well worth reproducing here. Alistair looks at the Roman custom of celebrating Candlemas in place by the end of the seventh century, and shows by careful argument how the practice was derived from goddess rites associated with Ceres and Proserpina, an admission first made by Pope Innocent III (1198–1216). This conclusion could cause us to overlook John McGuckin's caveat about failing to distinguish between goddess and Marian cults, but MacGregor does not do this; he is careful to show the evolution from the one to the other. The Church drew upon ancient classical customs, but it did not reproduce them.

In 'Pope John VII's Devotion to Mary: Papal Images of Mary from the Fifth to the Early Eighth Centuries', Eileen Rubery completes the book by examining the surviving early images of Mary in the basilicas and churches of Rome. The inclusion of two art historians in a book on the origins of the Marian cult needs no apology; art is a focal element of cult, expressing its beliefs and symbols. Eileen looks at the development of Marian art in Rome from the middle of the fifth century to the beginning of the eighth. She shows how these images developed from four sources or archetypes, only one of which was of the Mother of God, the other three being of women other than Mary, i.e. the Virgin saint, the Imperial Empress, and the Orant or praying woman. Eileen also puts the development of Marian art in Rome into its social and political context. This richly detailed and well-illustrated chapter ends the book.

There is a creative tension which ensures that this book as a whole embraces a range of informed views which may be held on this topic. Geri Parlby, Eileen Rubery and Richard Price all testify to the strength in the argument that the Marian cult, as a widespread phenomenon at least, is a late development in the first centuries of Christianity, and Alistair MacGregor's work lends support to that view. Nevertheless, Richard Price cautions that we should not follow the usual line in regarding Ephesus as a major turning point in its development.

Antonia Atanassova, on the other hand, sees Cyril's work as formative for Mariology. Stephen Shoemaker corrects assumptions that the fifth century is the earliest period when the Marian cult is demonstrable, while John McGuckin warns against arguing from silence for the lack of a cult. He, Margaret Barker and I focus on the influence of texts about Mary that derive from the first two centuries. The argument there is that, despite the lack of artifacts and imagery that would help us locate a *cult*, the textual evidence does suggest that Mary was of great significance to early Christian communities.

The contributors and I hope that this book will stimulate debate and research on this topic, and that, in parallel with other work being undertaken by the Centre for Marian Studies, it will ensure that Marian Studies has a very secure scholarly foundation.

I would like to thank the staff of York St John University for facilitating both the original conference and the editing of the book.

Chris Maunder
York St John University, November 2007

BIBLIOGRAPHY

Barker, M. (2003), *The Great High Priest*. London: T.&T. Clark.

Beattie, T. (2002), *God's Mother, Eve's Advocate: a Marian Narrative of Women's Salvation*. London: Continuum.

Benko, S. (2004), *The Virgin Goddess: Studies in the Pagan and Christian Roots of Mariology* (*Studies in the History of Religions* 59). Leiden: E. J. Brill.

Boss, S. (2000), *Empress and Handmaid: On Nature and Gender in the Cult of the Virgin Mary*. London: Cassell.

—— (2004), *Mary*. London: Continuum.

Boss, S. (ed.) (2007), *Mary: the Complete Resource*. London/New York: Continuum.

Bruce, S. (1996), *Religion in the Modern World: From Cathedrals to Cults*. Oxford: Oxford University Press.

Cameron, A. (2004), 'The Cult of the Virgin in Late Antiquity: Religious Development and Myth-Making', in R. N. Swanson (ed.), *The Church and Mary* (*Studies in Church History* 39). Woodbridge: Boydell & Brewer, 1–21.

Davidson, J. (2005), *The Odes of Solomon: Mystical Songs from the Time of Jesus*. Bath: Clear Press.

Elliott, J. K. (2005), *The Apocryphal New Testament*. Oxford: Clarendon Press.

Frazer, J. (1922), *The Golden Bough: a Study in Magic and Religion*. New York: Macmillan.

Graef, H. (1985), *Mary: A History of Doctrine and Devotion*. London: Sheed & Ward.

Johnson, E. (2003), *Truly Our Sister: a Theology of Mary in the Communion of Saints*. New York: Continuum.

McGuckin, J. A. (1994), *St Cyril of Alexandria: the Christological Controversy, its History, Theology, and Texts*. Leiden: E. J. Brill.

—— (2001), *St Gregory of Nazianzus: An Intellectual Biography*. New York: SVS Press.

Price, R. M. and M. Gaddis (2005), *The Acts of the Council of Chalcedon*. 3 volumes. Liverpool: Liverpool University Press.

Schneemelcher, W. (1992), *New Testament Apocrypha: Writings Relating to the Apostles Apocalypses and Related Subjects*, edited and translated by R. M. Wilson. Louisville: John Knox Press.

Shoemaker, S. J. (2002), *Ancient Traditions of the Virgin Mary's Dormition and Assumption* (*Oxford Early Christian Studies*). Oxford: Oxford University Press.

—— (2007), 'Marian Liturgies and Devotion in Early Christianity', in S. Boss (ed.), *Mary: the Complete Resource*. London/New York: Continuum, 130–45.

Smith, J. Z. (1990), *Drudgery Divine: On the Comparison of Early Christianities and the Religions of Late Antiquity*. Chicago: Chicago University Press.

Spretnak, C. (2004), *Missing Mary: the Queen of Heaven and her Re-Emergence in the Modern Church*. New York: Palgrave Macmillan.

Stark, R. and W. S. Bainbridge (1985), *The Future of Religion*. Berkeley: University of California Press.

Warner, M. (1990), *Alone of All Her Sex: the Myth and Cult of the Virgin Mary*. London: Pan/Picador.

Wilson, B. and J. Cresswell (1999), *New Religious Movements: Challenge and Response*. London: Routledge.

NOTES

1. Published by Continuum Press and Sheffield Academic Press, 2000–2003. It will be relaunched under the auspices of the University of Wales at Lampeter.
2. Boss 2000; 2004; Beattie 2002.
3. Boss 2007.
4. Warner 1990. The original was published in 1976, but the 1990 edition has an interesting epilogue, in which the author reflects on her arguments in 1976.
5. Johnson 2003.
6. Spretnak 2004.
7. *Ibid.*: 203.
8. *Ibid.*: 180.
9. Smith 1990.
10. Frazer 1922.
11. But see the critical review by Price (1996), *Journal of Higher Criticism* 3/1, 137–45.
12. See, for example, Warner 1990: 66: Ephesus was the 'first landmark in the cult of Mary, as mother of God'; Cameron 2004: 2 regards Ephesus as decisive in the Marian cult, especially as it was followed by the building of Santa Maria Maggiore (see Eileen Rubery's chapter).
13. See Geri Parlby's chapter. I have a postcard of the image which refers to it as the 'Madonna and Child and the Prophet Balaam', and apparently some staff at the site have referred to it as the oldest such image.

14. For the text, see Elliott 2005: 48–51.
15. Benko 2004: 200. The decree was entitled *Gelasianum de libris recipiendis et non recipiendis.*
16. The idea that Mary's physical state was unchanged by the birth of Jesus is also to be found in another early (first- to second-century) text, the *Ascension of Isaiah* (Schneemelcher 1992); the painlessness of the birth is suggested there and in an approximately contemporaneous text, the *Odes of Solomon* (Davidson 2005).
17. Benko 2004: 202.
18. The definition by the *Compact Oxford English Dictionary of Current English* (Oxford University Press, 2005) sums up different and contemporary usage of the word 'cult':
    (1) A system of worship directed towards a particular figure or object;
    (2) A small religious group regarded as strange or as imposing excessive control over members;
    (3) Something popular or fashionable among a particular section of society.
    Of these, (1) represents the original Latin usage (*cultus*), and is quite acceptable in Roman Catholic usage ('the Eucharistic cult'; the 'cult of the Virgin Mary'; the 'cults of the saints'). Sociologists in the middle of the twentieth century began to use the word in its more pejorative sense (2), as new groups with a focus on a particular object of devotion were often radical and small-scale, sometimes deviant. This led to the common, and sensationalist, media usage. More recently, sociologists have realized the dangers inherent in an evaluative definition that is inherently negative, and so have moved to a more neutral definition nearer (3) (e.g. Stark and Bainbridge 1985, for whom 'cults' are new but not sectarian movements; Bruce 1996, in which cults are regarded as loosely knit groups with common themes and interests), or have avoided the word altogether (e.g. Wilson and Cresswell 1999). My definition is derived from (1), but embellishes this because 'worship' is too general a term; for something to be called a 'cult', there needs to be an emphasis on visible devotional behaviour and community consensus.
19. Graef 1985 is still one of the best overviews of the history of references to Mary in theology and spiritual writing.
20. Shoemaker 2007: 130.
21. McGuckin 1994; 2001.
22. Elliott 2005.
23. Shoemaker 2002.
24. For example, Price and Gaddis 2005.
25. Cameron 2004: 5–6 points out the prominence of St Thecla by the fourth century, far more so than Mary. Eileen Rubery has told me that, in art, St Agnes is better represented than Mary on third- and fourth-century gold glass in Rome, and SS Agnese, Susanna and Cecilia have earlier representations in the catacombs than Mary, who, apart from the Adoration of the Magi scene mentioned in Geri Parlby's chapter, does not appear until the sixth century. Shoemaker 2007: 130 reminds us that it was *martyr* saints who were prominent before Mary, not saints in general.
26. For example, Barker 2003.

1

THE EARLY CULT OF MARY AND INTER-RELIGIOUS CONTEXTS IN THE FIFTH-CENTURY CHURCH

JOHN MCGUCKIN

It has long been a moot issue (and one that this volume of essays seeks to address through different angles of entry) as to precisely when one can sensibly talk about a visible 'cult' of the Virgin Mary. The posing of the question in a defensible academic way, however, demands a prior clarification of methodologies and the facing up to the chief problematic challenge: namely, what would one take as constitutive evidence of such a cult? Texts celebrating Mary? Graffiti? Tombal archaeological evidence suggestive of popular piety? Marian liturgical festivals or pilgrimage centres? Texts there are in abundance, of course. It is their interpretation on the external front (what the existence of such texts 'about Mary' says concerning the wider life of the Christian communities) which is where the hermeneutical friction begins to be felt. Hard, non-textual data also exists. This is not in abundance, certainly, but then again that 'paucity' is hardly (that is, only with immense difficulty) translatable in any direct sense into evidence of 'paucity of cult'. Too often this basic fact has been lost sight of and then, with a perhaps unjustifiable confidence, we might conclude that the fully functioning 'cult of the Virgin' is only a fifth-century phenomenon. By that stage, of course, there is no argument anyway; although that very fact demonstrates the circularity of argumentation that pervades the air – for the restriction of a cult of the Virgin to the fifth-century Church is tantamount to the admission that only the fifth-century cult of the Virgin meets the requirements of what a 'proper' Christian cult of the Virgin should be. There is undoubtedly a strong and vital flourishing of the Marian cult in the 'high patristic age',[1] and one that continues to develop in nuance and form throughout all the remaining centuries of Church history. The fourth-century Fathers build on earlier patristic writing and develop their theological reflection on the Virgin, predominantly in Christological contexts, and the fifth and sixth centuries witness an increasing focus on and interest in her species of glorification.

But what of the time before all this comes out into the light of day in extensive patristic texts – namely in the obscure second and third centuries? We ought to be able to trace the cult in the one place where cult ought to be evidenced – in the liturgical acclamations addressed to the recipient. But here is precisely the issue – the pre-history of the Christian liturgy is itself notoriously obscure. It is only in the late fourth century and on into the fifth that the very liturgy becomes more and more transparent to detailed external study: and thus it makes popular and communal piety as an avenue to the study of Marian devotion something of a cul-de-sac rather than a royal road. That being the case, the commentator is left with the necessity of looking longer and harder at the textual and epigraphic evidence, such as it is, that remains; and also at evidence from common religious practice in the ancient world (an awareness of goddess cult, for example). In reference to Mary, there is a heavyweight body of historical-textual data. It amounts to massive and unmoveable (if not extensive) evidence present in the first century (canonical texts), the second (apocryphal literature and the Irenaean corpus) and the third (where I would place the remarkable evidence of the *Sub tuum praesidium* prayer).[2]

If one were to take a parallel example of this historiographic problem, in a domain other than Marian studies, so as to serve as an illustration, we could note that with the exception of that very rare phenomenon of the Dura Europos finds, then before the fourth century one could actually be camping out within the archaeological remains of a Christian house-church yet not be able to recognize them for what they were. Lack of hard archaeological data in this case surely could not be taken as evidence that Christians occupied no special or particular dedicated buildings of any kind until after the Constantinian watershed. Mentions of special rooms in houses consecrated to Christian use are already to be found sprinkled in literature of the second century; and in the third century, in his *Treatise on Prayer*, Origen makes particular mention of which room in Christian houses ought to be used for sacred things in the domestic environment. The first 'hard' evidence, however, comes only from the sixth century, when inscribed crosses and frescoed domestic rooms make their appearance. This paucity of the 'hard evidence' is not in itself surprising. The survival of a consecrated Christian domestic room would actually have been the more surprising thing, unless it were the site of a martyrial shrine (such as the frescoed *Room of the Orans* in the subterranean shrine of SS Giovanni e Paolo on the Caelian hill in Rome, which only survived by virtue of becoming obsolete and covered over by later ecclesiastic building).

When we find the next 'unaltered' archaeological instance of a domestic prayer room with frescoes, it turns out unsurprisingly to be in Egypt. Mathews gives accounts of three such places of significance,[3] although only the first is unarguably 'lay' in character: the Kom el-Dikka (D) building which was a substantial villa in Alexandria, and the private quarters of the Coptic monks at Bawit and Saqqara. At Kom el-Dikka a Mother of God enthroned, flanked by an angelic guardian and donor, takes up a commanding position on a domestic wall, which must have marked a substantial 'prayer room'. In the domestic quarters of later Coptic monks, the *Virgo Lactans* was a favoured theme, by now firmly rooted as a eucharistic symbol. The paucity of the evidence, therefore, is no indication that there is nothing here to delay our attention. No more could the paltry textual evidence that survives of the liturgical form of pre-Constantinian Christianity be elevated as evidence that the 'liturgical concept' itself is a late patristic invention. Nevertheless, the silence the data presents one with, on so many fronts in ancient Christianity, gives rise to many dimensions of wonderment – and equally to many crazed speculations. The popular blog-land theme of Marian cult links to ancient paganism is one such area where common sense and apologetic zeal have clearly parted ways increasingly of late. The common thesis of such (numerous) websites is clearly the desire of zealous evangelicals to castigate modern Catholicism for its allegedly neo-pagan Marian devotions. One typically moves seamlessly in this strange and pseudo-scientific environment from the Isiac litanies to Pius XII, with little pause for thought – or for the sober adjudication of evidence, for that matter.

When there are few (remaining) peaks showing on the historical radar, what does register can either give a significant indication of the hardly visible remains of what was once a major topographical feature (records of a sandbank that was once a threat to navigation), or could well turn out to be merely an accidentally surviving 'blip' – one that has survived not because it was once a major sandbank at all, but rather because it was one of the details from an earlier age that 'struck the fancy' of a later time, which therefore invested in it the energy to retain it as a textual annotation for the (even later) contemporary record. Such accidents of preservation abound in all ancient history, and certainly in the course of the story of Christianity. For Christians, the desire to invest a movement of preservation in an antique element was usually related to a holy pilgrimage site. The Tomb of Jesus in Jerusalem is a prime example where Biddle has lately demonstrated the surprising fact that the present nineteenth-century edicule contains within its perimeter every archaeological level of Christian build on the site ever known, several in more or less complete states, like skins of an onion.[4] But in the case of the Marian cult, such pilgrim sites never became a dominant aspect until later Byzantine times (Jerusalem, Ephesus, Nazareth, Bethlehem). Even so, the Gospel records exercised the effect of the 'pull of the tidal moon' over Christian imagination, and an intense interest in the Mother of Jesus can be traced in every century of the early Church: and not just an incidental interest (such as later gave rise to the many legends about the majority of the apostles – about whom the primitive Church seemed to lose factual data at a very early stage), but rather a level of interest and excitement that left significant literary traces from earliest times onwards.

In relation to this, it is very important to note a fundamental rule: it is only the context of a living community of devotion that preserves such texts and adds to them. The very existence of second-century Marian Apocrypha (and such developed ones too) is proof positive of a community of interest. Let us take another example of the same process. Careless readers and commentators may often talk about the 'suppression' of Gnostic literature (but who had that level of censorial power in the second century?), when the perfectly natural process of 'remaindering' serves well enough to explain most of the question as to why the Church preserved a canon of four Gospels and did not preserve the Gnostic apocrypha. It was the sands that preserved the latter, and that mainly because the texts contained within them *nomina sacra* which were still hallowed in the later centuries that discarded the manuscripts by burial and not by incineration. It is only living communities that preserve the texts that are important to them: texts that are still alive, that is, will (generally) survive any degree of official disapproval, as long as there is a community there ready to invest time and money renewing the literature (and material fabric) of a previous age that still seems to it to be relevant and significant.[5] As another example of this remaindering and preservation dynamic, we can cite the Sinai monastery of St Catherine's. It is today one of the major repositories of most of the earliest surviving pre-Iconoclastic icons (sixth century being the earliest on site), not because it was a centre where ancient icons and their outmoded styles were furiously kept in current circulation, but precisely because it was one of the most out-of-the-way places on earth, and was a site where newer icons replaced the old ones, which were then remaindered into the kind of 'obscure archival storage by default' that explains their survival in history (again, just like the accident of the emergency infill that gave to us both the Dura Europos synagogue and house-church).[6] Within this universal process of historical reclassification, the Marian cult bears the marks more of the dynamic of 'preservation and extension' than of 'remaindering and archival storage', and that in itself is a very significant thing to note from the outset.

The history of the Marian cult, then, has ancient roots that are more than visible already in the New Testament records. If cult starts anywhere, it begins with a liturgical affirmation, or *acclamatio*, and we have a beautifully elaborated one staring us in the face in terms of the '*Benedicta tu*' of Lk. 1.42. The very appearance of Mary in the New Testament literature is a fact of major importance, given that the literary genre we witness across the various Gospels is one that elevates one central figure (Jesus) to a literary form 'merely approaching' two-dimensionality (three-dimensional characterization would be exaggerating it). In such a medium of presentation, when anyone else appears at all it is undoubtedly to be taken as very hard data indeed. Thus, to take but a few examples, the incredibly few evangelical texts that are hostile to Jesus (appearing to the casual reader almost *en passant*) are often underlined by historians as of primary significance in establishing the historical record of Jesus' own ministry. A chief example here is the hostile utterance of Mt. 11.19, the complaint that Jesus was a 'friend of tax collectors and harlots'. Such a viewpoint is generally taken to manifest the concern of the historical Jesus for a ministry of reconciliation, one that pre-dates the Gospel theology itself and that of the first-generation Church which so developed reconciliation theology around the concept of the Crucified Redeemer. Small indications ought not to be overlooked simply because they are small and *prima facie* insignificant. There are many other examples of this significance to historians of apparently small data. The enigmatic remark of Nathanael in Jn 1.46, 'Can anything good come out of Nazareth?' – for so long interpreted as a generic 'put-down' of provincial Galileans – takes on a dramatic new significance after the winter of 2005, when a grocer in Nazareth fell through his shop floor, and the Israeli archaeological service subsequently discovered, and excavated, the largest bath-house in Roman Palestine, making it clear that Nazareth (not Caesarea as had been thought) was the central hub and garrison station of the occupying Roman Legions in Palestine in the time of Jesus.

It is the same with the cult of Mary. Small, even isolated, data speak loudly – but only if they are heard in the correct context. In the case of the Marian cult, however, it is important to remember that it may not (indeed is not likely to) have the smooth linear development one might expect from seeing its 'developed' fifth- or sixth-century forms. It has long been a premise of patristic theologians that Christian theological utterance 'ought to have been perfectly smooth' (just as generations of dogmaticians coming from a patristic viewpoint used to believe that the Nicene movement gives the quintessential snapshot of the fourth century despite the existence of heretical dissidents). But hindsight is usually 20/20. Recent work on the shape of basic doctrinal presuppositions around the time of Nicaea has tended to argue a very different picture, and points up how extensively the Nicene victory leads to a reordering of the narrative of the earlier generations. The Church, that is, always tends to presume that the past leads up to its own door smoothly and in a familiar way. To facilitate this belief, the ancients (and many moderns too) were helped by two things: first, a radical un-familiarity with the past (generations quickly lost touch with the contextual world of previous generations who were cut off from them by too large a societal or cultural gap);[7] and second, a strong readiness throughout Christian history (despite its apparent 'style' of constant archaizing) to render the efforts of previous generations obsolete.[8]

It is only to be expected that the shape and features of the Marian cult will mutate through many quite different stages; so much so that if we overly expect a fifth-century type of 'acclamation', we may wholly miss what is actually going on in earlier times. It would be better to talk, therefore, of the Marian cults of early Christianity. The evidence of the Apocrypha (that great interest shown in the second-century 'Life of Mary' in the *Protevangelium of James*, for example) is generally and extensively subordinate to the material in the canonical Gospels. Generations of commentators have so presumed that its historical value is utterly worthless (a girl child brought up in the Temple Holy of Holies, to take but one example) that there has been accordingly next to no historical analysis of this important text – not even to consider again how the Herodian Temple func-tioned as a school for the families of priests, as a fabric workshop for cultic vestments staffed by members of priestly families and myriad other things (such as exchange mechanism and animal supply centre, as we so dramatically learn in the instance of Jesus' conflict with the money traders in the vast subterranean vaults of the Temple precinct). The concept of a dedicated virgin being brought up in the Temple precinct (admittedly not the Holy Sanctum) is far from a ridicu-lous notion, and certainly not the prohibitive detail that should lead us to dismiss the study of this text to the extent it has been neglected historiographically.

The predominance of the New Testament data in all forms of the later Marian cult has been sufficiently mulled over for me not to presume to do the same here; except to note that two significant things emerge from such a study of the New Tes-tament era: first, that Mary was apparently a figure powerful enough in the affairs of the early Church to have more than rivalled Peter or Paul, both of whom have 'cults' in the sense of disciples who subsequently elevate their lives and legends as examples of true piety and right theology. The Petrine tradition is manifested in what is arguably Peter's most significant theological work, the fashioning of the Transfiguration narrative with its implicit doctrine of the Petrine succession, a theme on which I have written at much greater length elsewhere.[9] The Pauline tra-dition is more fully known to the general Christian reader through its reworking in the Markan evangelical tradition (so misleadingly offered to us in patristic antiquity as a pro-Petrine narrative!), the (probably) second-century Acts of the Apostles, and not least the Pauline epistolary collection. The Lukan materials, so interesting for students of the earliest cult of the Blessed Virgin, were long thought to be thoroughly Pauline, but mainly because their author was seen as one and the same as the author of Acts. Today there is much less consensus that this is the case, and less confidence that Luke depends on Mark for theological perspective at all (as distinct from evangelical traditional materials).[10]

Both the Petrine and Pauline cults were developed in powerful ways that left their mark on canonical literature because both were closely associated with power bases in early Christian ecclesia-building. In the core Paulinist material, Mary is mentioned with some degree of hostility: not least because she is so closely aligned with the Jerusalem Church, which was known to have opposed the apostle to the Gentiles substantially in his own day. Mary in the Gospel of Mark, for example, is sidelined most interestingly. Mk 3.31-35 is a clear example. Luke also seeks to democratize what must even then have been a well-known Christian acclamation of Mary: 'Blessed are you'. For without an understanding of this *beata* tradition as it appears in Lk. 1.42, 45, 48, it is difficult to understand the point of the exhortation to faith in Lk. 11.27-28.[11] His motives for democratizing the Marian symbol, however, are a far remove from those of Mark 3.

At the same period, the end of the first century, Mary also features strongly in the (probably Egyptian) text which we now call the Gospel of John. Here in a much more positive fashion she is assigned, more than any other of the apostolic *dramatis personae*, a seminal role in facilitating not merely the mission of Jesus, but the manifestation of his Glory to the world. I refer, of course, tó the evangelical episodes of thc Wedding at Cana, 'where he allowed his glory to be seen' (2.1-11), and the episode of the Gifting of the Mother to the Beloved Disciple, as testamentary consignation of high authority over the Jesus movement to the Beloved Disciple in the Johannine Passion Narrative (19.26-27). Even earlier than this she features extensively in a tripartite infancy narrative that serves as the prelude to the Gospel of Luke, and whose triptychal shape is clearly designed to offset the possible claims of the Baptist to messianic status (claims that could only have been seriously mounted by contemporary disciples of the Baptist), all of which puts us squarely in the world of first-century Palestine. It is important to note, of course, that Mary did not necessarily 'have to' play a significant theolog-ical role in the Gospel infancy narratives. Comparing that of Luke to that of Matthew, we see how in the latter Mary is not elevated significantly. In Luke's hands, however, she is not merely the biological mother of the Messiah, but his prophetic interpreter; and therein lies the difference, and the evidence for what we must surely recognize as a significant 'cult'. None of these things are 'large monuments' taken in and of themselves. But each of them is monumentally important in establishing the earliest origins of the cult(s) of Mary and the ways in which those cults functioned for other ends, in the centuries pre-dating the Constantinian revolution. If our argument can, in some respects, be challenged as being of the form of drawing 'lines of prospective development' from paucity of remains, I can only make the answer that all commentators do exactly the same thing. The fault, if there be one, here lies not in the 'drawing in' of the lines, but in the judgement that one exercises in deducing which way the line is heading. If the textual (scriptural) development of the Marian cult seems to me to have left records sufficiently indicative that there was a substantial cultus of the Blessed Virgin from earliest times, it would stand to reason that research in other areas might suggest a similar pattern.

For reasons of comparison, therefore, we could fruitfully go elsewhere and look at aspects of the Marian cultus which have at one and the same time been massively 'considered' and yet (in my opinion) often not considered appropriately, because methodological presuppositions have blinded commentators. I refer to the incidences of the pre-Christian pagan cults of the goddess that so many have seen as parallels to the manner in which later Christians glorified Mary. It is hardly the case that Mary-Isis parallels have not been thought about to date. It remains a subject of wonderment, however, that they have been thought about so crudely, and with so little sense of discretion. The extensive and scholarly book by Witt, that put Isis scholarship on a new footing, has a remarkably poor final consideration of how much of all this actually ends up in the Marian cult of the fifth-century Church. His successors have rarely developed on this in terms of sophistication,[12] and even recent study gives us small grounds for comfort when the very terms of the comparison can be blandly, and rather ineptly, stated in terms such as: 'Links have been drawn between the Isis cult and Mariolatry . . .'[13] Let us take some of the issues surrounding the wider societal context of goddess-Marian devotion and, having considered some of the data, ask whether it offers us new perspectives on the extent and form of Marian cult already present before the Council of Ephesus in 431. Our prime set of examples is offered by the Isis cult. This has long been the playground for every wild speculation possible for many centuries past. It remains so to this day, and the innumerable Mary-Isis sites on the internet still offer ready material for much amusement, if not much enlightenment about history or theology.

Isis is the Greek name for the goddess Aset, an ancient Egyptian deity whose history will not concern us much here, except to state that she appears in a minor position in the Fifth Dynasty pantheon and her cult, like that of her husband-brother Osiris, was first centred at Abydos, but by the time of the New Kingdom (c. 1500 BC) it had universalized in Egypt and was destined to spread all over the ancient world in the centuries shortly before the appearing of Christ. It is in the Greco-Roman cult of Isis that we find material that will interest us in relation to Mary-Isis parallels.[14] By a few centuries before the time of Christ, Isis had become one of the great success stories of the exporting of the Egyptian cults across the Roman Empire. She is a ferociously syncretistic goddess absorbing, by a preferred style of her religion, most of the epithets of many other Greco-Roman goddesses, even those whose cultic myths and practices were alien to that of her own initial *mythos*. Isis can be and was 'many things to many'. As Witt puts it, 'She had absorbed the functions not only of the other Egyptian goddesses . . . but also those of Greece and Rome. Her votary could, therefore, be as eclectic as he wished.'[15] He goes on:

She could be worshipped as the Great Mother of all nature. She could be the personification of Wisdom and Philosophy. She could be said to establish her son Horus-Apollo as the youthful Pantocrator of the world. 'Voilà le culte oriental,' writes Gérard de Nerval, 'primitif et postérieur à la fois aux fables de la Grèce, qui avait fini par envahir et absorber peu à peu le domaine d'Homère.' Isis was all things to all . . . this was what made her so formidable a foe to Jesus and oecumenical Paul.[16]

Isis took her name originally from the hieroglyph depicting a woman with a stylized throne as her headgear. Aset thus means 'female of throne'. The link with the regnant Pharaoh is always of central importance to her. It is the link to her saving power. Her iconography as enthroned mother is thus integral to her *mythos*. In later times she was merged with Hathor's attributes and gains a head-dress of cow-horns with a lunar disc in the middle. The generic myth is complex and assumed many varied forms in the course of its ancient passage through history, but the basic shape can be briefly told.[17] Isis and Osiris are brother-sister lovers, children of the sun god Ra. Their sacred *mythos* tells that they bring the benefits of life, cereal cultivation and the sense of a just and artistic society to humankind. Osiris's brother Set, the god of the desert, is hostile to Osiris and arranges his abduction in a wooden chest, and his eventual death and dismemberment. From being the regnant god of life, Osiris thus becomes rendered into the gloom as a lord of the underworld. Isis his wife, skilled in magic and foresight, goes around Egypt in lamentation searching for her husband. Finding his dismembered corpse, she tries to assemble all the scattered parts and with the use of magic bring her dead spouse back to life. This she can do for the space of one day. But the resur-rected god lacks the essential phallus, the sole body part which could not be found. Isis thus makes a clay one with great magic power and conceives from Osiris their son Horus. He is a weakly child and in the arms of his wet-nurse appears to be dwindling away to nothingness. But Isis realizes that he must be fed with immortal ambrosia, not on mere human milk such as the nurse is giving him, so she suckles the child herself with the life-giving milk from her divine breast, and then Horus flourishes and grows strong. He becomes the symbol of regnant power and is the living Pharaoh (having eventually cast down Set in his just revenge, and set a bar to the powers of evil and violence). Osiris is the Lord of Underworld, Isis the great power of resurrection, fertility and magic, Horus the living symbol of divine power on earth. Isis was fre-quently depicted as seated with the child on her lap. She herself is the throne of the deity, and in some poses (though not the majority) she presents her divine child frontally for the cultic gaze of the worshipper. In other instances the child lies on her lap, as on a throne, and he sucks his finger – an allusion to the myth of the divine milk needed from his mother.

Around the time of the Christian era, the cult of Isis was immensely successful in absorbing the worship of other Greco-Roman deities. In the account of the rev-elation of Isis to Lucius, in the closing chapters of *The Golden Ass*, that bawdy pantomime of the ancient novelist Apuleius, the goddess Isis addresses the hero (symbolically transformed from a donkey into a man) in a way that manifests this 'missionary outreach' of the religion:

> You see me here, Lucius, in answer to your prayer. I am nature, the universal Mother, mistress of all the elements, primordial child of time, sovereign of all things spiritual, queen of the dead, queen also of the immortals, the single manifestation of all gods and goddesses that are, my nod governs the shining heights of heavens, the wholesome sea breezes. Though I am worshipped in many aspects, known by countless names . . . some know me as Juno, some as Bellona . . . the Egyptians who excel in ancient learning and worship call me by my true name . . . Queen Isis.[18]

The same readiness for absorbing can be seen in other surviving cult litanies. In Hellenistic times, indeed, one of her most distinctive cultic titles was 'Isis of the Myriad names'. The epithets 'many named' (*polynomos*) and 'many formed' (*polymorphos*) are both found in the Oxyrhyncus Isiac Litany. Plutarch is one of the many who designate her as the Many Named Isis.[19] Her titles are listed in this manner in shrines across the Roman world; not merely in Egypt, Asia Minor and Greece, but also in western inscriptions that show just how far she had travelled: in temple carvings from Cilicia, Latium, Cisalpine Gaul, Dacia, Germany and northern France.[20] The Oxyrhyncus Litany salutes her as protector of Horus and, accordingly, as 'Mother of the God'.

It is this phrase 'Mother of the God', of course, that catches our eye immediately in reference to ascription of the *Theotokos* title to the Virgin Mary by Cyril of Alexandria. Socrates Scholasticus tells us that it was a title first applied in Origen (once more we are in Egypt) and an attentive search shows that it is indeed in several places there, other than the 'First Book of his Commentary on Romans' where Socrates says he found it.[21] Though these instances are now in fragmented pieces of his much suffering *opus*, it is clear from the repeated iteration[22] (as well as from the list of subsequent theologians of his school who repeated the term[23]), though it is not extant in his surviving works. Cyril was an avid reader of Origen's works, though he pretended not to be, as was also true of his uncle Theophilus, the instigator of an anti-Origenian movement that was initiated in order to keep the allegiance of the simpler monks of Upper Egypt, who resented the growing influence of Evagrius and his circle at Kellia. It is very likely that the defence of the devotion to Mary as *Theotokos* originated in the Egyptian Church. Gregory of Nazianzus calls Mary the *Theotokos* explicitly, again a probable allusion to his mentor Origen, whom he quotes in the form of allusional citations at great extent.[24] If his text does represent to us the gist of the lost Origenian original, then the Christian theological point of defending the title was to argue against the Docetism of some of the Gnostics; a theme which Gregory reapplies as an argument against the Apollinarists who seem (to him at least) to think that the Logos did not derive his flesh from Mary, but from heaven. It is the same overall argument which Cyril applies in the slightly different environment of the fifth-century controversy with Nestorius.[25] Origen was not the Christian originator of the title (that distinction falls to Hippolytus of Rome, his contemporary and a theologian whom Origen greatly admired),[26] but it is Origen who surely makes the important link between the second and fourth centuries by developing the theological basis for Marian veneration in all its chief lineaments; for Origen had not only summarized all the Irenaean concern to depict Mary as Mother of the Faithful, but had extensively reflected on Mary's role as the model of Christian life and the 'first-fruits of faith' through her virginity and obedience.[27] Origen depicts Mary as uniquely sanctified because of her double consecration, first through the descent of the Holy Spirit, and then through the descent of the Divine Logos within her.[28] She is made into a great prophet[29] and an active channel of the Spirit who conveys to John the Baptist, in his mother's womb, the grace of the Holy Spirit, thus initiating his prophetic mission.[30] It was from this Origenian seed that the later Byzantine tradition developed its teaching that Mary and John the Baptist were the two supreme intercessors for the Church at the heavenly judgement seat of Christ, a theme which is abundantly witnessed in the iconographic tradition of the two figures standing at either side of the throne with arms raised in supplication (known as the Great *Deisis*).

Given close scrutiny, one sees that this early Egyptian tradition of *Theotokos* appears to work wholly within the biblical tradition, owing nothing whatsoever to the Isis cult. We must leave the world of conspiracy theory aside. Even though Origen himself bore a name that denoted 'Child of Horus', he himself is indebted to the Isis cult on no significant level anywhere in his voluminous writings, and certainly not for his doctrine of Mary as quintessential *Pneumatophor*.

The *Theotokos* title (God-Birther), after Ephesus in 431, quickly displaced the earlier designation of Mary as the Mother of God (*Mētēr Theou*). The prior antiquity of the latter title can be witnessed in the fact that it still retained its old place as the invariable superscription of the later Marian icons (that slow and conservative tradition of theological transmission). This title too, like that of the *Theotokos*, was resonant in many ways with contemporary pagan practice. The 'Mother of the Gods' was one of the most common cults of both Asia Minor and the West in the time of the Late Antique Empire.[31] In its original antiquity, the Great Mother had a cult centred on Asia Minor, but the cultus came to Rome much later and was there for more or less six centuries before the Christian emperors finally suppressed it, since it showed no signs of disappearing otherwise. Graeco-Roman mythology had, long before the time of Christ, brought in the cult of the Great Mother alongside the *mythos* of Artemis. This might give some explanation (at first sight such an improbability) as to how it was that two such opposite symbols as Isis and Artemis could become mutually absorbed in the late Hellenistic and early Christian eras.[32]

The symbiosis can be observed clearly, and one suspects that it was operable in Ephesus at the time of the Council there in 431, for Byzantine commentators more than 150 years later speak of still being able to witness the *Navigium* (the Ship procession) in Asia Minor, which was a ritual of lustration and a great public festival turning on themes common to both goddesses. The movement of absorption was not merely one way, though the Isiac religion certainly was the more powerful of the two cults in the end. Worship of Artemis arrived in Egypt first, where she was immediately subsumed under the guise of Hathor, the archetypal Mother of Egyptian religion who was symbolized by the cow. Artemis's secondary route of devotion was under the guise of Bastet, the cat goddess (an echo of her role as rider of the Lion in Asia Minor). Hathor and Bastet themselves, however, by the Hellenistic era had long been in the process within Egypt of assimilation into the cult of Isis, and so the linking began with a vengeance during the Roman period.

In the novel of Xenophon of Ephesus, Isis appears literarily as a fusion with Artemis the goddess of virginity. Isis, however, was the quintessential figure of the warm nurturing mother. It was this aspect that so appealed to the wide range of her female (and male) devotees. She was also the 'Giver of the Heart', the symbol of the warmest sexual relations and faithful bonding between spouses. In this latter role she also appeared as the 'Giver of the Breast' to her child Horus. In her iconography in this guise, Isis is shown pointing to her breast, indicating the *mythos* that she is the source of divine life, rescuing first her own child from wasting away, then her devotee, as their *Soter*. It is quite possible that this was the original subtext of the Marian icons of the *Hodegitria*. Presented by the Christians as Mary 'Showing the Way' to the cultic observer, it would have been widely interpreted as an explicit reference to Isis showing her breast as source of divine life. This is a typical instance of what I would like to come back to shortly, and argue that several of the associations between the Mary cultus and the Isiac religion (of which there are multitudes which are entirely incidental, part of the stock of all archetypal forms of religion, such as motherhood and femininity) were entirely understood by the Christians from the outset within their own cultural syntax, and used by them for missionary strategic reasons. A pagan approaching an iconic form of Mary *Platytera* (enthroned with child) or Mary *Hodegitria* (the severe Madonna pointing to her child) would find an immediate resonance, a point of contact with the Christians of his or her own town. If the Christian movement was in the ascendancy (as it certainly was in the late fourth and fifth centuries), then such assonance could lead to the easier transition of the pagans to the new cult of Christ and his Virgin Mother. If the Church was not in the ascendancy (as was the case certainly in Egypt in the third century, where some of the bloodiest suppression of Christian communities took place), such assonance might even serve to displace suspicion and hostility from Christians engaged in domestic cults which 'appeared to' their pagan contemporaries to be different from what they really were. But in no case from the Christian side is there any sign that symbiosis was taking place. Isis, in fact, disappears when she is absorbed by the Christian Marian iconography. Her form of virginity disappears too, and her regal *mythos* of patronage. What remains, in all Christian devotion as well as in all extant forms of Christian textual reflection, is the biblical narrative, expanded perhaps by some forms of peripheral and common religious imagery, and rooted in the concept of *Basileia* (itself rooted in the New Testament), but now mediated through that symbol as understood in early Byzantine imperial senses. In other words, even the symbol of Isis enthroned is 'made over', in relation to the post-fourth-century Marian cult, extensively in the light of the Byzantine concept of the significance of the regent *Basilissa*.

This latter notion was a Byzantine development of Roman imperial management theory that came to its most important instantiation in the succession of Theodosios II in the early fifth century. Arcadius' spouse Aelia Eudoxia (the 'Jezebel' whom Chrysostom rages against in his polemics against ostentatious luxury in the capital) had extraordinarily assumed the rare and exalted title of *Augusta*. In doing so she paved the way for her daughter, the princess Pulcheria, who in the next generation also demanded from the Senate the same title, using it (as well as her own self-dedication as a Christian virgin which thus precluded dynastic marriage attempts) to protect the minority of her younger brother Emperor Theodosius II. Mary understood as *Basilissa* represents the power of advocacy as entirely mediated through intercession: for thus it was in the Byzantine court, from which the impetus of the iconic symbol derives. Female *Basileia* in Roman imperial terms had no legal basis except that which it laboriously fashioned for itself in terms of influence, patronage and political manipulation; all of which made it an immensely powerful office by the early fifth century. But intercession, which was the stock in trade, from their devotee's point of view, of the *Basilissa* as well as the Virgin *Theotokos*, was not the *modus operandi* of Isis. Enthronement was integral to her *mythos* in a way that it simply was not in the Christian Marian conception. Isis was powerful in her own *mageia* and her devotees had no doubt on that score whatsoever. The conclusion is inescapable, to all who have any care for balance in the matter: the Marian cult uses incidental motifs from the iconography of the Isis cult, but the substantial connections are simply not there. The Marian iconography is driven exclusively by biblical symbols, and coloured by Byzantine imperial theory.

What connection there is between the Marian cultus and the world of the goddess, I suggest, exists as a bi-directional dynamic passage: first, the intense interest of the Isiac cult in 'absorbing' alternate (especially threatening) religious systems, by the device of renaming them as newly validated epiphanies of the goddess; second, the interest of several of the Christian hierarchs and theologians (more so than the ordinary people), from the third century into the fifth, of disarming Christian pagan interaction by appropriating many popular forms of festival to Christian usage. It goes without saying that this involved the resistance of the movements to assimilation initiated from the pagan side. Cyril's *apologia* against the Temple of Isis at Menouthi, the end point of the great processions of the goddess along the Canopic Way, is one example of this. The creation of the Akathist hymn naming Mary as protector (*Promacheia*, like Athena) of the city is another,[33] and the sermons of Proclus of Constantinople describing her as the 'Loom of God' yet another.[34] But Mary's primary title and cultic 'acclamation' in the theological literature (where she appears generally as first of the faithful disciples) is quite different from what we might call the more popular forms of Christian devotion (such as witnessed in the Apocrypha), where she is above all else simply 'the Virgin'. How could appeal to the Virgin be a point of reference for both Christians and Isis devotees at this period, when Isis is so clearly enshrined over a cult of tender and familial Eros?

The entry to this problem is given to us within the evangelical accounts, in the image of Mary as the tender Mother of the Lord; and also outside the Christian movement in the manner in which Isiac devotion had already collided with the Artemis cult long before the advent of the Christians. Yet how could the erotic Isis ever come to be associated with that ultimate virgin Artemis-Diana, patron of the chaste and the unmarried? The symbiosis with Isis was partly driven because, in a part of her *mythos* manifestation, Artemis presided over the underworld and monitored the birthing of children in her cult. Both these aspects were primary attributes of Isis too. Isis conceived Horus, from the magically reassembled body of Osiris, using the phallic substitute she herself had created. His conception and birth were thus 'out of the normal run of affairs' (to say the least!), and did not deny her the right to claim to be both virgin and mother. Both Isis and Artemis were protectors of children. Artemis, in her role as helper of women who were giving birth, was known as Artemis-Eileithyia. Both Isis and Artemis were also rendered as moon goddesses.

Moreover, Isis is not merely a symbol of erotic love, while Artemis merely stood for chastity. The Great Mother's cult, at least at Ephesus, featured a remarkably potent cultic statue where her torso is draped with countless bulls' testicles (formerly read as breasts); and we should not forget poor Attis, bleeding to death for his heavenly lover. Isis herself could also be a symbol of chastity in the form of faithfully devoted spouse. Though very much a goddess of eroticism and magical procreation in common usage, Isis was also widely known for the rituals of chastity she demanded of her votaries. Virgins had a high place in her liturgical rites (especially when mimicking the roles of Isis and Nepthys, the divine sisters who lamented the death of Osiris during the sacred festival of 'the Seeking').[35] For married devotees, regular days of abstinence were set out for observance, as can be seen, for example, in the humorous complaints of Propertius against his lover Cynthia, when she devoted herself to Isiac ritual and turned him away from her bed for the required ten nights of celibate single-sleeping and ritual ablutions.[36] In the Roman calendar these were known as the *dies puri*.[37] One inscription from Chaeronea, a few miles away from Delphi, records the votary prayer of a young girl who dedicated perpetual chastity to Isis.[38] And Tertullian also records this aspect of the chastity required of African devotees of Isis-Ceres, another form of Isis symbiosis with Demeter.[39]

The cult statues of both Artemis and Isis in Hellenistic times show them as holding in their hands a lighted torch, symbolizing their roles as moon goddess, bringer of light, and bringer of children into the light. Their devotees, women who valued the goddess's protection over the home and the female in labour, carried lighted torches in procession to honour them. Witt describes the assimilation of Isis and Artemis as the most important single instance of all the many examples of syncretism that the Isiac cult demonstrated.[40] It was this fusing of the 'Great Virgin' with the 'Universal Mother' that made of the late Isiac cult a major force that contended with early Christianity for the allegiance of the masses. It cannot be incidentally insignificant that when the bishops emerged from what was already called the 'Mary Church' at the docks in Ephesus, and which was an extensive basilica, having accepted that it was legitimate to designate Mary as *Theotokos*, they were escorted home by women bearing lighted torches. Now, significant men retiring to their lodgings late at night would surely command a lighted torch in their retinue, but this large procession of women bearing the lighted *lampadas*, that Cyril of Alexandria so delights in telling his readers was a sign of the devotion they had to the Virgin Mary, was actually an inescapable symbol of women associated with the Isis-Artemis cult. Women bearing lighted torches were an integral part of her processional ritual. The figure of priests carrying a lighted torch and an open scroll is also one of the iconic synopses of the Isiac cult on a surviving altar from Rome. Readers coming at the history of the Council of Ephesus have generally concluded (following Cyril's suggestive lead) that the crowd was largely composed of Christian women.[41] But we have no hard evidence for this. The local bishop Memnon (who was placed under house arrest after the Council of Ephesus for having disbursed sums of money from his church in the blatant support of Cyril) was the one who apparently supplied a local crowd from all and any sources. In this light, the crowd could as easily have been a gathering of Artemisian devotees, or pagan women mixed in with Christians, among whom the Artemisians were celebrating the welcome advent of a large group of high-ranking visitors to their town, as well as their belief that the Christians had appeared to them finally to be making some ground in allowing what they themselves had long claimed anyway – that Mary, the recent Christian 'goddess', was yet another form of the Isis *Polynomos* whom they worshipped. Such syncretic blurring of the boundaries was absolutely typical of the Isiac-Artemisian traditions; just as it was *not* absolutely typical of the Christians.

What is at issue here, once again, is cross-religion perceptions, rather than real influences and indebtedness. The Artemisian hopes, perhaps that this common procession at Ephesus (if indeed it were of mixed Christian and pagan women) might briefly manifest a more tolerant attitude from the Christian side, were not to be realized, either at Ephesus or anywhere else in the Byzantine world. Ephesus was fast silting up, its harbour was becoming landlocked, its glory days were numbered. In the next century it fell into economic ruin, and religiously the writing was on the wall when Justinian destroyed the Great Artemision in order to provide columns and ballasting for his great Temple of Divine Sophia at Constantinople, and also for his Church of the Evangelist John on the Ephesian Acropolis. It is the century of Justinian that finally saw the cults of the Great Mother and Isis herself lapse into history.

Cyril stands as the witness of the Ephesian torchlight procession, and it was the same interpreter who stood, a few years earlier, as the central protagonist in the episode of the shrine at Menouthi, an important healing temple of Isis along the Canopic Way. Menouthi was located at the present bay of Aboukir; the very name shows the success of Cyril's strategy, for it still bears in Arabic the title of the ascetic Unmercenary healer-saint Abba Kyros. He was one of two sets of relics that Cyril was instructed in a 'dream-vision' to take to the desert where a black female demon, named Menouthi, had been terrorizing the local inhabitants.[42] Removed of its rhetorical wadding, it is clear to the percipient reader that the 'demon' is none other than Isis, as worshipped in the form of her familiar black basalt cult statue, adorned with the moon insignia, aligning her with Artemis and Astarte, the Queen of Heaven. The Isis temple at Menouthi in the time of Cyril was still a major site for incubational healing presided over by a medical priesthood. Its temple walls were filled with votive inscriptions giving thanks for innumerable healings. With the passage of another two centuries (and historical memories and senses of context were very short in antiquity), the patriarch Sophronios of Jerusalem, temporarily resident in Egypt, paid a visit to the site, which was now the shrine of the Unmercenary saints Cyrus and John, and in all innocence recorded some of the inscriptions as testimonies to the salvific intercessions of the martyrs.[43] The juxtaposition of many themes makes this an especially interesting incidence of inter-religious apologetic at the time of the Council of Ephesus. Isis devotees, especially the priesthood, were regularly called upon to 'see' the goddess.[44] Vision played an immensely important part in the 'apprehension' of the divine. By contrast, one only needs to glimpse into the literature of the Desert Fathers, for example, or throughout more or less the whole gamut of third- to fifth-century patristic writing, to find a resounding silence about the notion of religious vision as an appropriate path to divine sensibility. The *Alphabetical Collection of Apophthegms of the Desert Fathers*, in the story listed as Omicron, under an attribution to Abba Olympius, describes the consternation of two hermit monks in Egypt who of necessity have to give overnight shelter to some travelling priests of Isis.[45] The pagan priests marvel at their ascetic lifestyle, but are even more astounded to hear that even in spite of it they do not claim to have regular visions of their God. The monks are so disturbed by the import of their words that they soon afterwards leave the hermitage and return for the guidance of the elders who, meeting in a synaxis, evidently decided that visions were not the proper thing for ascetics, who rather must work and pray for purity of heart with dedicated perseverance.

Gregory Nazianzen, it ought to be said, at roughly the same time as the setting of this tale, has a famous appeal in some of his poetry to a 'dream vision' in which he is found between two female heavenly visitors.[46] This sagacious Christian rhetor tells how he was thus inducted into the ascetic life. The figures are Temperance and Prudence, patronesses of his dedication to a life of single chastity. Any literate reader of his verse, however, would recognize a learned allusion to the Eleusinian *mythos* of the deification of Triptolemos standing between the goddesses Demeter and Kore. A great marble frieze from the cult precincts depicting just this scene exists in the Archaeological Museum in Athens, having been removed from Eleusis.[47] The goddesses, in Gregory's redaction, have been neatly re-formed into angelic abstractions. The vision he claims, however, is of the type of 'dreaming initiation' (*oneira*) for which he finds an authority in Scripture; and his audience is an élite group of litterateurs in late fourth-century Constantinople who could be presumed to be a mixture of pagans and Christians, ready to appreciate his tactful 'classicizing' of the new monastic movement which seemed barbarous to so many of them, pagan and Christian alike. Even Gregory is not willing to advocate that Christians should experience *oramata*.

In Cyril's case, the societal paradigm is much closer at hand: a Christian hierarch who could not claim direct contact with the heavenly world seemed a poor second to the Isiac cult where the priests who did not see the goddess during the previous week were not expected to take a leading role in the worship for that coming week. Manifestation (*epiphaneia*) and Sight (*orama*) were key

15

factors in this religious approach, in a way in which they simply were not in a religion that declared blessed 'those who have not seen'.[48] Cyril was aware that he could not afford to allow his religious opponents to 'have all the best tunes', as it were, and so we find him too appearing as a religious visionary (an archetype that is signally missing from all his other writings after the time he becomes internationally noteworthy and draws hostile fire from Christian Syria). In his festal sermons which survive from this occasion, Cyril tells us that a prophetic dream warned him to seek for relics of a great martyr saint under the cathedral church's altar (a pretty safe place to dig if one knew the church was originally a *martyrium*).[49] There the martyr was waiting to gird up his loins once again and do battle with the demon in the desert, who was seducing so many people. To his surprise, Cyril tells us in his festal sermon, he found not one set of relics but two, and 'not knowing which one was indicated in the dream', he took both, wrapped in silk and laid in a jewelled casket in a triumphant chariot ride down the Canopic Way, to deposit them in a newly built martyr shrine adjacent to the site where the demon 'was still appearing'. There he instructed monks to staff the church and see to it (robustly if necessary) that the martyrs could do their work without disruption. His specification that their medical solicitude would come free indicates to us that the ministrations of the Isis temple nearby were probably paid for. This alone would account for a lively interest in the Christian holy place; but the temptation must have been a lively one for devotees, both pagan and Christian, to pay a visit to both shrines once they were in the vicinity, paying homage to Cyrus and John on the way to Isis (much like the modern secular tourist who passes so easily from Abu Simbel and Karnak to the Coptic desert monasteries).

Cyril, in his *Paschal Epistles*, complains loudly that there was too much permeation of congregations between the Synagogue and the Church in the Alexandria of his day. We might suspect it was the same between some of the pagan festivals and the Christians, and especially so in that religion of all religions which so elevated the principle of syncretism. Was not Osiris risen from the dead 'the same as' Christ resurrected? Was not Isis *Theotokos*, 'the same as' Mary? But, for all the famed easy and all-inclusive attitude of the Isis cult, there were limits. It has rightly been said that ecumenical dialogue with Buddhists is all plain sailing and liberally inclusivist until one touches upon metaphysics, and there one finds a massive dogmatic brake quickly applied. So it was with Isiac universalism. The one thing that would not be tolerated at her temples was ritual defilement. This was specified in many distinct ways and the Isis priests policed it heavily. Chief among the worst of all defilements was contact with dead things. So strictly was this enforced that pilgrims seeking Isis's healing could not enter her precincts wearing leather sandals (dead animal skins). To have initiated a Christian healing shrine in rivalry to Menouthi, where the kissing of the relics of martyrs' bones was an integral part of the rite, *de facto* introduced a massive wedge between the two cultic centres.

Cyril, therefore, in bringing the rival healers alongside Isis, far from mimicking her religion, is actually initiating another example of what his uncle did before him at the time of the destruction of the Serapeum; he is setting in motion a deliberate attempt to stop religious fusion, but this time by offering more subtle methods of missionary deconstruction than his uncle did when he let loose forces that looked to many like civil war. Not being in a position himself to initiate forceful moves against the continuing practice of the Isiac religion (Cyril had been severely censured by the imperial administration only a few months before-hand for 'retaliatory' actions taken against local synagogues and had seen his personal 'bodyguard', the *parabalani*, drastically reduced in size), he is clearly determined to undermine it by missionary strategies that involved subtle cultic dislocation. If any Christians came to the shrine of Isis after visiting their own church of Abbas Cyrus and John, they would be turned away, not by Cyril's monks, but by the Isis priests themselves. If any pagans did likewise, they too would be deprived of the benefit of Isis's consolations, and perhaps led to consider joining the Christian ascendancy instead, which must have seemed in these circumstances to offer comparable benefits in a more accessible and democratized style. Cyril's festal homily, delivered *circa* 427 or 428 when he had set up the martyrs in their new shrine, gives us proof (if we ever doubted it) that the motive was as far removed from 'ecumenism' as we could possibly go:

> These holy martyrs Cyrus and John have come out to do battle for the Christian religion . . . As their reward for the love of Christ they received power to trample on Satan and to expel the force of evil demons.[50] Now that those who were once going astray have turned to the true and Unmercenary Healer,[51] none of us need now make up dreams; none of us need cry out to the pilgrims: 'The Mistress has Spoken!' or 'She commands you to do this and that.' How can one be a Mistress and also a god demanding worship? Among demons there is neither male nor female. Anyway, what kind of characters must they have when they want to be called by girly names?[52] But nowadays the people trample on these brainless myths and worn-out deceptions of divination. Instead they are coming to the true and heavenly healers, those to whom the All-Powerful God gave the authority to be able to effect healing when he said:[53] 'Go and heal the sick. You received without charge, give without charge.'[54]

There is a great current of religious interaction going on at this period, when the Byzantine Christian ascendancy was first beginning to realize the extent of the missionary possibilities for the extension of Christianity, after the years of persecution and the previous century of disunity around the storm-centre of the Arian crisis. Although we today often see the Christological crisis Cyril presides over in the fifth century as a time of division among the churches, it in no way compared with the chaos of the fourth-century theological crises. Cyril helps along what increasingly gains momentum in his generation as the establishing of a vast international form of ecumenical synthesis and consonance among the Christians. The Christological ascent of Logos mysticism is a large part of this, but so too is the cultus of the Blessed Virgin. All aspects of it can be traced across the known world, from Rome to Antioch, from Nubia to Constantinople. Mary indeed absorbed iconic aspects of previous goddess cults, but in each instance they are absorptions on a wholly different level of operation than the syncretism witnessed in the pagan cults themselves. Even in the most significant forms of assonance (such as the iconic forms of Isis enthroned, and Isis *Lactans*), the appearance of such themes in relation to Mary is entirely subordinated to Gospel paradigms, and never plays the essential part either of these icons played in terms of the fundamental *mythos* of Isis.

Mary as a symbol of cultural assonance is far from being a sign of religious inter-penetration between Christianity and late Hellenistic paganism, but in fact always stands as a symbol of the dramatic missionary strategy of dislocation and replacement which Christianity initiated in its attitude to pagan cult and theology. If, as we may suspect, it was the Isiac religion and the Artemision cult at Ephesus which themselves were the first who saw the opportunities to gain a purchase on an 'unfriendly' religion such as Christianity, then this itself is important subsidiary witness to the fact that the Marian cultus was much more established among the Christian rank and file than it might appear from the records of the literary elite. But at the same time the end result shows that Mary was more than capable of repelling the pirate boarders.[55] As the paradigm of the *Pneumatophor* and faithful disciple, the protecting Mother and Regent, she served as a repulsion of the goddess cult among Christians in the ancient world. For Mary enthroned is not Isis, 'she whose name is the throne', rather the paradoxical *Platytera* whose small human womb is 'greater than the heavens' themselves because of the divine condescension to human limitation. Neither Mary the *Theotokos*, nor Mary *Lactans*, is giving divine ambrosia to a divine child, but rather a human mother nursing her son in human fashion because of his need for human milk. Mary the Virgin is not the magical seductress who fashions for herself a new child from the dismembered corpse of a god, but rather a young maiden whose courage to give assent to God's demands upon her signifies to all Christian generations afterwards that she stands first in the ranks of disciples. The ancient Marian cultus, in short, owes nothing beyond peripherals to pagan devotion, and everything to the Gospel records. Hopkins put his finger on it exactly when he described her as:

> Merely a woman, yet
> Whose presence, power is
> Great as no goddess's
> Was deemèd, dreamèd; who
> This one work has to do –
> Let all God's glory through . . .[56]

BIBLIOGRAPHY

Barber, E. A. (1960), *Scriptorum Classicorum Bibliotheca Oxoniensis*. Oxford: Clarendon Press.

Benko, S. (1993), *The Virgin Goddess: Studies in the Pagan and Christian Roots of Mariology* (*Studies in the History of Religions* 59). Leiden: E. J. Brill.

Bergman, J. (1968), *Ich Bin Isis*. Uppsala: Uppsalenis Academia.

Biddle, M. (1999), *The Tomb of Christ*. Gloucester: Sutton.

Blanc, C. (ed.) (1970), *Origen: Commentaire sur Saint Jean II* (*Sources Chrétiennes* 157). Paris: Éditions du Cerf.

Constas, N. (1995), 'Weaving the Body of God: Proclus of Constantinople, the Theotokos, and the Loom of the Flesh', *Journal of Early Christian Studies* 3, 169–94.

—— (2003), *Proclus of Constantinople and the Cult of the Virgin in Late Antiquity: Homilies 1–5, Texts and Translations* (Supplements to *Vigiliae Christianae* 66). Leiden: E. J. Brill.

Crouzel, H. (ed.) (1962), *Origen: Homélies sur Saint Luc* (*Sources Chrétiennes* 87). Paris: Éditions du Cerf.

David, R. (2002), *Religion and Magic in Ancient Egypt*. New York: Penguin.

Dunand, F. (2000), *Isis Mère des Dieux*. Paris: Evrance.

Festugière, A. J. (ed.) (1982), *Éphèse et Chalcédoine: Actes des Conciles*. Paris: Beauchesne.

Friedrich, H. (ed.) (1990), *Tertullian: De Exhortatione Castitatis*. Stuttgart: Teubner.

Gallay, P. (ed.) (1969), *Gregor Von Nazianz. Briefe* (*Die Griechischen christlichen Schriftsteller der ersten Jahrhunderte* 53). Berlin: Akademie Verlag.

Girod, R. (ed.) (1970), *Origen: Commentaire sur L'Évangile selon Matthieu I* (*Sources Chrétiennes* 162). Paris: Éditions du Cerf.

Hansen, G. C. (2004), *Socrate de Constantinople: Histoire Ecclésiastique I* (*Sources Chrétiennes* 477). Paris: Éditions du Cerf.

Hopkins, C. (1979), *The Discovery of Dura Europos*. New Haven: Yale University Press.

Lane-Fox, R. (1987), *Pagans and Christians*. New York: Knopf.

Langener, L. (1996), *Isis Lactans-Maria Lactans. Untersuchungen zu koptischen ikonographie*. Altenberge: Oros Verlage.

Limberis, V. (1994), *Divine Heiress: The Virgin Mary and the Creation of Christian Constantinople*. London: Routledge.

Mathews, T. (2006), 'Early Icons of the Holy Monastery of St Catherine', in R. S. Nelson and K. M. Collins (eds), *Holy Image, Hallowed Ground*. Los Angeles: J. P. Getty Museum, 38–55.

McGuckin, J. A. (1987), *The Transfiguration of Christ in Scripture and Tradition*. New York: Mellen Press.

—— (1992), 'The Influence of the Isis Cult on St Cyril of Alexandria's Christology', *Studia Patristica* 24, 191–9.

—— (1994), *St Cyril of Alexandria: the Christological Controversy, its History, Theology, and Texts*. Leiden: E. J. Brill.

—— (2001), *St Gregory of Nazianzus: An Intellectual Biography*. New York: SVS Press.

McGuckin, J. A. (ed.) (2004), *The Westminster Handbook to Origen of Alexandria*. Louisville: Westminster John Knox Press.

McKenzie, N., and W. Gardner (eds) (1977), *The Poems of Gerard Manley Hopkins*. Oxford: Oxford University Press.

Migne, J. P. (1857–1866), *Cursus Completus Patrologiae Graecae*. Paris: Éditions Garnier. Referred to in the notes as *PG*.

Peek, W. (1930), *Der Isishymnus von Andros*. Berlin: Weidmannsche Buchhandlung.

Peltomaa, L. M. (2001), *The Image of the Virgin Mary in the Akathistos Hymn* (*The Medieval Mediterranean* 35). Leiden: E. J. Brill.

Rahner, H. (1935), 'Hippolyt von Rom als Zeuge für den Ausdruck *Theotokos*', *Zeitschrift für katholische Theologie*, 59, 73–81.

Showerman, G. (1969), *The Great Mother of the Gods*. Chicago: Argonaut.

Simon, M. (ed.) (1973), *Les Syncrétismes dans les Religions Grecque et Romaine* (*Actes du Colloque du Strasbourg 1971*). Paris: Presses universitaires de France.

Solmsen, F. (1979), *Isis among the Greeks and Romans*. Cambridge, MA: Harvard University Press.

Takacs, S. A. (1995), *Isis and Sarapis in the Roman World*. Leiden: E. J. Brill.

Valdes, M. G. (1995), *Testi e Commenti*. Volume 13. Pisa: Università de Urbino, Istituto di Filologia Classica.

Vanderlip, V. F. (1972), *The Four Greek Hymns of Isidorus and the Cult of Isis*. Toronto: A. M. Hakkert.

Vidman, L. (ed.) (1969), *Sylloge Inscriptionum Religionis Isiacae et Sarapicae*. Berlin: De Gruyter.

Ward, B. (ed.) (1975), *Sayings of the Desert Fathers*. London: Mowbray.

Witt, R. E. (1971), *Isis in the Graeco-Roman World*. Ithaca: Cornell University Press.

NOTES

1. Stephen Shoemaker's article in this present collection gives a strong case for the fourth-century materials that would demonstrate the continuity of the fifth-century type of cult already present in the fourth-century praxis. His exegesis of Epiphanius is particularly persuasive; and I would only add on a footnote that his use of Gregory Nazianzen's acquiescence to the demands of his Constantinopolitan audience of aristocratic women for a celebration of the feast of Cyprian (in which he makes reference to the well-known protection of the Virgin Mary) is evidence that the Marian devotion is not only recognizable in the capital city, but also relevant for the majority of his congregation at the Anastasis church, which at this time were Egyptian sailors from Alexandria and the Nile Delta. The evidence from his hand alone ties in three points of reference for the Church: Egypt, Cappadocia and Constantinople, with Syria playing a dissident role.

2. An extraordinary juxtaposition already of the four major Marian titles: 'Only Chaste', 'Only Blessed', 'Mother of God' and 'Protector of those who invoke you'. Those who argue that this prayer 'has to be' fourth century because it uses the *Theotokos* title found at Ephesus 431 neglect to notice the tightly associated quadrant of titles found within it. Close to the 'Only Chaste' is the *Aeiparthenos* (Ever-Virgin), which was 'formally' ascribed to the Virgin Mary only at the Fifth Oecumenical Council of Constantinople in 553.

3. Mathews 2006: 38–55.

4. Biddle 1999.

5. Despite the sixth-century imperial and synodical condemnation of Origen, his texts survived extensively; the lesser-known Evagrios also survived (for his best and most significant works) by the process of re-ascription of authorship (Neilos of Sinai in his case).

6. The occupying Roman garrison, alarmed by the imminent collapse of the city wall during a siege by the Sassanian armies in 256, broke the roofs of all the houses in the adjacent street and infilled them with debris to buttress the defence perimeter. It was simply a happy accident that the Jews and Christians both had their meeting places in that outermost ring of the last suburb, otherwise we would have happily continued to the present believing such nonsense as the idea that no Jewish synagogue in antiquity 'ever' had pictorial representations (the Dura Europos synagogue is massively decorated), or that a frescoed baptistery of the Christians was 'impossible' at such an early date. For more information see Hopkins 1979.

7. There are quintessential moments of the 'loss of cultural context' in Christian history,

such as the manner in which the Gentile Church of the second century predominantly lost the colour palette of the Semitic Church of the first century. To illustrate this, contrast the manner in which Paul theologizes in his authentic letters with the manner in which he appears in the *Apocryphal Acts*; or the manner in which the twentieth-century liturgical revival attempted to 'appropriate' the *Leitourgia* of the patristic era.

8. One can think of such things as the rapid dislocation of the ancient offices of Christian prophet, deaconess or widows, by bishops and monastic ascetics; the extensive elaboration of sacramental and eucharistic rituals in the late third and fourth centuries; or the absorption of the primitive structure of local ecclesial synodical authority into the system of the primacies of 'Great Sees'.

9. McGuckin 1987.

10. In other words, the very publication of Luke was intended as a correction of Mark's biases.

11. Many commentators (predominantly Protestant with deeply invested 'Paulinist' attitudes) have taken this in the negative (censorious) Markan sense, that is as paralleled with Mk 3.31-35; but if one does not parallel it with those Markan verses (and why should one, since this is a Lukan *hapax*?), one ought to read it rather in line with the earlier *beatae* of Lk. 1.42-43. In this light, Mary (as biological Mother) is not contrasted with the 'person of faith', but rather highlighted as person of faith: that is, she was able to suckle the child precisely because she was the obedient disciple who gave her *fiat* to God despite the danger in which it enveloped her.

12. Important exceptions would be the works of Benko 1993 and Limberis 1994.

13. David 2002: 343.

14. See especially Witt 1971; Bergman 1968; Dunand 2000; Langener 1996; Peek 1930; Simon 1973; Solmsen 1979; Takacs 1995; Vanderlip 1972.

15. Witt 1971: 31.

16. *Ibid.*: 20.

17. Plutarch describes it in his *De Iside et Osiride*, critical edition by Valdes 1995.

18. Apuleius of Madaura, *The Metamorphoses of Lucius* (*The Golden Ass*) 11. As cited in Witt 1971: 19.

19. Plutarch, *De Iside et Osiride* 53.

20. Witt 1971: 286 n. 58.

21. Socrates Scholasticus, *Ecclesiastical History* 7.32, critical edition in Hansen 2004.

22. *Selecta in Deuteronomium* 22–3, in *PG* 12.813; the title reappears in Origen's *Commentary on the Psalms* 21.1; *Fragments of the Homilies on Luke* nos. 41 and 80; *Homily On Luke* 7. See W. Rusch, 'Mary', in McGuckin 2004.

23. Cyril of Alexandria pointed out its appearance in a whole raft of earlier Fathers when Nestorius made the claim in 430 that it was a recent neologism. Cyril was able to cite the instances in Peter, Alexander and Athanasius of Alexandria, Eusebius of Caesarea, Gregory of Nazianzus and Gregory of Nyssa. For the list of references, see McGuckin 1994: 22 n. 52.

24. Perhaps his most famous phrase from Letter 101, attacking Apollinaris, 'What is not assumed is not saved', was one such slightly altered citation of Origen. The *Theotokos* title is found in the same letter, *Epistle* 101.5, critical edition in Gallay 1969.

25. As, for example, in his *Letter to the Monks of Egypt* (*Epistle* 1.4). Text in Festugière 1982: 27–44.

26. Rahner 1935: 73–81.

27. Origen, *Commentary on Matthew* 10.17, critical edition in Girod 1970.

28. Origen, *Homilies on the Gospel of Luke* 7.2–4, in Crouzel 1962; *Commentary on Matthew* 10.17, in Girod 1970.

29. Origen, *Homilies on the Gospel of Luke* 8.11, in Crouzel 1962.

30. Origen, *Commentary on the Gospel of John* 6.49, in Blanc 1970; *Homilies on the Gospel of Luke* 7.1–3, in Crouzel 1962.
31. Showerman 1969.
32. Witt 1971: 145.
33. Peltomaa 2001.
34. Constas 1995: 172–6; see also Constas 2003.
35. An interesting description of this can be found in the British Museum Egyptian papyrus 10.188.
36. Propertius, *Carmina* 3.31.1, critical edition in Barber 1960.
37. *Ibid.* 5.5.34; 2.28.60–61; cf. Witt 1971: 143–4.
38. Vidman 1969: no. 62.
39. Tertullian, *De exhortatione castitatis* 13, Friedrich 1990.
40. Witt 1971: 151.
41. The carrying of the sistrum and sistula, rattle and pitcher, was more commonly found, but the torch and scroll, the Apis bull and the devotee form the iconic syntax of the Roman Isiac altar illustrated as fig. 50 in Witt 1971: 226.
42. I have discussed this at greater length in an earlier piece: McGuckin 1992: 191–9.
43. Sophronios, *The Praises of Saints Cyrus and John*, in *PG* 87.3380–424, esp. 3412–13.
44. Lane-Fox 1987: chs 4–5, 8.
45. Ward 1975: 160.
46. Gregory of Nazianzus, *Carmina* 2.1.1, *De Rebus Suis*, vv. 194–204, 210–12, 452–6, *PG* 37.985–6; see also *Carmina* 2.1.45, *Carmen Lugubre*, vv. 191–204, *PG* 37.1367. For an exegesis, see McGuckin 2001: 62–9.
47. A good copy is in the Greek and Roman gallery of the Metropolitan Museum in New York.
48. Jn 20.29. For John, the Incarnate Word alone is the Lord and mediator of divine vision (cf. Jn 1.18; 5.37; 6.46; 8.38; 14.9), a key element which testifies to his profoundly biblical inspiration and his aversion to the contemporary pagan world view.
49. Cyril of Alexandria, *Homiliae Diversae* 18, *PG* 77.1100–6.
50. Ref. Mk 3.15; Lk. 10.17.
51. This refers to Christ.
52. A mocking allusion to the ritual of the Isis/Artemis festival of *Navigium*, or ship-carrying, when it was the custom for male devotees to masquerade as women (a less drastic measure popular in Late Antiquity than undergoing castration as a priest of the Great Mother).
53. Ref. Mt. 10.8.
54. Cyril of Alexandria, *Homiliae Diversae*, *PG* 77.1105.
55. Retrospectively, looking from the eighth century backwards, John Damascene muses on how useful the Marian cult was for re-educating pagans and weaning them from the veneration of idols (*On the Holy Icons* 2.11, *PG* 94.1293–6).
56. G. M. Hopkins, 'The Blessed Virgin Compared to the Air We Breathe', in McKenzie and Gardner 1977: 94.

2

ORIGINS OF THE CULT OF THE VIRGIN MARY
IN THE NEW TESTAMENT

CHRIS MAUNDER

INTRODUCTION

As the papers in this volume will demonstrate, there is little evidence to suggest that there was anything like a fully developed 'cult of Mary' until at least the late fourth century: Geri Parlby warns against deducing it from the figures in the catacombs, for example. However, John McGuckin comments that, while it is dangerous to speculate from silence, it is also unhelpful to state categorically that there *cannot* have been elements of a cult – prayers, hymns and devotions to Mary – before the fourth century. The importance of Mary the mother of Jesus in texts such as the *Protevangelium* (see J. K. Elliott's chapter), which is likely to have originated in the second century, show that certain early Christian communities *did* regard Mary as an important exemplar of holiness. Likewise, second-century theologians such as Justin Martyr and Irenaeus, describing Mary as the 'Second Eve', did not coin this term in a writer's garret, but as members of communities in which there would have been discussion, speculation and interpretation, all focused on early Gospel narrative traditions.

To discover anything approaching devotion to Mary in the New Testament period is next to impossible, of course. Nevertheless, major themes can be identified which characterize the portrait of Mary in the Gospel narratives, suggesting that *some* first-century Christian communities regarded these themes as worthy of integration into the texts.

Recent insights into Gospel narrative as literature, and the mythological themes present in it, add insight into the way in which the Gospel texts about Mary may have been constructed. However, two contrasting observations should be made as caveats. They emerge from a reading of the Marian material and its development in the post-Gospel period.

1. First, it is inadvisable to distinguish too strongly between a Gospel picture of Mary and a later mythological accretion based on Marian devotions and rivalry with pagan goddesses; elements of myth and allusions to classical goddesses can be found in the New Testament itself.
2. Second, the concerns of the later Christian churches – the virginity of Mary as a physiological phenomenon; Mary as *Theotokos*; the beginning and end of Mary's life – cannot be traced back to the New Testament period.

WOMEN IN THE LITERATURE OF THE NEW TESTAMENT

In the 1980s and 1990s there was some optimism amongst feminist interpreters that in the Gospels we have a glimpse of an early egalitarian community which, while it was centred upon the person of Jesus, held women and men in an equal regard very unusual for the period. For these writers, although the New Testament is shaped by patriarchal concerns, it does not completely suppress this older spirit. Elisabeth Schüssler Fiorenza's *In Memory of Her* (1983) was seminal in this respect.[1] Later, Schüssler Fiorenza was to write about 'the "dangerous memory" of the young woman and teenage mother Miriam of Nazareth, probably not more than twelve or thirteen years old, pregnant, frightened, and single, who sought help from another woman'.[2] Although Schüssler Fiorenza's main area of interest was the use of these narratives by contemporary feminist movements, the implication here is that the text points us back to a community which included Mary, and which proclaimed a prophetic and liberating message.[3]

In the 1990s Carla Ricci suggested that some of the Gospel passages could be based on a 'women's tradition'.[4] She cited Lk. 8.1-3 as an example; this is the text which recalls the presence of Mary Magdalene, Joanna, Susanna and 'many others' in Jesus' community. The presence of so many prominent women in the letters of Paul, for example, does make such an idea attractive, i.e. that the women in the early Christian communities were contributors to the Gospel narratives, and some sections record their memories, concerns and theologies. Sandra Schneiders in 1999 went as far as to suggest that John's Gospel may have had a female author, at least in an earlier version; the 'Beloved Disciple' could originally have been a woman, perhaps even Mary Magdalene.[5]

The general picture that one could have held, towards the end of the 1990s, was that the portrayal of Mary in the Gospels could have been partly based on women's traditions about her, a portrayal which kept alive the memory of her as a member of an egalitarian community. Whilst the texts were overlaid with a patriarchal emphasis, i.e. theological and scriptural shaping by male authors or editors, nevertheless the powerful image of Mary – fleeing through occupied territory as a single mother in danger, or proclaiming the subversive Magnificat – was at least true to the lives of some women believers in Jesus for whom Mary was a role model, even if it does not record a memory of actual events.

However, there is a contrasting view that has been emerging as more persuasive. This is that the images of women in the New Testament do not really give us an insight into real women in the first-century Mediterranean context or their life experiences. They are literary constructions, and serve patriarchal interests. Whilst Schneiders was positing a female author for John, in 1998 Adeline Fehribach claimed that the women in John's Gospel are included as foils to heighten the image of Christ as Bridegroom.[6] In 1999 Ross Kraemer doubted whether the Christian community was attractive to women on account of its egalitarian principles, as it would not have been especially unusual in that respect; in 2002 Deborah Sawyer downplayed the possibility of any historical basis for the female characters in the Gospels, while Kathleen Corley wrote about the 'feminist myths of Christian origins'.[7] The tenor of these writings is that the evidence does not suggest that Jesus' community was as radical as might have been hoped. Corley critiqued the Schüssler Fiorenza thesis, for example. Nevertheless, she concluded by conceding that there is some evidence for the fact that 'women played a role in Jesus' movement, in the development of gospel and liturgical traditions, and vied for authority in the aftermath of Jesus' death'. This does not mark out early Christianity: 'both Jewish Palestinian and larger Greco-Roman contexts . . . were far more open to women's involvement in religion and society than has previously been supposed'.[8]

The literary criticism of the Bible strengthens the view that, in looking at Gospel images, one should be cautious in linking them to actual historical persons; they are role models and ideal figures. The treatment of the Gospels as literature has been a prominent feature of biblical scholarship in recent years.[9] Burridge has shown that, despite many years during which commentators regarded the Gospel genre as unique, the Gospels can in fact be compared to classical biographies and be included in that genre.[10] As mentioned above, Fehribach's study of women in the Gospel of John concludes that this Gospel portrays women as subordinate to the central figure of Jesus. They are characters in literature, and conform to literary codes of the time. Mary at Cana, according to Fehribach, fulfils the role of the 'mother of an important son', 'only important to the extent that she furthers the role of her son'. The depiction is not all positive: 'a first-century reader, who was reading John's Gospel for the first time, would have initially perceived the mother of Jesus as a non-believer who is simply not aware of her son's importance.'[11]

How might this image accord with classical literary codes concerning women? Zeitlin's book on women in classical drama is not concerned with biblical texts at all, yet her descriptions of women in tragedy strike chords when considering Mary as the mother intimately involved with the life and ministry of Jesus.

> Gods (frequently goddesses, as previously noted) sometimes appear 'in person' on stage, although most often they operate from afar as inhabiting that other, unknown dimension of existence that mortals may only grasp dimly and generally too late. But it is remarkable how often that energy is channelled through the feminine other, who serves as the instrument of the gods even when she acts or seems to act on her own terrain and for her own reasons, and even when she acts out of ignorance or from partial knowledge of the tragic world she inhabits. Women frequently control the plot and the activity of plotting and manipulate the duplicities and illusions of the tragic world.[12]

The Gospel 'tragedy' is, of course, preface to the final victory of the resurrection. In that sense it is not tragedy, at least not from the perspective of the believer. Its hopeful message overcomes the 'duplicities and illusions of the tragic world'. However, the role of Mary, for example in Luke 2 or John 2, does have parallels to this classical view of the woman as literary character. Compare Keener's comment about Cana: '. . . despite her shortcomings, Jesus' mother ultimately also functions as a model of faith.'[13] Women act out the will of the gods and bring the divine plan to fruition, sometimes unknowingly. Zeitlin's research associates women in classical literature with visions; birth and death; darkness and chaos; sexuality and passion as opposed to reason.[14] Mary Magdalene, in her most enduring recasting, came to serve the Christian tradition with its classical stereotype: anointer foreseeing the death of Jesus; witness to that death; seeker in the tomb and darkness of the garden; the woman associated with skulls; reformed prostitute; passionate weeper.[15] Mary the mother of Jesus is distanced from sexual passion, but her sexual status is nonetheless important; she sees angels; gives birth; attends the death of her son.

In first-century Christian literature, therefore, Mary fulfils the roles that the reader might have expected her to: she is the mother of an important son; she is the one who sees and reflects (Luke 1, 2); she initiates momentous events (Jn 2.1-11); she is present at the moment of tragedy (Jn 19.25-27). The story of her giving birth (Luke, Matthew – see below) has precedents in Hebrew literature and classical legend.

There seems to be a spectrum of views as to how far women's lives and traditions may have fed into the Gospel texts, even among feminists. Certainly, socially prescribed roles for women, such as involvement in funerary rites, will have shaped the Gospel narratives.[16] However, it is less likely that the heroic aspects of the images of women reflected real lives, and they were probably constructed as ideal types. Sawyer argues that this does not correspond to a strong role for women in early Christian communities. The Mary of faith is a literary figure, rather than a real woman. Ideal feminine figures in Gospel stories may have served to encourage the faith of *male* readers: '. . . the type of submission embodied in traditional female behaviour is more preferable in the sight of God than male autonomy.'[17]

It is probably prudent to remain agnostic on the matter as to how far the stories about Mary yield a glimpse into some kind of historical reality. Certainly, the New Testament narratives about Mary are drawn from literary types and cultural expectations. Whether they also bear traces of earlier oral traditions about Mary will remain an open question. However, we do not have to resolve it to provide an analysis of the main themes operative in the Gospel portrayals of Mary, which are the only clues as to the views of first-century Christian communities about her. These themes can be divided into four main categories: the Virgin Birth stories, the visionary image in Revelation 12, Mary as eyewitness, and the mothers at the cross.

VIRGIN MOTHER

There have been many debates about the historicity of the virginal conception of Jesus; David Jenkins in 1984 became famous for expressing his own doubts just before being consecrated Bishop of Durham. However, in the academic circles from which Jenkins came (he had been Professor of Theology at Leeds University), the belief that the virgin conception/birth stories were legends, without a basis in history, had a long history stretching back two hundred years. It is illustrative that Richard Bauckham, who argues in his recent work *Jesus and the*

Eyewitnesses that many of the characters in the Gospels may really have been eye-witnesses to the ministry of Jesus, does not examine Mary's involvement in the events of Jesus' birth in this respect.[18] When he wrote about her in a previous book, *Gospel Women*, his focus upon her was as a literary character, the Hebrew Scriptures being used as prototypes in the construction of the Gospel birth narratives.[19] A few years earlier Raymond Brown, who – as a Roman Catholic priest – refused to give up on the *possibility* that the Virgin Birth story was histori-cal, nevertheless worked only with the Hebrew scriptural precedents as building blocks in the versions in Matthew and Luke.[20] These, among others, argue that the Annunciation is not so much an account of a real experience, it is a literary *genre*.[21]

If these relatively conservative interpretations of New Testament history concede that the birth stories are a construction, then more liberal commenta-tors take it as a fact. The Hebrew scriptural foundations for this material are important, and include Mary cast as a representative of the faithful of Israel.[22] However, other classical and non-Jewish influences can be identified. The theme of miraculous birth is not uncommon in stories about gods and famous historical figures, and the first-century Mediterranean reader would have expected stories about that part of a hero's life which occurred before they entered the public phase of their work.[23] Yet why did Jewish and Christian writers use pagan motifs? Bovon writes, 'Jewish messianism – as can often be shown to be the case with minorities – expressed its identity polemically, in foreign categories.'[24] In sketch-ing the outlines of such a polemic, Crossan notes how Jesus is contrasted to the Emperor Augustus, for whom a miraculous birth was also claimed.[25] The famous words in Lk. 2.1, 'In those days a decree went out from Emperor Augustus . . .' contain a good measure of irony, which is much more the point of the text than establishing the date. Augustus was the first of the line of emperors to be pro-claimed divine; under his reign, the imperial cult was established. The writer of Luke wants to tell us how the imperial cult is mistaken: the divine image is indeed on earth in human form, but is to be found in the manger at Bethlehem rather than the splendour of Rome. The emperor may send out decrees, but the God of Abraham, Isaac and Jacob is actually the master of events, and Augustus his unwitting puppet.

The divine child as peace-bringer was prefigured in cults of the sun, Isis-Horus and royal theologies in Egypt and Mesopotamia. Virgil's *Fourth Eclogue* poetically described the great Virgin (the astrological sign Virgo) as a harbinger of a new age of peace because of the child that she carried.[26] Borgeaud shows how the virgins of classical myth, like Hecate, were regarded as mediators between the heavenly and earthly realms.[27] While direct 'borrowings' cannot be established in any particular case,[28] it is not possible to ignore the fact that all these ideas were extant in the first-century Mediterranean context at the time that the Gospels of Matthew and Luke were written. Of course, there were important contrasts between the classical and Christian versions of the myth. Talbert shows how, if we accept that the Virgin Birth is a construction of the early Christian community, it had to have the form that it takes in the Gospel texts: a human mother and divine father. Other possibilities available at the time (human mother and father; divine mother, human father; divine mother and father) would not have been consistent with the Hebrew scriptural tradition.[29]

Therefore, the cult of Mary, which is so often associated with goddess cults in the post-Constantinian period, has classical goddess connotations from its very origin in the narratives about the birth of Jesus. Other symbolic ideas concerning the motherhood of Jesus can also be found in relatively early Christian apocrypha. The *Odes of Solomon* seem to identify Jesus' mother as Wisdom, while the belief that the Holy Spirit was Christ's mother can be found in Gnostic literature such as the *Gospel of Philip*, and also in the *Gospel of the Hebrews*, in which Mary is described as an incarnation of the archangel Michael.[30] Some of these traditions are Jewish Christian, and may therefore have early precedents. The later concern to demonstrate the true nature of the incarnation by referring to the *human* mother of Christ is prefigured neither in the Gospel birth narratives, with their legendary and mythological allusions, nor in these examples of the apocryphal literature.[31] Even the greatest New Testament witness to the incarnation, the Gospel of John, speaks of a spiritual birth for believers, 'who were born, not of blood or of the will of the flesh or of the will of man, but of God' (1.13), and Jesus refers to the crucifixion as his 'hour' (2.4; ref. 16.21).[32] The use of symbolic forms referring to birth, then, is common in both classical and Jewish literature (from where Matthew drew upon Isa. 7.14 as a proof text). Classical and Jewish traditions come together in the Logos-Wisdom imagery of John 1, and this is also the case for the Gospel narratives describing the Virgin Birth.

WOMAN OF REVELATION

The New Testament contains another maternal theme that is certainly associated with classical myth. The woman of Revelation 12 – clothed with the sun and threatened by a great dragon as she gives birth – is a mythological figure, as has been demonstrated in most scholarly interpretations of the book.[33] First of all, she is an astrological figure, with sun, moon and zodiac combined in the image; as mentioned above, Virgo was a zodiacal sign and also, for Virgil, a woman in heaven, coming to earth carrying the peace-bringer.[34] Secondly, in Egyptian mythology, Isis gives birth to Horus despite the threat of Typhon-Seth. Thirdly, there is a parallel in Greek myth with Leto, fleeing from the Python to give birth to Apollo who, when born, will defeat the monster. Here again we find polemic: Nero associated himself with Apollo, and the Queen of Heaven was Roma, the patroness of the imperial cult. In Revelation, however, the symbolism is subverted: the emperor (Nero or Domitian, or any persecutor of the Church) becomes the dragon instead, and Roma is Babylon, the queen of harlots.[35]

Most modern commentators note that the woman of Revelation 12 was associated with Mary in *later* tradition, assuming that this occurred due to the observation that both she and Mary gave birth to the Christ. The original figure (and this is supported by many interpretations in the early Church) was more likely to have been interpreted as a type of the Church,[36] symbolized in the form of a woman, using Hebrew scriptural precedents such as the Daughter of Zion.

This has parallels in classical Greco-Roman ideas (Athene as the protectress of Athens; Roma, the Great Mother of Rome).

Therefore a nexus of symbols evolved: Woman-Mary-Church. However, there is another less obvious link between the woman clothed with the sun in Revelation and Mary in the Gospel birth narratives. This consists in the sequence: giving birth – marriage, i.e. a woman giving birth first, her marriage occurring second. In a human life, in a heavily regulated society at least, this is problematic. The Gospels of Matthew (in particular) and Luke deal with this by acknowledging its controversial nature and stressing the role of the Holy Spirit.[37] This led to the debate in the first centuries of the Church about Mary's integrity (which has recently been revisited in Schaberg's work).[38] In Revelation, however, the sequence is wholly unproblematic, as it is mythological. No one is concerned about the marital status of the woman giving birth, or that the woman as Church seems to become the bride of her son in Revelation 21 (thus prefiguring later ideas about Mary),[39] with its connotations of incest. Such narratives were common in the mythological schemes of the ancient Near East and classical Greco-Roman culture. What distinguishes the orthodox Jewish and Christian traditions from their contemporaries is that the figure is regarded as wholly symbolic, and not worthy of devotion or ritual enactment. The figure of Wisdom (Proverbs; Wisdom; Ben Sirach) is regarded in the same way. Whether or not there is also a hidden countercultural trend in ancient Judaism which preserved the feminine aspect of the divine is beyond the scope of this chapter (see Margaret Barker's contribution).

The motif of the woman as Church giving birth to the Redeemer, and then transforming into the Bride, has its roots in (a) birth/labour imagery, as applied to the situation of the crucifixion of Jesus and persecution of his followers, and (b) nuptial imagery, as applied to the *parousia* or second coming. These themes can be found in the Gospels too, particularly John. Because the imagery can be so clearly located in the thought world of very early Christianity (as evidenced in the apocalyptic material found in the letters of Paul or sections of the Gospels), it is likely to have been prior to the Virgin Birth narratives. The fact that the theme of giving birth before marriage appears in both Revelation *and* Matthew/Luke suggests that it reflects a pre-Gospel tradition, which also found its way into Revelation.[40]

INTIMATE EYEWITNESS

The presence of the mother of Jesus occurs at critical moments in two of the Gospels. She encompasses the life of Jesus in Luke-Acts (she gives birth to him in Luke 2, and is present in the post-Ascension community in Acts 1.14), and his ministry in John (its beginning in Cana, John 2; its end on the cross, John 19). Is this significant? In a recent work, Richard Bauckham claims that certain major characters in the Gospels are portrayed as authentic eyewitnesses.[41] The Gospels, then, are *testimonies*. Bauckham compares the Gospels to other classical biographical literature by showing that the eyewitness to events was traditionally identified by the use of the *inclusio*. The *inclusio* is a literary device in which events are sandwiched between interconnected pieces of narrative. The eyewitness appears at the very beginning and end of those events; this indicates that they were regarded as reliable narrators of all that occurred in between. The classic examples given by Bauckham are Peter in Mark's Gospel (the first disciple to be called, Mk 1.16, and the last to be mentioned, 16.7) and the Beloved Disciple in John (identified as the disciple who replaces Peter in the synoptic tradition as Andrew's companion in Jn 1.35-40, and is the first to believe in the resurrection, 20.8, as well as the last mentioned, 21.24). The other examples are the women in Luke as witnesses from the ministry in Galilee to the tomb (Lk. 8.1-3; 23.49; 24.1-11; Acts 1.14).[42] However, Mary the mother of Jesus is not discussed by Bauckham, although she provides a clear example of the *inclusio* in both Luke-Acts and John. If we were to follow Bauckham's reasoning, we might argue for Mary's role as eyewitness, as was the traditional view, especially with regard to Luke's Gospel ('Mary treasured all these words and pondered them in her heart', Lk. 2.19; also 2.51). Yet he is likely to have overlooked this because of his presumption that, in the birth and childhood narratives, she represents a literary figure rather than an historical one.

The *inclusio* is important to the later devotion to Mary, as it singles her out as a particularly important figure in Jesus' life. She is an intimate companion of Jesus, the one who knows most about him, a role also assigned to Mary Magdalene in some apocryphal and Gnostic literature. In tradition, she is portrayed as the one who comes to recognize the significance of the whole story of Jesus, his life from birth to resurrection (Luke-Acts) and his ministry from Cana to the cross (John).[43] She is the only one who has an insight into the totality of that life. As Coleridge says of the faithful Mary of Luke's birth and childhood stories, 'she is privileged over all human characters in what she knows'.[44]

In Mark's Gospel, there is no *inclusio* for Mary, and Bauckham is right to identify Peter as the key eyewitness. In Matthew, Mary does appear at the beginning, but her role is neither active nor reflective as it is in Luke, and her presence at the Gospel's end is at best debatable. However, in these two Gospels, there is another *inclusio* involving a woman, which does have structural parallels to the role of Mary in Luke and John. This is the anonymous anointing woman of 14.3-9, whose action foreshadow the death and burial of Jesus.[45] She is contrasted to the disciples: they object to the ointment because they do not understand its significance (anticipating the disciples' objections to Mary Magdalene in the apocryphal literature).[46] She, consciously or unconsciously (the text does not make this clear), knows Jesus' intended destiny, to die and be buried. The positioning of this story is deliberate; as Hengel notes, it introduces the Passion.[47] The women, with their jars of ointment at the empty tomb, end the *inclusio*; we are not told whether the woman of 14.3-9 is among them, but the fact that she was identified as Mary Magdalene throughout much of Western tradition is hardly surprising, given the obvious link between 14.8 and 16.1. It is not surprising, either, that given the importance of this role, John fleshes out this story and names two Marys: Bethany and Magdalene (the fact that the author of John does not identify them as the same person may reflect uncertainty as to whether the anointing woman of Mark 14 is also present at the tomb in ch. 16).

There are reasons to believe that this too is a motif important in understanding the role of Mary in the Gospels of Luke and John. The structural parallels between the roles of the anointing woman of Mark, and Mary in Luke and John, are given in Table 1.

Table 1: Structural parallels between Mark, Luke and John

Theme	Mk 14.3-9; 16.1-8 (*inclusio*)	Lk. 1–2; Acts 1.14 (*inclusio*)	Jn 2.1-12; 19.25-27 (*inclusio*)
Knowledge of Jesus' Messiahship	Anointing on the head[48]	Angelic annunciation	Awareness of Jesus' miraculous powers
Taking the initiative	Anointing despite objections	'Let it be to me according to your word'	'Do whatever he tells you'
Foreknowledge of tragedy	Anointing anticipates burial	'A sword will pierce your heart'	'My hour has not yet come'
Praise and reward	'What she has done will be told in her memory'	'All generations shall call me blessed'	'This is your mother'
Openness to new life after the events	Witnesses to the male disciples	Amongst gathered community in Acts 1.14	Adoption of the Beloved Disciple ('This is your son')

Thus the absence in Mark of Mary's *inclusio* in Luke and John is compensated for by the shorter span of the *inclusio* of the anointing woman. The theme is utilized in two different ways. In Mark, an unknown woman takes up the thematic structure, which reflects the fact that Mark downplays the role of Mary and of Jesus' family in general.[49] On the other hand, Luke and John use it in stories about the mother of Jesus.

The discovery of parallels between Gospel themes could be regarded as evidence that real historical events lie behind different traditions, their memory having been developed in contrasting ways. On the other hand, the common 'core' could reside in literary developments, in the portraying of ideals for Christian discipleship.

MOTHERS AT THE CROSS

A possible clue to a pre-Gospel understanding of Mary can be found in the tantalizing question of the identities of the women at or in sight of the cross (in all four Gospels). Of course, accessing the literary codes that we have utilized above will suggest that the reader might expect Mary to be there, as an important female 'character': women were present at births and deaths, and key players in tragic scenes in literature and drama. This does not help us any further with pre-Gospel history. However, the fact that the Marys at the cross have such a perplexing array of names has caused much debate, and may suggest that the Gospels had access to earlier strata of tradition; otherwise, it is difficult to know why the Gospel writers would have included such variable information.[50] The Marys at the cross are mentioned in connection with their sons or husbands: mother of James and Joses or Joseph, at Mk 15.40 and Mt. 27.56; (mother?) of James in Luke (here the women are only named at 24.10, in the story of the empty tomb); mother of Jesus at Jn 19.25, although unnamed; (wife?) of Clopas also at Jn 19.25.[51] The Marys are identified as (to use Fehribach's phrase, above) 'mothers of important sons'. Jesus was the most important son of them all. James, if it is the brother of Jesus who was intended in the synoptic versions, was the leader of the Jerusalem Church. According to Hegesippus, Clopas was the brother of Mary's husband, Joseph (a detail that could be deduced from John's text), and the father of its second leader, Symeon.[52] The mother of Jesus also became the mother of the Beloved Disciple, another prominent apostle. Albeit without the name Mary, another woman at the cross, in Matthew's version, was the 'mother of the sons of Zebedee', also 'pillars' (ref. Gal. 2.9; Acts 12.2) of the early Church.

The names cannot be incidental to the story. Their inclusion in the narrative marks them out as leading figures in the Church that remembered the Passion. Whilst John's Beloved Disciple is the only male disciple mentioned as being present, the other prominent disciples are represented by their mothers or wives, this being true to the synoptic tradition that women were present within sight of the cross while the men had fled.

As far as can be determined, like the Passover in the Jewish tradition, the Passion will have been recounted in the early Church, and its telling associated with the Eucharist (this still occurs today in Holy Week services, of course). Hengel suggested that Jesus' saying in Mk 14.9, that the anointing woman would be remembered wherever the gospel was preached, was an allusion to the fact that this story remained part of the oral telling of the Passion story in the liturgical setting.[53] The names of the women at the cross, too, would have been part of this 'retelling' tradition. On the evidence of the Gospels, the names of their sons will have varied, according to the community that was passing on the story. Clopas's inclusion may have come later than James's, as his prominence seems to have become important with the establishment of his son as Jerusalem leader after James's death.[54]

Therefore we may have more than just a literary, mythological and scriptural basis for the figure of Mary that we find in the Gospels. We may also have a liturgical one. While literary or mythological themes *may* suggest something of a primitive 'devotion' to Mary, in the Jewish and Christian traditions this would most likely have been strongly counterbalanced by a concern not to reproduce pagan patterns of goddess worship. The liturgical possibility is therefore more suggestive of something approaching a 'cultic' aspect, namely, the inclusion of famous mothers and in particular the mother of Jesus in the eucharistic cult itself. Whether the early communities would have understood their own mystical presence at the cross symbolized by the 'mother' of their prominent apostle (mother = Church), we cannot tell, but it is tempting to suggest it, given the symbolic link between women and Churches suggested in the second epistle of John and Revelation 12.[55]

CONCLUSION

We have no evidence for any cultic elements with a Marian connection in the first two centuries of the Church, and certainly not in the first century. However, Mary is an important figure in the Gospel texts, and any embryonic devotion to her that existed in that period would have reflected Gospel themes. The themes that were important to the writers of the Gospels were:

1. Mary as a virgin mother (Matthew and Luke). This has parallels in ancient Mediterranean myth and symbolism, although the Gospel version has its distinctiveness. The Virgin Birth sequence of giving birth before marriage can also be found in Revelation, which has related mythological precursors. The fact that the sequence appears in two different textual traditions may suggest that it was an early motif. However, the New Testament does not have the later concern for the physiological basis for Mary's virginity, which begins to figure from the *Protevangelium* onwards.

2. Mary as the intimate eyewitness to the events of Jesus' life, and prominent at pivotal moments (Luke and John). This may have structural convergences with the figure of the anointing woman in Mark. What is clear is that the name 'Mary' became synonymous – from the time of the Gospels (Mary mother of Jesus; Mary Magdalene; Mary 'of Bethany' in Lk. 10.38-42 and Jn 12.1-6; note also Acts 12.12; Rom. 16.6) and into the apocryphal tradition (*Thomas* 114 and many examples following) – with female faithful discipleship, sometimes in the face of the opposition of male disciples (probably deriving from Mk 14.4-5). This led to confusion between the various 'Marys'.[56]

3. Mary as a mother at the cross. The confusion over the identity of the women at or near the cross does suggest an earlier pre-Gospel stratum to this tradition. The fact that women were normally associated with death and burial does not necessarily diminish the significance of the names which, linked to various important apostles, may have held special liturgical meaning for certain early Christian communities.

We can go as far as suggesting that the primitive themes we have identified – giving birth before marriage; the *inclusio* of the faithful woman; the mother representing the son at the cross – were part of an embryonic Marian tradition in the New Testament period. This 'Marian' tradition appears not to have been restricted to the mother of Jesus alone, however. It is best not to speculate on the relationship between these motifs and actual historical women. It is perhaps more plausible to see these themes as traditions emerging in some early Christian groups. Feminist criticism of classical literature, both Graeco-Roman and Jewish, suggests that women usually functioned as ideal figures in literature, and that will act as a caution against any theorizing on history as lived in Jesus' community, and the very earliest post-Easter Church.

As a final point, we could add that any nascent beginnings of special honour paid to Mary in the first-century Church (as might be reflected in Lk. 1.42, 45, 48; Jn 19.27) may have been deliberately resisted in the Markan tradition, with its lack of emphasis on Mary and apparent rejection of her importance (Mk 3.31-35 and parallels). The Markan concern to play down the family of Jesus seems to have been a foil to its dominance in the early Church, perhaps to resist, with the Pauline tradition, the family's continued faithfulness to the Jewish law. If that is the case, the strong Marian images in Luke may have been a rebuttal of Mark's negativity.[57] This reminds us that a plurality of traditions existed in the earliest Christian communities, which is likely to be reflected in their varying assessments of the importance of Mary.

BIBLIOGRAPHY

Abrahamsen, V. (2005), 'Human and divine: the Marys in early Christian tradition', in A-J. Levine, with M. M. Robbins (eds), *A Feminist Companion to Mariology*. Cleveland: The Pilgrim Press, 164–81.

Aune, D. E. (1998), *Word Biblical Commentary Volume 52B: Revelation 6–16*. Nashville: Thomas Nelson.

Bauckham, R. (1990), *Jude and the Relatives of Jesus in the Early Church*. Edinburgh: T.&T. Clark.

—— (2002), *Gospel Women: Studies of the Named Women in the Gospels*. London: T.&T. Clark.

—— (2006), *Jesus and the Eyewitnesses: the Gospels as Eyewitness Testimony*. Grand Rapids: Eerdmans.

Bechtel, L. M. (1996), 'A symbolic level of meaning: John 2.1–11 (the marriage in Cana)', in A. Brenner (ed.), *A Feminist Companion to the Hebrew Bible in the New Testament* (*The Feminist Companion to the Bible* 10). Sheffield: Sheffield Academic Press, 241–55.

Benko, S. (2004), *The Virgin Goddess: Studies in the Pagan and Christian Roots of Mariology* (*Studies in the History of Religions* 59). Leiden: E. J. Brill.

Bernheim, P-A. (1997), *James, Brother of Jesus*, trans. J. Bowden. London: SCM Press.

Borgeaud, P. (2004), *Mother of the Gods: From Cybele to the Virgin Mary*, trans. Lysa Hochroth. Baltimore/London: John Hopkins University Press.

Boss, S. (2007), 'Editor's Introduction', in S. Boss (ed.), *Mary: the Complete Resource*. London/New York: Continuum, 1–7.

Bovon, F. (2002), *Luke 1: A Commentary on the Gospel of Luke 1:1–9:50*, trans. C. M. Thomas. Minneapolis: Fortress Press.

Boxall, I. (2006), *The Revelation of Saint John*. London: Hendrickson/Continuum.

Bradshaw, P. F. (2002), *The Search for the Origins of Christian Worship: Sources and Methods for the Study of Early Liturgy* (rev. edn). London: SPCK.

Brown, R. E. (1993), *The Birth of the Messiah: a Commentary on the Infancy Narratives of Matthew and Luke*. London: Geoffrey Chapman.

Brown, R. E., K. P. Donfried, J. A. Fitzmyer and J. Reumann (eds) (1978), *Mary in the New Testament*. London: Geoffrey Chapman.

Burridge, R. A. (1992), *What are the Gospels?: a Comparison with Graeco-Roman Biography*. Cambridge: Cambridge University Press.

Chilton, B. and J. Neusner (eds) (2001), *The Brother of Jesus: James the Just and his Mission*. Louisville: Westminster John Knox.

Coleridge, M. (1993), *The Birth of the Lukan Narrative: Narrative as Christology in Luke 1–2* (*Journal for the Study of the New Testament* Supplement Series 88). Sheffield: Sheffield Academic Press.

Corley, K. E. (2002), *Women and the Historical Jesus: Feminist Myths of Christian Origins*. Santa Rosa: Polebridge Press.

Crossan, J. D. (2005), 'Virgin mother or bastard child', in A-J. Levine with M. M. Robbins (eds), *A Feminist Companion to Mariology*. Cleveland: The Pilgrim Press, 37–55.

D'Angelo, M. R. (1999), 'Reconstructing "real" women in gospel literature: the case of Mary Magdalene', in R. S. Kraemer and M. R. D'Angelo (eds), *Women and Christian Origins*. Oxford: Oxford University Press, 105–28.

Davidson, J. (2005), *The Odes of Solomon: Mystical Songs from the Time of Jesus*. Bath: Clear Press.

Edwards, M. (2004), *John*. Oxford: Blackwell.

Elliott, J. K. (1974), 'The anointing of Jesus', *Expository Times* 85, 105–7.

Eusebius (1965), *The History of the Church from Christ to Constantine*, trans. G. A. Williamson. Harmondsworth: Penguin.

Fehribach, A. (1998), *The Women in the Life of the Bridegroom: a Feminist Historical-Literary Analysis of the Female Characters in the Fourth Gospel*. Collegeville: Michael Glazier/The Liturgical Press.

Foskett, M. F. (2002), *A Virgin Conceived: Mary and Classical Representations of Virginity*. Bloomington/Indianapolis: Indiana University Press.

Gaventa, B. R. (1999), *Mary: Glimpses of the Mother of Jesus* (new edn). Edinburgh: T.&T. Clark.

Haskins, S. (2005), *Mary Magdalen: Myth and Metaphor*. London: Pimlico.

Hengel, M. (1985), *Studies in the Gospel of Mark*. London: SCM Press.

Jones, F. S. (ed.) (2002), *Which Mary?: the Marys of Early Christian Tradition*. Atlanta: Society of Biblical Literature.

Keener, C. S. (2003), *The Gospel of John: a Commentary, Volume 1*. Peabody: Hendrickson.

Klauck, H-J. (2003), *Apocryphal Gospels: an Introduction*. London: T.&T. Clark.

Koester, C. R. (2003), *Symbolism in the Fourth Gospel: Meaning, Mystery, Community*. Minneapolis: Fortress Press.

Kovacs, J., and C. Rowland (2004), *The Apocalypse of Jesus Christ*. Oxford: Blackwell.

Kraemer, R. S. (1999), 'Jewish women and Christian origins: some caveats', in R. S. Kraemer and M. R. D'Angelo (eds), *Women and Christian Origins*. Oxford: Oxford University Press, 35–49.

LiDonnici, L. R. (1999), 'Women's religions and religious lives in the Greco-Roman city', in R. S. Kraemer and M. R. D'Angelo (eds), *Women and Christian Origins*. Oxford: Oxford University Press, 80–102.

Lieu, J. (1996), 'Scripture and the feminine in John', in A. Brenner (ed.), *A Feminist Companion to the Hebrew Bible in the New Testament* (*The Feminist Companion to the Bible* 10). Sheffield: Sheffield Academic Press, 225–40.

—— (1998), 'The Mother of the Son in the fourth gospel', *Journal of Biblical Literature* 117/1, 61–77.

Maunder, C. (2007), 'Mary in the New Testament and Apocrypha', in S. Boss (ed.), *Mary: the Complete Resource*. London/New York: Continuum, 11–46.

Miller, R. J. (ed.) (1994), *The Complete Gospels: Annotated Scholars Version*. San Francisco: Harper/Polebridge Press.

Moloney, F. J. (2004), *Mark – Storyteller, Interpreter, Evangelist*. Peabody: Hendrickson.

Osborne, G. R. (2002), *Revelation*. Grand Rapids: Baker Academic.

Ricci, C. (1994), *Mary Magdalene and Many Others: Women who Followed Jesus*, trans. P. Burns. Tunbridge Wells: Burns & Oates.

Sawyer, D. (2002), *God, Gender and the Bible*. London: Routledge.

Schaberg, J. (1995), *The Illegitimacy of Jesus: a Feminist Theological Interpretation of the Infancy Narratives*. Sheffield: Sheffield Academic Press.

—— (2002), *The Resurrection of Mary Magdalene: Legends, Apocrypha, and the Christian Testament*. New York: Continuum.

35

Schneiders, S. M. (1999), *Written that You May Believe: Encountering Jesus in the Fourth Gospel.* New York: Herder & Herder/Crossroad.

Schüssler Fiorenza, E. (1983), *In Memory of Her: a Feminist Theological Reconstruction of Christian Origins.* London: SCM Press.

—— (1992), *But She Said: Feminist Practices of Biblical Intepretation.* Boston: Beacon Press.

—— (1995), *Jesus, Miriam's Child, Sophia's Prophet: Critical Issues in Feminist Christology.* London: SCM Press.

—— (2006), 'Babylon the great: a rhetorical-political reading of Revelation 17–18', in D. L. Barr (ed.), *The Reality of Apocalypse: Rhetoric and Politics in the Book of Revelation.* Atlanta: Society of Biblical Literature, 243–69.

Streete, G. C. (1999), 'Women as sources of redemption and knowledge in early Christian traditions', in R. S. Kraemer and M. R. D'Angelo (eds), *Women and Christian Origins.* Oxford: Oxford University Press, 33–54.

Talbert, C. H. (2003), *Reading Luke-Acts in its Mediterranean Milieu.* Leiden: Brill.

Zeitlin, F. I. (1996), *Playing the Other: Gender and Society in Classical Greek Literature.* Chicago: University of Chicago.

The Bible version used is the *New Revised Standard Version* (Anglicized edn). Oxford: Oxford University Press (1995).

NOTES

1. Schüssler Fiorenza 1983.
2. Schüssler Fiorenza 1995: 187.
3. Schüssler Fiorenza 1992: 80–1 accepts that 'feminist historical reconstruction cannot distil "factual truth" from discursive representations'. It can, however, 'examine the exclusions and choices that constitute historical knowledge'.
4. Ricci 1994.
5. Schneiders 1999.
6. Fehribach 1998.
7. Kraemer 1999: 35–49; Sawyer 2002; Corley 2002.
8. Corley 2002: 146.
9. For example, a literary approach to Mary can be found in Gaventa 1999.
10. Burridge 1992.
11. Fehribach 1998: 42.
12. Zeitlin 1996: 356–7. Sawyer 2002: 103 gives Herodias as an example of how women in biblical literature can often be represented as devious and manipulative.
13. Keener 2003: 506. For Bauckham 2002: 76, Mary in Luke 1–2 is God's agent.
14. Zeitlin 1996: 112–14. Streete 1999: 33–54 notes how women were regarded as conduits to divine knowledge in both ancient Judaism and paganism.
15. D'Angelo 1999: 105–28 shows how difficult it is to recover the 'real' Mary Magdalene. For the development of the Mary Magdalene tradition, see Schaberg 2002 and Haskins 2005.
16. Corley 2002: 107–39 examines the Gospel traditions about the tomb of Jesus; although women will have been integral to funerary traditions in the ancient world, there are points of departure between the texts and what we know of history, particularly in the lack of lamentation by the Gospel women. LiDonnici 1999: 80–102 also reviews the divergence between the real and the ideal portrayed in classical literature.
17. Sawyer 2002: 103.
18. Bauckham 2006. Mary is listed among named characters in the Gospels, but nowhere does Bauckham expand on her possible role as an eyewitness.
19. Bauckham 2002: 47–76.

20. Brown 1993: 698.
21. Also Bovon 2002: 43–4. See Boss 2007: 2–4 on Luke's depiction of Mary as the Ark of the Covenant, and the association with Wisdom (for which also see Margaret Barker's contribution to this volume).
22. Thus reinforcing the view that Mary is presented as a literary type, rather than being the subject of biography. For Mary representing Israel, see Foskett 2002: 129–30, and as the *anawim* or poor of Israel, Brown *et al.* 1978: 142–3.
23. Talbert 2003: 73. See Bovon 2002: 45–6 on the virgin birth of Isaac as allegory in Philo, and conceptions by gods in other classical mythologies.
24. Bovon 2002: 47.
25. Crossan 2005: 53–5.
26. Bovon 2002: 45; Benko 2004: 108–15.
27. Borgeaud 2004: 127. Foskett 2002: 128–32 points out the link between virginity and the gift of prophecy, in classical representations.
28. Benko 2004: 113–14 notes that the first known Christian reference to the link between Virgil's poem and the Virgin Birth dates from the fourth century.
29. Talbert 2003: 87–8. In addition, Bovon 2002: 49 thinks virginity is important to the early Christians, giving Acts 21.9; 1 Cor. 7.25; Rev. 14.4 as references.
30. *Odes of Solomon*: Davidson 2005; *Gospel of Philip*: Klauck 2003: 123–34; *Gospel of the Hebrews*: Klauck 2003: 38–42.
31. The one place where the mother of Jesus is important to the incarnation in the New Testament is, of course, Gal. 4.4, but Paul does not identify Mary or accord any significance to her individually.
32. Edwards 2004: 183 cites Augustine, *Homily* 119.1, as identifying the 'hour' in Jn 2.4 as the crucifixion; Lieu 1998: 67 explores the links between John 2 (Cana) and 19 (the crucifixion), and looks at birth metaphors in John (Lieu 1996: 237–8); Keener 2003: 508 compares other classical usage of the idea of the 'hour' as the fated time.
33. For example, Aune 1998: 667–74; Boxall 2006: 126–7; Osborne 2002: 454. See also Barker's contribution to this volume, as she puts more emphasis on the Jewish Wisdom/Temple background to the Revelation vision.
34. Benko 2004: 108–15 looks at the astrological and zodiacal connotations of the woman of Revelation 12; Boxall 2006: 178 prefers to link the stars to the twelve tribes of Israel. Of course, these may not be mutually exclusive.
35. Boxall 2006: 181; Koester 2003: 118; Schüssler Fiorenza 2006: 265.
36. Boxall 2006: 179; Benko 2004: 131–6; Kovacs and Rowland 2004: 136–7. The first suggestion of a Marian association with the woman of Revelation 12 is made by Epiphanius (fourth century); after this, it is not explicit until the sixth century.
37. Of course, I do not mean to imply that the inclusion of the Holy Spirit is only meant to avoid controversy; the theology is far more positive (see e.g. Boss 2007: 3).
38. Schaberg 1995.
39. Kovacs and Rowland 2004: 294.
40. There are no obvious precedents in the intertestamental pseudepigrapha or Qumran literature for the sequence: giving birth – marriage. It can only be found in the New Testament, and so one would have to posit an early Christian provenance for it. The most likely influence is an allegorical interpretation of Isa. 7.14, as reflected in Mt. 1.23. There is, of course, a possibility that the same sequence of birth – marriage lies behind the positioning of the Cana story in John's Gospel, at an early point in the ministry. The birth theme would then relate to the ideas in the prologue, on the incarnation of the Word and the spiritual birth of believers. Edwards 2004: 36 cites Augustine, *On the Trinity* 8.4, as believing that the marriage at Cana prefigured the heavenly nuptials of the eschatological marriage.
41. Bauckham 2006.

42. *Ibid.*: 124–47.
43. Although the mother of Jesus is not named in John's Gospel, of course. Koester 2003: 240 does see an *inclusio* in John 2 and 19.
44. Coleridge 1993: 218.
45. On anonymity, various interpreters do not necessarily see it as derogatory. For example, the mother of Jesus and the Beloved Disciple are anonymous in John's Gospel. Bauckham 2006: 183–201; Moloney 2004: 186–7; Keener 2003: 502 see its use in Mark and John as helping to bring the reader into the story, identifying with the anonymous figure.
46. For example, the *Gospel of Thomas* 114 (Miller 1994: 322) and the *Gospel of Mary* 10.30-4 (*Ibid.*: 365).
47. Hengel 1985: 54.
48. The messianic symbolism of the anointing on the head in Mark's and Matthew's (26.6-13) versions was noted by Elliott 1974 and Schüssler Fiorenza 1983: 152–3. Both John's (12.1-6) and Luke's (7.36-50) very different versions have the anointing on the feet.
49. On Markan negativity about Mary and the family of Jesus: Brown *et al.* 1978: 286–7. Recent works on James and other relatives of Jesus (Bauckham 1990; Bernheim 1997; Chilton and Neusner 2001) demonstrate how much their importance was played down in the Gospel tradition. There is the possibility that Mark's Gospel speaks about the distance between Jesus and his family (3.21, 31-5) in order to encourage Christians disowned by their families (ref. 13.12). In the same vein, the faith of the brothers of Jesus is also portrayed negatively in John (7.1-9), but Keener 2003: 705 thinks that this story challenges Jesus' disciples generally to have faith. Nevertheless, the split between Paul and James (Gal. 2.11-14) may have meant that the influential relatives of Jesus came to represent a conservative holding to the Jewish law in the eyes of the Gospel communities.
50. For discussions about the identity of the women at the cross, see Brown *et al.* 1978: 68–72 and Bauckham 2002: 203–23. I am in agreement with Bauckham 2006: 49: 'The divergences among the lists [of women at the cross and tomb] have often been taken as grounds for not taking them seriously as naming eyewitnesses of the events. In fact, the opposite is the case: these divergences, properly understood, demonstrate the scrupulous care with which the Gospels present the women as eyewitnesses.' I am emphasizing the maternal status of several of the prominent women more than Bauckham does here (but see his 2002: 213).
51. The uncertainty about whether the relationship is 'mother', 'wife' or even 'daughter' is because the Greek genitive does not specify in these cases.
52. Eusebius 1965: 123–4 = 3.11; 142–3 = 3.32; 181–2 = 4.21. Bauckham 2002: 209–11 therefore deduces that Mary of Clopas was Symeon's mother.
53. Hengel 1985: 54. I am not making any exaggerated claim to know anything about the form of the Christian liturgy of the New Testament period (agreeing with the caution of Bradshaw 2002). My suggestion is modest and follows Hengel: the names of people who were important eyewitnesses to the Passion and Easter events may have been recounted in the retelling of the stories which probably was, at certain times, liturgical.
54. I have discussed elsewhere (Maunder 2007: 20–3) the possibility, assumed by some writers in the early Church and gaining support again today, that Mary, the mother of James and Joses, is to be identified as another name for Mary the mother of Jesus. Certainly, a person with no familiarity with New Testament interpretation would conclude so on the basis of comparing Mk 15.40 with 6.3. A comparison with Jn 19.25 may go even further to suggest that Mary of Clopas was also the same person. The best explanation for a variety of relationships associated with one woman is that the combination of her name with that of an important apostle or apostles meant something to early

Christian communities as they remembered the crucifixion. The adoption of the Beloved Disciple in Jn 19.26-27 may be linked to this. If that is the case, then the argument for some kind of devotion to Mary in the New Testament period would be considerably strengthened.

55. Bechtel 1996: 248, 254–5 explores the symbolism of Mary at the cross, reiterating older interpretations in which she is seen as representing Judaism.

56. The collection of papers in Jones 2002 examines the name Mary in the apocryphal literature, and notes how the usual identification of her as the Magdalene can be debated (although the general consensus is that it is correct). Because of 'Mary of Bethany', the lack of clarity about who is intended by the name 'Mary' is already present in the New Testament, as Abrahamsen 2005: 164–81 rightly observes.

57. A point made by John McGuckin in his chapter (n. 10).

3

THE ORIGINS OF MARIAN ART IN THE CATACOMBS AND THE PROBLEMS OF IDENTIFICATION

GERI PARLBY

Over the past decade, scholars from a variety of different disciplines have started to turn their attention to the early centuries of Christianity in their search for the real origins of the cult of the Virgin Mary. Texts are being re-examined, theological controversies reconsidered and pictorial evidence rediscovered.[1]

One of the most inspiring developments of this growth in early Marian studies has been the launch of the International Early Mariology Project, an initiative dedicated to producing a database of textual and archaeological evidence relating to Mary up to the Council of Ephesus.[2] The image that adorns the website of the Project is a sketch of one of the most iconic portraits of early Christian art, a third-century fresco of a mother and child from the Catacomb of Priscilla (Figure 1). The official guidebook to the Catacombs of Priscilla published by the Pontifical Commission for Sacred Archaeology tells us unequivocally that this fresco is the oldest known portrait of the Virgin Mary and dates it to the beginning of the third century, so it is perhaps understandable that the Project would have chosen it as their logo.[3]

The guidebook is not alone in confidently labelling it as the earliest image of Mary; most books on early Christian and Marian art include details of the fresco.[4] When used as an illustration, the image is usually reproduced in the same manner, a closely cropped photograph with no indication of the fresco's size or position, so unless the reader had actually seen the image *in situ* they would be excused for thinking that it was a large and very prominent portrait of the holy couple.

In fact, far from commanding pride of place in the underground cemetery, this relatively small image was originally painted vertically in an inconspicuous corner of one of the oldest parts of the Catacomb of Priscilla. As we can see from the sketch of the whole tomb in Figure 2, it plays second fiddle to a far more prominent stucco image of a good shepherd figure that once formed part of a pair.

Yet in spite of its odd angle, the overall composition of this fresco does indeed provide us with an acceptable and even comforting image of Mary as a practical-looking mother, her head loosely veiled, her sleeves rolled up to reveal a sturdy arm as she holds a chubby infant at her breast. In front of the seated mother and child stands another figure dressed in an off-the-shoulder *pallium*, holding a scroll in one hand, who appears to be pointing to a faint outline of a star above their heads. Although this figure has been identified as representing a variety of

Figure 1: Mother and Child fresco from the Catacomb of Priscilla – Pontifical Commission for Sacred Archaeology.

Old Testament prophets, the most favoured choice is Balaam, who is said to have foretold the birth of Christ when he uttered the fateful words, 'A star shall come forth out of Jacob and a sceptre shall rise out of Israel' (Num. 24.15-17).[5]

Overall, this tableau is a familiar and reassuring image that – taken at face value – appears to provide pictorial evidence that the Christian community in Rome venerated Mary from at least as early as the first half of the third century. Unfortunately, few things in early Christian art are quite that straightforward and I suggest that several anomalies need to be reviewed before accepting such a sweeping interpretation of the meaning of this fresco.

It is helpful that a thorough analysis was undertaken in 1992 when Professor Fabrizio Bisconti and a team from the Pontifical Commission of Sacred Archaeology conducted some emergency restoration work on the fresco.[6] The fluorescent lights in the catacombs had started to create the growth of algae on the plaster that was seriously damaging the paint. Bisconti discovered much about the decorative scheme of the whole tableau during the restoration. Firstly, he analysed the surviving shepherd who takes centre stage in the tableau, dating it to between 220 and 230. This image is actually a stucco figure, an unusual decorative scheme within the catacombs as the damp atmosphere caused a rapid degeneration in plasterwork. Indeed, it seems that large chunks of the figures fell off the wall almost as soon as the work had been created, leaving only one shepherd still in place.

A few years after the creation of the shepherds, Bisconti suggests that the burial niche was enlarged and turned into an arched recess known as an *arcosolium*. During this extension, the artists decided to abandon the use of stucco and revert to traditional fresco technique. Bisconti deduced that between 230 and 240, two frescoes were painted at the end of the arch. On the left side the faintest traces of yellow ochre remain and on the right side is the mother and child image we see today.

The final stage of the development probably took place around the middle of the third century and that included a painting of a pointing figure on one side of the burial niche and two *orans* or praying figures on the other side. The nineteenth-century drawing of the tomb in Figure 2 gives some idea as to how the full tableau may have looked originally.

There are, of course, no inscriptions to indicate whom the figures in the tableau are supposed to represent and yet the fresco was confidently identified as Mary and the child Jesus when it was rediscovered and documented by the

Figure 2: Drawing of the original decorative scheme of the Priscilla Arcosolium (from Northcote and Brownlow 1879).

Maltese explorer Antonio Bosio, the man responsible for the first systematic exploration of the catacombs in the sixteenth and seventeenth centuries. Over several years, Bosio recorded almost every fresco, sarcophagus and artefact discovered in the many catacombs he explored. After his death in 1629, his records and drawings were published and still form one of the most important sources of reference for scholars studying early Christian art.[7]

Bosio's discoveries in the aftermath of the Counter-Reformation could not have been more timely; the Catholic Church had already reaffirmed the importance of the veneration of the Virgin Mary at the Council of Trent. The rediscovered wall paintings were cited by Catholic scholars as evidence that art had always been an integral part of early Christian practice, but more importantly that the early Christians had revered Mary in the same way as the Church still did. As Leonard Rutgers has pointed out: 'the fact that catacomb archaeology originated in counter-reformist Europe has had an enormous impact on the way it has been interpreted.'[8]

Because of the lack of inscriptions on the wall paintings, Bosio and his fellow archaeologists developed a method of interpretation using biblical and patristic literature as their source. Where possible the images were linked to a scene from the Bible or from the writings of the Church Fathers. No thought was given to the many artistic traditions that were already in place in funerary art of the late antique period.[9]

This tendency to see only what they wanted and expected can be found in the disturbingly inaccurate sketches made by earlier explorers and their copyists. Alphonso Chacon, a sixteenth-century Spanish Dominican also known as Ciacconio, and two Flemish laymen, Philip de Winghe and Jean L'Heureux, commissioned artists to copy some of the frescoes that had been discovered. Carried away with religious enthusiasm, the copyists appear to have misinterpreted what they saw and transposed the images into an almost contemporary setting. A good shepherd figure was transformed into a girl in a farmyard and Ciacconio described the fresco as representing 'St Priscilla feeding the preachers of the gospel, represented as cocks, and the faithful Christians as sheep'.[10]

Yet strangely enough, a sketch that Bosio made of the Priscilla mother and child fresco seems surprisingly accurate (Figure 3). It shows the seated woman with coiled and braided hair set into a high bun with her veil pinned loosely on top. This is a style of coiffure popular in the third and fourth centuries, and closely resembles several other frescoes of women found in the catacombs. In this instance, Bosio seems to have drawn accurately what he saw on the wall of the catacomb and yet this image bears little resemblance to the way the fresco looks today (Figure 1). It could be suggested that the change has come about through the natural wear and tear of time, but in my opinion the difference has been brought about by what is best described as 'creative restoration' work which seems to have been conducted within the last two centuries.

Bosio's sketch (Figure 3) includes two more anomalies. There is no star above the head of the woman and the figure standing in front of them is clearly pointing at them and not up into the sky.

The drawing in Figure 2 was taken from the Vatican-sponsored magazine, the

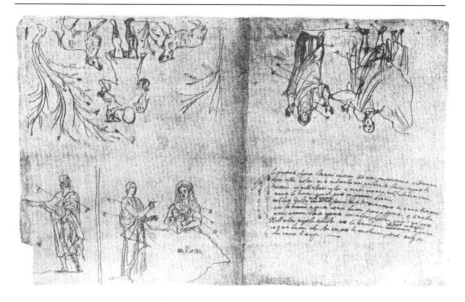

Figure 3: Drawing of the original decorative scheme of the Priscilla Arcosolium *from Antonio Bosio's sketchbook.*

Bullettino di Archaeologica Christiani, published in 1865 by the Italian archaeologist Giovanni de Rossi, and reprinted in 1879 in an English two-volume interpretation of de Rossi's work also entitled *Roma Sotterranea*, compiled by Revs J. Spencer Northcote and William Brownlow (Figure 4).[11]

This drawing provides us with a very clear impression of the layout of the *arcosolium* and the position of the Virgin, child and prophet image. Here once again we have no obvious star, but the prophet's finger seems now to be pointing up rather than across, and the head of Mary has changed dramatically, something shown even more clearly in a close-up featured later in the book (Figure 4). In both illustrations, she has lost her elaborate hairstyle and seems to be wearing a simple veil fitting closely to her head. She also appears to be bending her head towards the child, very unlike the upright pose adopted by the Bosio Virgin and more in keeping with the maternal images of Mary not seen in Christian art before at least the sixth century.[12]

This anomaly becomes even more puzzling when we look at the work of Father Josef Wilpert, a pupil of de Rossi who had adopted photography as a way of recording his work. His groundbreaking study of the catacombs, *Die Malereien der Katakomben Roms*, published in 1903, included several colour plates of the *arcosolium* in Priscilla. There is no doubt that Father Wilpert was a resolute scholar; he was a German Jesuit priest who had devoted himself to the study of the catacombs. He was also a skilled restorer and we have him and his team to thank for revealing some of the most beautiful paintings of the catacombs, such as the 'Fractio Panis' fresco in the Catacomb of Priscilla, lost for centuries under whitewash and calcification.[13]

Figure 4: Engraving of Mother and Child fresco from Catacomb of Priscilla (from Northcote and Brownlow 1879).

However, many modern scholars describe much of Wilpert's work in disparaging terms, blaming him for creating a huge gulf between the diverse Christian and non-Christian traditions.[14] Indeed, he was immoveable regarding his identification of images in the catacombs. In the early part of the twentieth century, there was a growing sense of unease amongst non-Catholic archaeologists as to the way Roman Catholic archaeologists were interpreting the catacomb art; Wilpert had regular battles with anyone who dared to question his findings.[15] One area where he was especially protective was in his identification of Marian images. He once informed a critic that:

These paintings . . . better than any written document from the period of the persecutions, characterise the position of Mary in the Church of the first four centuries and show that, in terms of substance, she was the same person then that she would later become.[16]

His use of coloured photographs revolutionized the study of early Christian art and the methods he used to produce his colour plates were an art form in their own right. Using photographs printed onto special paper, he would return to the catacomb with a watercolour artist who would handpaint the prints. The publishers then sent the painted photos to a graphics firm to match the exact colours for printing.

Wilpert published two painted photographs of the complete fresco in *Die Malereien der Katakomben Roms*. The first image shows Mary in a pose almost identical to the Bosio sketch. Her head is upright and she wears her hair piled high covered with a light veil. However, on the next page we are confronted by what could easily be described as a completely different image. The colours are lighter, but more importantly the woman's head is now very definitely inclined to the left and she is wearing a closely fitting veil which follows the contours of her head. Rather puzzlingly, this image appears far more like the de Rossi sketch published by Brownlow and Northcote two decades earlier (Figure 2) than the first photograph.

Things become even more confusing when we then compare the first Wilpert photo with a more recent photograph of the complete tableau taken by the Pontifical Commission of Sacred Archaeology (PCSA) in Rome. In this photograph, although the stucco of the shepherd is clearly the same, the fresco is very different. Wilpert's version shows the reddish-brown colour of the paint used to create the border patterns and the fruit on the trees as being of a similar shade to the fresco, whereas in the more recent photograph the fresco is a paler, pinker shade. However, what is even more noticeable is the difference between the two female figures, with the PCSA photograph featured in Figure 1 looking identical to the second of Wilpert's images.

One possible reason for the disparity between the images could be that between the time the first and second photographs were taken Wilpert had the outline of the head of the women re-traced.[17] When confronted by the rapidly deteriorating fresco and with his total commitment to the presence of Marian images, he may have felt justified in engaging in some judicious touching up, perhaps even using the earlier de Rossi drawing as his inspiration. In the process he produced a far more idealized view of Mary, an image more in keeping with the ideas of some of the contemporary artists of the nineteenth century such as Jean-Auguste-Dominique Ingres.

Bisconti certainly uncovered evidence of changes in the painting: whereas the mother and child tableau is painted fresco style, parts of the standing figure and the star were painted dry onto false plaster and in an entirely different artistic style. This seems to indicate that the design of the fresco was first changed at some point after Bosio sketched it in the sixteenth century and in the process the standing figure's hand was redirected upwards and a dazzling star painted into the sky above.

Bisconti also suggests that the praying figures illustrated in Figure 2 that once decorated the other side of the tomb were intended to represent a dead husband and wife, with the figure on the opposite wall pointing towards them to indicate their presence in the tomb.[18] If this was the case, then rather than pointing to the star as evidence of the prophecy of the arrival of Christ, the original purpose of the 'prophet' figure may have been to point to the mother and child as earlier occupants of the tomb.

Instead of being the oldest image of the Madonna and child, the fresco in the Catacomb of Priscilla may be nothing more than a poignant funerary portrait of a dead mother and child. Indeed, I would suggest that this same interpretation could be applied to the other so-called early images of Mary within the catacombs.

Outside the narrative setting of the Annunciation and the Adoration of the Magi, there are only two other wall paintings found in the catacombs that have been identified as representing Mary and Jesus. Up until as recently as the early 1990s, an image of a seated mother and child dated to the end of the third century and also found within the Catacomb of Priscilla was regularly cited as being one of the earliest images of the Madonna and child (Figure 5). However, as with the first example, this image formed part of a more detailed tableau. When Bosio discovered the fresco around the beginning of the seventeenth century, he described it as representing the patron of the cemetery 'the holy matron St Priscilla' standing in a praying pose. The scene to the left of 'Priscilla' he identified as depicting her daughter Praxedis or Pudentiana taking the veil in a ceremony conducted by Pope Pius with the assistance of the deacon pastor.

In the nineteenth century Wilpert seems to have agreed with Bosio's interpretation and was confident that the seated woman and child were Mary and Jesus and that the bishop or Pope is pointing towards the seated Mary, suggesting to his new initiate that she should emulate her. As we have already seen, Wilpert was not without his critics and some of his contemporaries were sceptical of his interpretation, suggesting instead that this tableau represented the traditional style of funerary art with narrative scenes from the life of the deceased.[19]

In spite of this scepticism, the identification of the seated figure as Mary holding the baby Jesus continued throughout the last century. John Beckwith's *Early Christian Art*, first published in 1970, identified the fresco as 'possibly a very early Virgin and Child' and this photo caption was still in place in the 1993

Figure 5: Engraving of the Presentation of the Veil and Mother and Child fresco from the Chamber of the Veiling in the Catacomb of Priscilla (from Palmer and Northcote 1859).

Figure 6: Engraving of the fresco of the praying Mother and Son from the Coemeterium Maius Cemetery (from Bosio 1632).

reprint.[20] Nowadays most scholars acknowledge that it probably is a narrative scene from the life of the deceased, although it does still appear in some mainstream publications as an early image of Mary.[21]

The next contender for the title of earliest image of the Virgin Mary is in the lunette of an *arcosolium* in the Coemeterium Maius cemetery not far from the basilica of Sant Agnese (Figure 6). The painting shows a richly dressed, lightly veiled woman, her arms outstretched in prayer, with the head and shoulders of a boy resting against her chest. On either side of her are painted Chi-Rho monograms.[22] Bosio and de Rossi identified the image as a fourth-century painting of the Madonna and child, although not everyone was convinced.[23]

Once again, to understand the concept of the image we need to look at the fresco in context and it is Bosio's illustration that gives us the best sense of the original setting of this tableau. The central figure is the mother and child and the figure on the ceiling is usually identified as Christ. However, on the sidewalls facing each other are two praying figures of an older man and woman. In the light of these accompanying images, I would suggest that this chamber is far more likely to be a family crypt with individual portraits of the occupants.

So if the previous frescoes are not early portraits of Mary, where else should we be looking to discover the prototype of the first image of Mary in Christian art? Catacomb artists favoured narrative scenes from both the Old and New Testaments and one of the key Marian scenes that inspired later artists was of course the Annunciation, usually depicted with Mary seated and being approached by the angel Gabriel. However, this imagery does not feature in Luke's version of the story, but comes instead from the apocryphal *Protevangelium of James*, generally dated to the second century. In this text, Mary is first approached by the angel while she is drawing water from a stream; startled, she runs to her house, sits down and starts nervously to unravel a skein of thread, whereupon the angel approaches her for a second time.[24] Rather surprisingly, the stories from the *Protevangelium* do not seem to have inspired the catacomb artists in Rome and in fact the earliest example of an image said to illustrate the apocryphal description of the Annunciation comes from the lid of a sarcophagus found in the catacomb of San Giovanni in Syracuse, dated to around 340.[25]

Even so, the two examples of the Annunciation that have been identified by scholars both feature a seated woman being confronted by a pointing man. The oldest of these images can be found on the ceiling of a chamber in the Catacomb of Priscilla. The 'angel' is dressed in the robes of a Roman senator and he stands before a seated woman with his right hand raised as a sign that he is speaking. Bosio discovered the fresco during his work on the catacombs and his sketch in *Roma Sotterranea* is of a seated woman veiled and looking downcast (Figure 7). However, the surviving fresco shows a far more regal-looking figure seated upright and confidently meeting the eye of the male figure opposite her. Conservation work carried out in 1996 observed that there had been a considerable amount of damage done to the fresco by 'high humidity, vandalism and previous works of conservation', so it is hard to know accurately how the scene was first designed.[26]

Figure 7: Engraving of the 'Annunciation' scene from the Catacomb of Priscilla (from Bosio 1632).

Figure 8: Engraving of sarcophagus featuring the Adoration of the Magi (from Bosio 1632).

As with our first Madonna and child fresco in the Catacomb of Priscilla, perhaps the seated woman was intended to represent an image of the deceased. In his analysis of the Priscilla Madonna and child, Bisconti describes this artistic style as part of a range of 'figurative situations in the funerary space like those of commendation, with the deceased seated solemnly on a throne, in dramatic and suspended conversation with the survivors/living'.[27]

The only other example of the Annunciation, also dated to the fourth century, shows a couple in a similar pose and was first discovered by the intrepid Wilpert in the Catacomb of SS Peter and Marcellinus. As the catacomb was enlarged and embellished by Pope Damasus in the fourth century and then again in the fifth, sixth and seventh centuries, it is hard to be sure how much of the original decoration is still intact, and so an accurate interpretation of the scheme is beyond the scope of this paper.

The sparseness of Annunciation scenes and indeed the complete absence of Nativity scenes in the catacomb frescoes seem to be more than made up for by the vast array of Adoration of the Magi images in both frescoes and sarcophagi carving.[28] The iconography of this tableau is standard and depicts a woman seated in a high-backed chair holding a young child on her lap (Figure 8). The couple are usually facing a group of figures varying between two and four men who are approaching on foot and holding a variety of objects they are preparing to present to the seated child. The figures are normally dressed in pointed

Phrygian caps and wear leggings and tunics in the style of eastern barbarians. To show they have travelled a distance, they are often portrayed with their cloaks billowing as if they are still in motion.

Since the days of Bosio, these scenes have almost without question been interpreted as the Adoration of the Magi, an episode that appears only in the Gospel of Matthew. The Gospel does not specify how many wise men there were and the traditional number of three is probably based on the number of gifts mentioned.

The Adoration was one of the most popular pictorial narrative scenes in early Christian art in Rome and one of the oldest paintings of this tableau can be found on the archway of the Greek chapel in the Catacomb of Priscilla. Although the numbers and the gifts they carry may vary, the Magi are almost always identically dressed in the type of clothes contemporary Roman artists used to illustrate barbarians from the east. Matthew tells us that the wise men came from the East, so it seems logical to portray them in the generic dress of the region, an artistic tradition that is well illustrated amongst the sculpted friezes of the triumphal arches of Rome.

There are many different theories as to what the Adoration scene is meant to represent; these vary from Christ in the role of emperor triumphant over the pagan religions of the East to Christ the magician receiving tribute from the eastern magicians the Magi.[29] From a theological point of view, the Adoration scene is usually interpreted as a representation of the conversion of the first Gentiles to Christianity. Another possible reading is that it was a propaganda exercise against Gnostic and heretical sects. Iconography played a very important part in the religious rivalry that was growing in the Roman East in the early part of the third century. Whether or not the Adoration message was spiritual or political, it would seem logical to assume that the seated mother and child are indeed the earliest images of the Madonna and Child. There is certainly no question that these early Adoration scenes heavily influenced the development of images of the enthroned Mary and Jesus in apse mosaics and icons from the sixth century.

However, when these images were first created two centuries earlier, I believe they were more symbolic than iconic. Rather than a portrait of Mary introducing her baby son to the approaching wise men, what we may be seeing is an allegorical representation of Christianity, the seated figure a personification of *Ecclesia* or the Church presenting Christianity to the Gentile nations.

Indeed, it seems apparent that the Christians who were burying their relatives in the catacombs did not regard the Adoration figures as holy images. One of the engravings in Bosio's *Roma Sotterranea* shows part of an Adoration of the Magi scene on the arch of an *arcosolium* in St Callistus Catacomb (Figure 9). A new *loculus* has been cut directly into the fresco carelessly obliterating the heads of the seated woman and child. If these figures had been regarded as portraits of Mary and Jesus, then this type of vandalism would surely have been regarded as unacceptable by the early Christian community.[30]

Having searched the passageways of the catacombs, it seems we may have been chasing only phantoms of Mary in the early centuries of the Church. However, times were changing, and with Christian art emerging triumphantly from the shadows, Mary's artistic persona was finally taking shape. Key moments from her

uefte fono le figure, che ftanno nella facciata principale del Cubicolo incontro alla Porta, fegna-

Figure 9: Engraving of a fresco from an arcosolium *in St Callistus Catacomb featuring the Adoration of the Magi, Prophecy of Micha and Moses striking the rock with Orpheus taming the wild beasts below (from Bosio 1632).*

life appear billboard-style on the monumental mosaics of Santa Maria Maggiore, the church built in Rome in her honour after the Council of Ephesus in 431. Its triumphal arch is not only a tribute to Mary as the Mother of God, but it also provides us with the first indications of the woman she will become – no longer an elegant *femina clarissima*, but instead a heavily veiled and draped image of the triumphant Church.

BIBLIOGRAPHY

Appell, J. W. (1872), *Monuments of Early Christian Art: Sculptures and Catacomb Paintings.* London: Chapman & Hall.

Beckwith, J. (1993), *Early Christian and Byzantine Art.* New Haven: Yale University Press.

Belan, K. (2001), *Madonnas from Medieval to Modern.* New York: Parkstone Press.

Bisconti, F. (1996), 'La Madonna di Priscilla: Interventi di restauro ed ipotesi sulla dinamica decorativa', *Rivista di archeologia Cristiana* 72, 7–34.

Bosio, A. (1632), *Roma Sotterranea: opera postuma di Antonio Bosio Romano, antiquario ecclesiastico singolare de' suoi tempi. Compits, disposita, et accresciuta dal M. R. P. Giovanni Severani da S. Severino.* Rome: Guglielmo Facciotti Press.

Cameron, A. M. (2000), 'The Early Cult of the Virgin', in M. Vassilaki (ed.), *Mother of God, Representations of the Virgin in Byzantine Art.* Milan: Skira, 3–15.

Carletti, S. (2005), *Guide to the Catacombs of Priscilla,* trans. A. Mulhern. Vatican City: Pontifical Commission for Sacred Archaeology.

Cumont, F. (1922), 'L'Adoration des mages et l'art triumphal de Rome', *Memorie della Pontifica Accademia Romana di Archeologia* 3, 81–105.

Elliott, J. K. (2005), *The Apocryphal New Testament.* Oxford: Clarendon Press.

Grabar, A. (1969), *Christian Iconography: a study of its origins.* London: Routledge.

Katz, M. R. and R. A. Orsi (eds), (2001), *Divine Mirrors: The Virgin Mary in the Visual Arts.* Oxford: Oxford University Press.

Lombardi, A. (ed.) (1998), *Et Lux Fuit: Le catacombe e il sarcofago di Adelfia.* Palermo and Syracuse: Lombardi.

Mancinelli, F. (1981), *Catacombs and Basilicas, The Early Christians in Rome.* Florence: Scala.

Mazzei, B. (1999), 'Il cubicolo dell'Annunciazione nelle catacombe di Priscilla. Nuove Osservazioni all' luce dei recenti restauri', *RAC* 75, 233–80.

Nicolai, V. F., F. Bisconti, and D. Mazzoleni (2002), *The Christian Catacombs of Rome; History, Decoration, Inscriptions* (trans. C. C. Stella and L. A. Touchette). Regensburg: Schnell & Steiner.

Nordhagen, P. J. (1985), 'Working with Wilpert. The Illustrations in "Die römischen Mosaiken und Malereien" and their Source Value', *Acta ad Archaeologiam et Artium Historiam Pertinentia Institutum Romanum Norvegiae* 5, 247–57.

Northcote, J. S., and W. R. Brownlow (1879), *Roma Sotterranea Volume 2.* London: Longmans.

Palmer, W., and J. S. Northcote (1859), *An Introduction to Early Christian Symbolism.* London: Longman, Green, Longman & Roberts.

Partner, P. (1999), *Two Thousand Years, The First Millennium: The Birth of Christianity to the Crusades.* Granada Media (accompanying ITV's 1999 series on the history of Christianity).

Peltomaa, L. M. (2001), *The Image of the Virgin Mary in the Akathistos Hymn* (*The Medieval Mediterranean* 35). Leiden: E. J. Brill.

Rutgers, L. V. (2000), *Subterranean Rome.* Leuven: Peeters.

Schaepman, A. C. M. (1929), *Explanation of the Wallpainting in the Catacomb of Priscilla.* Utrecht: Lekker en van de Vegt.

Shoemaker, S. J. (2002), *Ancient Traditions of the Virgin Mary's Dormition and Assumption* (*Oxford Early Christian Studies*). Oxford: Oxford University Press.

Snyder, G. F. (2003), *Ante Pacem: Archaeological Evidence of Church Life Before Constantine.* Macon: Mercer University Press.

Soper, A. C. (1937), 'The Latin Style on Christian Sarcophagi of the Fourth Century', *The Art Bulletin* 19.2, 148–202.

Stevenson, J. (1978), *The Catacombs: Rediscovered Monuments of Early Christianity.* London: Thames & Hudson.

Swanson, R. N. (ed.) (2004), *Mary and the Church* (*Studies in Church History* 39). Woodbridge: Boydell Press.

Trexler, R. C. (1997), *The Journey of the Magi: Meanings in History of a Christian Story.* Princeton: Princeton University Press.

Vassilaki, M. (ed.) (2005), *Images of the Mother of God: Perceptions of the Theotokos in Byzantium.* Aldershot: Ashgate.

Wilpert, J. (1895), *Fractio Panis: Die älteste Darstellung des eucharistischen Opfers in der 'Capella greca'.* Freiburg: Herder.

—— (1903), *Die Malereien der Katakombem Roms.* Freiburg: Herder.

—— (1930), *Erlebisse und Ergebnisse im Dienste der christlichen Archäologie: Rückblick auf eine fünfundvierzigjährige wissenschaftliche Tätigkeit in Rom.* Freiburg: Herder.

NOTES

1. See Cameron 2000: 3–15 and the Introduction of Vassilaki 2005: xxvii–xxxii; Swanson 2004; Shoemaker 2002; Peltomaa 2001.

2. The International Early Mariology Project was initiated in 2002 by Prof. Pauline Allen and Dr Leena Mari Peltomaa in collaboration with a group of international scholars. Since its inception, it has started to build a database of all reliably dated Greek, Latin and Syriac texts containing references to Mary up to the Council of Ephesus, as well as an alphabetical list of all Marian epithets. See http://www.cecs.acu.edu.au/mariologyproject.htm.

3. Carletti 2005: 23.

4. The most recent example can be found in Katz and Orsi 2001.

5. Other suggestions as to the figure's identity have included Isaiah, Micah, David, Joseph, or even a generic personification of a prophet intended to emphasize the prefiguring of the New Testament by the Old. Nicolai *et al.* 2002: 124–5; Bisconti 1996: 22 nn. 17, 18, 19, 21.

6. Bisconti 1996: 7–34. Translation by the author.

7. Bosio 1632.

8. Rutgers 2000:14.

9. For a critique of the history and methodology of early Christian archaeology, see the revised version of Snyder 2003.

10. Stevenson 1978: 48; Schaepman 1929: 12–13. Unfortunately we are no longer able to study the original frescoes as the rediscovered catacomb was plundered to such an extent that by the end of the century almost every trace of the images had disappeared.

11. Northcote and Brownlow 1879: 138, 139, 226.

12. Cameron 2000: 5.

13. In 1895 Wilpert published a monograph. This was translated into French the next year, and illustrated with photogravures of the fresco. Because the details were difficult to discern, Wilpert included a coloured reproduction in his 1903 two-volume work.

14. Bisconti describes the methodology used for the study of catacomb art at the beginning of the twentieth century as being 'impregnated with powerful apologetic aims, clear confessional character, to a considerable extent defined by speculation, preconceived hermeneutic methods and heavily dogmatic interpretations' (Nicolai *et al.* 2002: 132–3).

15. Wilpert believed his plates of catacomb frescoes and earlier mosaic work to be far superior to any other reproductions of the time and in 1930 published *Erlebisse und Ergebnisse im Dienste der christlichen Archäologie*, in which he rather immodestly praised his painstaking techniques. See Nordhagen 1985: 247–57.

16. Wilpert 1903: 197.

17. Wilpert does appear to have been involved in some restoration work on the tomb. In *Die Malereien der Katakombem Roms* (1903) he also includes a black-and-white photograph of a fragment of stucco showing part of the second shepherd. This fragment appears to have been missing in the Northcote and Brownlow sketch and is not evident in Wilpert's full-colour photo. The missing pieces of stucco may have been replastered onto the ceiling during Wilpert's restoration work. Clear evidence of fresh plaster can be seen in the most recent PCSA photograph.

18. During his restoration work Bisconti uncovered two inaccuracies in the earlier plates created by Wilpert that also featured in the de Rossi drawing used by Northcote and Brownlow. He discovered a small capsule between the two praying figures on the left of the *loculus*, and the third figure illustrated in both books he found to be part of the border stripe (Bisconti 1996: 7–34).

19. See Schaepman 1929. This paper gives a detailed explanation of the various alternative interpretations of the 'veiling' fresco.

20. Beckwith 1993.

21. Examples include Partner 1999; Belan 2001.
22. These monograms are unusual in that the right-hand 'P' is transposed. It is possible that the Chi-Rho symbols were added at a later date, although they were recorded by Bosio.
23. Writing in 1872, Dr J. W. Appell, the assistant keeper of the South Kensington Museum, refers to the fresco as being 'assigned to the eighth century' and describes it as 'a much obliterated painting of the half figure of a woman, with her hands outstretched in prayer', and the half figure of a child placed in front of her, supposed to be intended for the Virgin Mary and the Infant Saviour (Appell 1872: 57). See also Mancinelli 1981. André Grabar was also uncertain of the identity of both this and the fresco in Priscilla (Grabar 1969: 9).
24. Lk. 1.26-55 is the only Gospel to describe the Annunciation. The *Protevangelium of James* 11.1 expands the description following on from the moment when Mary was given the purple thread by the priests of the Temple in order to spin a new veil (the text is translated in Elliott 2005).
25. There is still some debate as to the exact interpretation of the scenes on the lid of the Adelfia Sarcophagus. The most recent analysis can be found in Lombardi 1998, the catalogue of an exhibition at Syracuse.
26. Mazzei 1999: 233–80.
27. Bisconti 1996: 7–34.
28. The Adoration scenes were also depicted in other media such as liturgical silver vessels and textiles. The great hoard of broken silver vessels discovered at Traprain Law in East Lothian in 1919 includes a vase featuring the Adoration of the Magi, and has been dated to around 400.
29. The Belgian scholar Franz Cumont is one of the earliest researchers to link the religion of Mithras with the Christian Magi (Cumont 1922: 81–105). For a more extensive review on the different theories about the origins of the Magi story, see Trexler 1997.
30. Towards the end of the fourth century, Christians were competing to be buried near martyrs in the catacombs. The *fossores* were charging high prices for prime burial sites and many frescoes were destroyed in the process; however, I have yet to find an image of Christ that has been defaced in this way.

4

MARY IN THE APOCRYPHAL NEW TESTAMENT

J. K. ELLIOTT

INTRODUCTION

The term 'The Apocryphal New Testament' is given to a range of amorphous texts that seem to have originated from the second (some would even argue the first) century onwards. These earliest examples of this literature spawned many imitations, rewritings and expansions. For instance, the five earliest apocryphal *Acts* (those of Peter, Andrew, Paul, Thomas, John) were followed by countless later imitations, such as the *Acts of Xanthippe and Polyxena*, the *Passion of Matthew* or the *Acts of Philip*. Most of the famous texts, like the *Apocalypse of Peter* or the *Gospel of Thomas*, were composed in the second and third centuries.

The term 'The Apocryphal New Testament' is not ideal: the definite article wrongly implies that one is dealing with a fixed and agreed collection, comparable to the Old Testament Apocrypha, the contents of which are generally known and accepted by modern scholarship and to be found as a recognizably fixed entity in Bibles. Recent editions of the Apocryphal New Testament differ considerably, ranging from the very extensive collections in Erbetta or Moraldi to smaller selections such as those in Hennecke-Schneemelcher or Elliott. Not only is the use of the definite article in the title 'The Apocryphal New Testament' misleading, but the adjective 'apocryphal' is wrong if taken in its primary meaning of 'hidden'. Very few of the so-called apocryphal texts claim to have been hidden immediately after having been written close to the events they relate, only to be miraculously revealed in later times.[1] (If the meaning of 'apocryphal' is 'spurious' or 'secondary' then it may well be allowable.)

Even the use of 'New Testament' in the title is not ideal. It is true that many of the 'apocrypha' are concerned with the characters or events that appear in the canonical texts (i.e. those texts that were to be accepted as the approved, authorized New Testament), but not all are. There is, moreover, a tendency in modern scholarship to collect the apocryphal texts into the conventional New Testament subheadings (Gospels, Acts, Epistles and Apocalypse), but certainly not all such texts match those categories.

What we should perhaps be calling this genre of writing is something far more open-ended like 'early non-canonical Christian writings'.[2] 'Unorthodox' and 'heretical' are also to be avoided in describing this literature; these terms are anachronistic of the earliest period. Precision requires that we should define our terms rather pedantically as something like 'texts that were later to be accepted by the Church as orthodox' (of the canonical texts), or as 'writings castigated by the Church as unorthodox' (of the apocryphal texts) – but it is perhaps simpler to follow convention and use 'canonical' and 'apocryphal' anachronistically when referring to the writings of the earliest Christian centuries.

In the syncretistic world of second-century Christianity it would be surprising if all writings were monochrome. Certainly modern readers may rightly judge that the canonical texts have a greater spirituality, a developed theology and more refined literary qualities compared with most of the apocrypha. These later texts are uncritical, superstitious and represent the 'popular' or entertaining reading matter of the faithful but simple man and woman in the pew. But it is because they are examples of early Christian popular reading matter that in them and through them we may have an insight into contemporary beliefs, practices and theological concerns.

One of the dominant motives behind the composing of these secondary texts seems to have been the filling in of perceived gaps in the canonical, biblical narrative; another is the completing of the biographies of its *dramatis personae*.

It was the natural curiosity of those reading the texts that became the canonical Gospels that led to the need to amplify the story of Mary. Anyone attempting to tell her life based only on the New Testament comes across many tantalizing gaps. Outside the Nativity stories, the New Testament includes Mary in the story of the miracle at Cana (Jn 2.1-11); then she appears in the fourth Gospel at the foot of the cross (Jn 19.25-27). She reappears after Easter among the followers of Jesus reassembled in Jerusalem (Acts 1.14). And that is about all we read of her later life.

Biographical queries then arose about Mary: Where was she born? Who were her parents? How was she reared? What about her death? Others are theological: Why was that woman chosen to be the mother of Jesus? What was special and unique about her? What example can she set?

It was in order to answer questions such as these that, by the second century, Christian imagination and piety produced many (apocryphal) tales about Mary. Some of these survived, despite official disapprobation.

Likewise, artists responsible for illustrative series such as cycles of Mary's life (for example in Chartres Cathedral) had to look beyond Scripture to complete their narrative.[3] Giotto's famous sequence of scenes from Mary's life in the Scrovegni Chapel in Padua (the Arena chapel) needed to use apocryphal stories to tell of her early life and background.

We divide the stories into (i) those dealing with Mary up to the time of Jesus' birth, and (ii) her death.

MARY'S PARENTAGE, BIRTH, UPBRINGING AND BETROTHAL

The Texts

A. The *Protevangelium of James*

The third- to fourth-century Bodmer MS V contains this text and entitles it 'The Birth of Mary; the Revelation of James'. Normally, however, because it tells of events prior to Jesus' birth and concerns Mary's parents, Anna and Joachim, her birth and upbringing, and because the purported author (according to its final paragraph) is James of Jerusalem, it is known as the *Proto-Gospel* or *Protevangelium of James*. Its stories reflect the developing tradition that was ultimately expressed in Christian teaching regarding the perpetual virginity of Mary. In addition it gave support and impetus to feasts such as the Immaculate Conception of Mary and the Presentation in the Temple, about which see below. Chapters 22–4, the so-called *Apocryphum Zachariae*, may have been added later or have come from a different source; those chapters tell of the death of John the Baptist's father. Once again, prominence is given to a character who, in the New Testament, has only a small role and in that sense his story is completed.

The text, which was probably originally composed in the second century, was particularly popular in the East. Over 150 manuscripts of it in Greek have survived. These are dated from several centuries, thus indicating its long-standing popularity. It was translated into several early versions (Coptic, Syriac, Georgian, Armenian, Ethiopian and Slavonic), showing that it was also popular in a wide geographical area. Latin versions also exist, albeit not in great numbers.[4] In the West the later *Gospel of Pseudo-Matthew* (see below) was the main vehicle in Latin for propagating stories that had originated in the *Protevangelium*. However, the Gelasian Decree (of the sixth century) appears to have condemned this writing as apocryphal.

The Greek text has been edited in various collections (for example by Tischendorf). The oldest manuscript, found in Bodmer V, edited by Testuz in 1958, forms the basis for Émile de Strycker's French translation and commentary.[5]

The work is sometimes seen as apologetic in tone. One motive seems to have been the defence of aspects of Christianity ridiculed by Celsus. To combat charges of Christianity's humble origins, the *Protevangelium* is at pains to show us that Jesus' parents were not poor: Joseph is a building contractor; Mary spins, but not for payment. Another motive may be to defend Jesus' conception against charges of sexual irregularity: the pregnant Mary's virginity is vindicated before Joseph (14.2) and the priests (16). Similarly, the Davidic descent of Mary is stressed (10.3), a significant detail once Joseph is described only as the putative father of Jesus. Jesus' siblings, well known from the canonical Gospels, are now explained as Joseph's children from an earlier marriage. (Later, Jerome, objecting to such an apologia, preferred to say the siblings were in fact cousins.)

But Ronald Hock, probably correctly, defines the *Protevangelium* as an encomium, that is, an extended homily to Mary, praising her, describing her origins and character and extolling her virtues and accomplishments.[6] Throughout the *Protevangelium* the destiny of Mary is known from the beginning: for example, at 4.1 when Anna is told that her as yet unborn child will become world famous (cf. 6.7, 9; 7.7; 12.2, 6). At Mary's first birthday the parents make a feast at which the priests and people ask God to 'bless the child and give her a name eternally renowned among all generations'. Prior to the story of Mary's visit to Elizabeth in the *Protevangelium* Mary is blessed by the high priest (not by Elizabeth as is the case in Lk. 1.42) with these words: 'Mary, the Lord God has magnified your name, and you shall be blessed among all generations of the earth' (and cf. Lk. 1.48).

Mary Foskett writes:

> In comparison to the Lucan Mary, the virgin of the *Protevangelium* is presented in rather an austere light. From beginning to end, she is the holy one of God destined to give birth to a son who, in turn, will be called holy. Miraculously given to Joachim and Anna, she is preserved for the Lord. From the day that she is born, Mary functions less as an active subject and more as an object of exchange and offering. Her birth is guaranteed in angelic announcements (4.1, 4); she is vowed to the Lord by her parents (4.2, 7); protected by them in their home (6.3; 7.4-5); placed under the protection of the Temple priests (7.7–8.2); removed from the Temple and placed under the guardianship of Joseph (8.3-12); and subjected to a series of accusations and tests (13.6-7; 15.10; 16.5; 20.1-2). She is often cherished by those who bear responsibility for her, yet she also poses a burden. Finally, she is a passive character whose bodily integrity is of paramount concern.[7]

B. The *Gospel of Pseudo-Matthew*

As indicated above, the *Protevangelium* was popularized, especially in the West, by *Pseudo-Matthew*. Over 130 manuscripts containing this text have been listed. This Latin text, originating in the sixth to seventh centuries, is close to a Latin version of the *Protevangelium* (for chs 1–17) and to the *Arabic Infancy Gospel* (in chs 18–24). Our oldest extant manuscript is eleventh century. (The chapters which Tischendorf included in his edition (25–42) and called *Pars Altera* are attached in some medieval manuscripts to *Pseudo-Matthew*, but do in fact belong to the *Infancy Gospel of Thomas*, with which they need to be considered both from a literary and textual point of view.)

Pseudo-Matthew popularized legends about Mary's early life in Latin-speaking Christendom in the Middle Ages. What encouraged its wide circulation and acceptance were prefatory letters from bishops Cromasius and Heliodorus to Jerome and his reply to them. Those spurious letters, which are found in other apocryphal texts too, were added here to provide this gospel with appropriate credentials. The motive for its compilation seems to have been to further the veneration of Mary, not least by the inclusion of stories about the Holy Family's sojourn in Egypt.

As far as differences between *Pseudo-Matthew* and the *Protevangelium* are concerned, Anna's father, Achar, is mentioned only in *Pseudo-Matthew*, Abiathar is high priest during the time of Mary's espousal to Joseph – in the *Protevangelium* it is Zacharias. Other changes to the story are the protracted absence of Joachim and the reduction of Anna's lament (probably in order to enhance the figure of Joachim); there is no visit by Mary to Elizabeth. In *Pseudo-Matthew* the birth occurs in a cave, as in the *Protevangelium*, but mother and son soon move to a manger, thereby assimilating the text to the canonical account. *Pseudo-Matthew* adds the ox and the ass to the scene there and the fulfilling of prophecy when these animals worship Jesus. For the Annunciation the event is now divided into two scenes: one at the well, the second indoors.

C. The *Gospel of the Birth of Mary*

The text known as *De Nativitate Mariae* (sometimes, less accurately, called the *Gospel of the Birth of Mary*) was popular. Over 130 manuscripts of this apocryphon have been catalogued. The text appears in two main types, one the more original, the other a grammatically or stylistically revised form. The gospel probably arose in the ninth century; in chapters 1–8 it is a free adaptation of *Pseudo-Matthew*, while chapters 9–10 follow the canonical Gospels of Matthew and Luke. The motive for its composition was to enhance devotion to Mary, but without some apocryphal accretions found in *Pseudo-Matthew* that were doubtless deemed inappropriate or offensive. Much attention is paid to angelic apparitions. The problematic tradition about Joseph's former marriage is eliminated.

The influence of this apocryphon was spread by its having been used in the thirteenth century by Jacob of Voragine for his chapter 131, 'The Birth of the Blessed Virgin Mary', in *The Golden Legend*.[8] Once the Feast of the Nativity of Mary was established, readings from *De Nativitate Mariae* were used liturgically. The Dominicans seem to have held the book in high regard and versions of the text were used by the order from the thirteenth century onwards.

The use of scriptural citations in *De Nativitate Mariae* betrays a more faithful acceptance of the biblical narrative than is the case in many earlier apocryphal writings. The author of *De Nativitate* has deliberately avoided the more picaresque elements (i.e. the more characteristically *apocryphal*) in his retelling of the story about Anna and Joachim and of Mary's upbringing. The story is more restrained and is more of a hagiographical than an apocryphal story.

The lament of Anna (*Protevangelium* 3) and Anna's conversation with her maid are avoided. Surprisingly, perhaps, less is said about Mary's daily routine in the Temple (such as is found in *Pseudo-Matthew* 6–7) – 'surprisingly' because *De Nativitate* is concerned to show Mary, the ward of the Temple, as an exemplary religious in a convent: her arrival at the Temple at the age of three betrays a precocious spirituality; her being succoured by an angel (a detail carried over from the *Protevangelium*) implies her asceticism; at the Annunciation she is unafraid of the vision because she is accustomed to the 'faces of angels and to celestial light' (9.2).

My *Apocryphal New Testament* suggests a fifth- to sixth-century date for its composition. However, the recent exhaustive textual analysis of this work by Rita Beyers[9] favours a later date, because of the apparent Carolingian influence she detects there. The Carolingians' interest in the patristic exegesis of earlier centuries, especially of Matthew, is said to have rekindled this interest in scripture. For example, the linking of Mary's ascent of the fifteen steps to the Altar of Burnt

Offerings in the Temple is said to parallel the fifteen Gradual Psalms (Pss. 120-134);[10] 3.7 makes an appeal to scripture absent from the earlier accounts; 4.8 is seen as due to Carolingian exegesis. The naming of Mary at 3.8 and the divine promise that she will be 'made eminent by name and work' is compatible with such teaching. Hence it is not surprising that docetic or magical elements in the *Protevangelium*, such as the catalepsy of nature, were dropped. The more restrained and theological tone shows that whenever the apocryphon was composed, the age of the unbridled, magical, superstitious features of many apocryphal writings of earlier centuries had passed.

The condensing of *Pseudo-Matthew* and by extension the *Protevangelium* in *De Nativitate Mariae* had the effect of concentrating the narrative on Mary. Emphasis on her virginity both reflected and itself fuelled belief about her perpetual virginity; virginity itself was proclaimed as the most sublime form of chastity (see below under 'Virginity').

Among differences from earlier accounts, the planned betrothal of Mary to the high priest Abiathar's son in *Pseudo-Matthew* 7 becomes a planned betrothal to Abiathar himself; there is a greater emphasis on angelic appearances – to Joachim, Anna, Joseph and Mary; Anna's Magnificat is not reproduced; in *De Nativitate Mariae* Mary's and Joseph's marriage is a real, albeit unconsummated, marriage; there is no flight to Egypt in *De Nativitate*, perhaps because Celsus centuries earlier had said that Jesus had learned magic arts there.

D. Arundel 404

This is but one Latin manuscript that belongs to what is now being referred to as the 'J' Compilation, so called after Montague Rhodes James who had discovered and published it. Another Latin manuscript is the Hereford MS, also originally published in part by James.[11] The Arundel manuscript (British Library Arundel 404) is fourteenth century; the Hereford Cathedral manuscript O.3.9 is thirteenth century.

Like the gospel of *Pseudo-Matthew*, the Arundel manuscript and its allies provide another means whereby the stories of the *Protevangelium* were popularized in the Latin West. Jean-Daniel Kaestli's and Martin McNamara's recent researches show how the Irish traditions about the Nativity and the original form of the 'J' compilation seem to have had an existence prior to their 'contamination' by *Pseudo-Matthew*.[12] If so, the text in the Arundel, Hereford and allied manuscripts has a good and early pedigree.

Other texts

This literature had many successors and followers. Other texts include the *Arabic Infancy Gospel*, the Irish *Leabhar Breac*, the *Infancy Gospel of Thomas* and the *History of Joseph the Carpenter*.[13]

The Teaching in the Texts

A. Monasticism

At the time Anna conceives Mary, she and Joachim vow that, if they are granted to be parents, their offspring would be dedicated, like a religious, to the service of the Lord (*Protevangelium* 4: 'I shall offer (the child) as a gift to the Lord and it will serve him its whole life', thereby echoing 1 Sam. 1.11, 28).

The monastic origin of some of the Mary materials may be seen in *Pseudo-Matthew*, even at the beginning of the narrative (*Pseudo-Matthew* 1), where Joachim is introduced as a pious man whose almsgiving is exemplary: he even supports pilgrims as many a monastic house did. Later, Mary too practises almsgiving.

Mary's monastic upbringing begins even prior to her third birthday, when she is presented in the Temple where she is to remain until she is twelve. From her earliest days in the parental home she is nurtured constantly in the 'sanctuary of her bedroom', as her feet must not be contaminated through contact with the earth. The *Protevangelium* stresses the undefiled nature of that domestic sanctuary where Mary is attended by 'the pure daughters of the Hebrews'. In the Temple, later, Mary is attended by fellow virgins and she undertakes monastic rituals. Only *Pseudo-Matthew* 6–7 gives the daily routine of the virgin during her nine years cloistered in the Temple. Are we to see here the influence of the Benedictine Rule? Day and night her life is characterized as righteousness and prayer: 'From the morning to the third hour she remained in prayer; from the third to the ninth she was occupied with her weaving; and from the ninth she again applied herself to prayer. She did not retire from praying until there appeared to her an angel of the Lord, from whose hand she used to receive food.' *Pseudo-Matthew* 6.1 refers to perpetual adoration (*laus perennis*) by Mary. Her communicating with angels and her being nurtured by a dove occur here, as they do in other Marian gospels. The *De Nativitate Mariae* also mentions Mary's divine visions in the Temple.

Throughout her life she had been at home in the company of the 'undefiled daughters of the Hebrews' and later as a ward of the Temple; when Mary leaves the Temple to be the ward of Joseph, other virgins (religious) accompany her. Her life is therefore described as having been in a monastic community until she sets off to Bethlehem to give birth to Jesus.

B. Virginity

As soon as Anna conceives, her child is destined to be the mother of the Son of the Most High. The pregnancy is divinely ordained. The repeated angelic proclamations to Joachim and to Anna make that clear. Mary's own destiny is spelled out: she is to be reared in the Temple and later, without the stain of sexual contact, shall, as a virgin, bear a son. *Protevangelium* 9.7 uses the title 'Virgin of the Lord' for the first time, but that is how she is constantly referred to thereafter in this literature.

Mary's reaction to the proposal by the high priest Abiathar that she marry his son is to defend her status as a true religious, saying that her own virginity is in itself worship: 'God is first of all worshipped in chastity . . . I from my infancy in the Temple of God have learned that virginity can be sufficiently dear to God. And so, because I can offer what is dear to God, I have resolved in my heart that I should not know a man at all' (*Pseudo-Matthew* 7).

The theme of virginity continues with Joseph being appointed merely as Mary's guardian. *Pseudo-Matthew* emphasizes that Joseph is only the ward, not a husband. In this gospel he is said to have grandchildren older than Mary. Doubtless, that is intended to show not only Joseph's great age, but the improbability that he would have any desire for Mary as a woman. Once he takes her to his home she is once again in a monastic setting and her virginity is preserved. Her companions are other virgins and she is to remain a virgin. Mary's vow in *De Nativitate Mariae* reminds us that she is 'dedicated to the Lord'. In *De Nativitate Mariae* wedding preparations are made, but Mary goes off with seven virgins to her parental home. Those two later texts are thus still faithful to a tradition that is seen as early as the *Protevangelium* that the marriage is not consummated. Immediately after the marriage – and a genuine wedding seems not to be understood in the *Protevangelium* – Joseph goes off surveying his buildings immediately upon taking Mary as his ward, until he returns months later to find Mary pregnant. Her time at home is spent chastely preparing the wool work for the Temple. In *Pseudo-Matthew* her fellow virgins (five in that gospel) recognize her special qualities and they call her Queen of the Virgins – apparently the earliest recorded instance of the use of that title for Mary.

Mary's perpetual virginity is emphasized after the pregnancy: the strange story of the administration of the 'water of truth' in the *Protevangelium* serves to emphasize her ongoing virginity, while physically her womb is great. Similarly in *De Nativitate Mariae* 8.5, although Joseph's and Mary's is a real marriage, Augustine stated that it was not consummated.[14] Throughout the Marian gospels Mary is only ever called 'the virgin', not ever 'daughter', 'wife', or 'mother' (with only one exception at *Protevangelium* 21.11).

The midwife in *Pseudo-Matthew* 13.3 makes a significant declaration about Mary's perpetual virginity by stating, having observed that the birth of Jesus occurred without the spilling of blood: 'Virgo peperit et postquam peperit virgo esse perdurat' ('A virgin has conceived, a virgin has brought forth and as a virgin she remains', cf. the Lateran formulation of 649).[15] The physical examination by the disbelieving midwife confirms she is virgo intacta.

C. Immaculate Conception

The development that was later to be defined as the Immaculate Conception of Mary may be seen most vividly in the *Protevangelium*. The angel tells Anna she *will* conceive, but at 4.4 when an angel speaks to the absent Joachim, he tells him his wife *is* pregnant, implying a miraculous conception. At 4.9 too the present tense is found, although some manuscripts, conscious of the difficulty, both here and at 4.4 have substituted a future tense. Even if the present tense is likely to be the original reading, nonetheless it is, as it were, a 'prophetic' present and points to a future state, but that is not how the scribes who adjusted the present tense in the manuscripts they were copying viewed it. Defenders of the future tense take

Joachim's 'resting' at home after his return for a euphemism that is intended to say that this is when the conception occurred.

In *Pseudo-Matthew* 3, Anna is told she has conceived of Joachim's seed, but, as the story progresses, that detail seems to have been forgotten. Joachim is absent for five months and takes thirty days to reach home. That Anna has conceived without sexual intercourse is implied when Joachim sees in the priest's frontlet that he has not sinned (*Protevangelium* 5.1), the only 'sin' possible being concupiscence.[16]

D. Annunciation

The Annunciation, the location of which is unspecified in Luke, is said in *Pseudo-Matthew* to have been out of doors at a fountain. The message is repeated on the following day in *Pseudo-Matthew* when Mary this time is indoors, either spinning or reading. Later iconographical representations of the scene in Western art typically prefer the studious Mary, busy with her books. Eastern traditions prefer to portray her spinning. Mary's reaction to the apparition is far more phlegmatic in *De Nativitate Mariae* because it is said there that her life in the Temple meant she was well accustomed to such visions. The angel's explanation of Mary's impending pregnancy in *De Nativitate Mariae* again emphasizes Mary's sinlessness. The Son of God requires this priority and privilege.[17]

E. Anti-docetic teaching

What needs to be emphasized here is that throughout the traditions Mary is visibly pregnant. Elizabeth, Joseph and the priests all observe her swollen womb. The *Protevangelium* has this at six months; *Pseudo-Matthew* at nine months; *De Nativitate Mariae*, still calling her a fiancée, refers to four months; *The History of Joseph the Carpenter* has three months.

However apparently docetic some descriptions of the actual birth of Jesus seem to be, e.g. in Arundel 404 and *Protevangelium* 19.16, which speak of the light in the cave withdrawing until the baby 'appears', and the bloodlessness at the parturition in *Pseudo-Matthew*, and the painlessness of the childbirth in *Leabhar Breac*,[18] the main message is that Mary's pregnancy is real enough. The reality of the birth is also evident in Mary's lactating. Her breasts are 'gushing' according to *Leabhar Breac*, and she suckles Jesus in *Arabic Infancy Gospel* 3 and even in Arundel 404 (which is often pointed to as having encouraged a docetic understanding of the birth).[19]

F. Intercession

Soon after the birth in the *Arabic Infancy Gospel* (ch. 3), Mary encourages a sick woman to touch the baby and be healed. Mary as intercessor is a prominent motif through the Holy Family's sojourn in Egypt. The *Arabic Infancy Gospel* as well as the *Infancy Gospel of Thomas* in Latin and also the *Leabhar Breac* have numerous stories in which the 'Lady Mary' is an intercessor. In *Pseudo-Matthew* 6 we learn that Mary herself is also a healer and not merely a mediatrix ('If anyone who was unwell touched her the same hour he went away healed'). After the end of her life she heals on her own account too: in the Dormition account of Pseudo-Melito, Mary heals the Jew whose hands were evulsed when he attacked her bier.

G. Liturgy

After the Council of Ephesus in 431, when Mary's status as *Theotokos* was proclaimed, the Eastern Churches began to celebrate Marian festivals. The feast of her birth, based on the *Protevangelium*, seems to have originated in Constantinople in the sixth century, the Presentation of Mary in the Temple perhaps in the century following, the Conception of Anne from the ninth, as well as the Feast of Anna and Joachim a century later. The West imported from the East some of these, thanks in part to Augustine's influence. Those include the Purification and the Assumption as well as the Annunciation and Nativity.[20]

MARY'S DEATH AND ASSUMPTION

Other apocryphal narratives tell of Mary's death. Just as believers and writers in the post-New Testament period began to reflect on why it was that Mary, of all people, was chosen to be the one to bring Jesus into the world, so too they reflected on her death. Her birth and upbringing had to be special, her virginal life increasingly emphasized. Her death also needed to emphasize her unique status. The Assumption, or Dormition, or 'Falling asleep', or 'Transitus', or 'Obsequies', appeared in written forms somewhat later than stories of her family and upbringing; Epiphanius of Salamis towards the end of the fourth century claims he can find no record of how the Virgin's life ended. Only from the fifth century do the stories of Mary's departure from the earth emerge. The day to commemorate Mary's death, 15 August, seems to have originated from the end of the fifth century, according to Mary Clayton.[21] Before that date writers merely mention her end only in the context that she remained a virgin until her death. Stephen Shoemaker, however, argues that some of the traditions in these earliest accounts may go back to the third century.[22] The later, i.e. fifth-century, traditions did not emerge throughout Christendom *ex nihilo*! Whatever their possible early history, it is clear that nothing substantial emerges in writing on this theme until the end of the fifth century. Before then the death itself was not of relevance – only her perpetual virginity. But by the sixth century the Gelasian Decree denounces an apocryphal book named the *Transitus Sanctae Mariae*, by which Pseudo-Melito, *Assumption of the Virgin*, may be meant.

There is a large number of accounts of her death and Assumption into heaven (or paradise) composed in various languages including Greek, Latin, Coptic, Ethiopic, Georgian, Armenian, Arabic and Syriac. There is also an Irish tradition with close links to the Syriac. The history of those traditions is largely uncharted, although Simon Mimouni has argued for an organic growth of the differing extant traditions.[23] That view has, however, recently been criticized by, among others, Stephen Shoemaker.

Although it seems impossible to edit a single Assumption account that takes into account all variant forms in the different languages,[24] one can detect certain roughly defined differences between two main areas. In the Coptic tradition, Mary's corporeal ascent is a feature: there is a long interval between her death and her Assumption. That tradition knows nothing of the summoning of all the apostles – only Peter and John are present. Mary is warned of her death by Jesus.

In the tradition represented by the Latin, Greek and Syriac, Mary's death is announced by an angel (who in the Latin brings a palm branch), the apostles are summoned from all parts of the world and Mary's Assumption occurs soon after her death. In the Latin narrative attributed to Joseph of Arimathaea, Mary dies and Jesus takes her soul to heaven. Her corpse is placed in her tomb, but is then immediately transported to heaven by angels to be reunited with her soul. During that translation into heaven Mary throws her girdle to Thomas.[25] The Greek narratives may have been used liturgically on the commemoration of Mary's death, and as a consequence are somewhat shorter. The Latin narratives are smoother, suggestive of a later date. The Syriac tradition is perhaps the earliest.

But in all the accounts it seems that Mary actually dies, even though that detail is glossed over – as indeed it is in the difficult papal dogmatic decree of 1950 *Munificentissimus Deus* with reference to the Assumption. Inevitably, since that decree was issued, much discussion of the history of the Assumption has been conducted along either Roman Catholic or anti-Catholic lines, especially where that declaration states: '. . . [Mary] was not subject to the law of remaining in the corruption of the grave and she did not have to wait until the end of time for the redemption of her body.'[26]

M. van Esbroeck over many years has contributed a number of articles to learned journals in which he has analysed many of the oriental versions of the Assumption.[27] He is concerned to explain how such narratives arose especially in Greek, Georgian and Armenian. The key to understanding the development of the tradition is, according to van Esbroeck, the relationship with the imperial policies of the Byzantine emperors and their attitudes to Chalcedon. Pulcheria's influence on Theodosius II is one of the better-known examples of how Mary as *Theotokos* was vigorously promoted. However, one needs to remember that the various apocryphal Assumption tales are remarkably neutral regarding Chalcedon.

How far we should link the origins of written stories about the Assumption and the flowering of pre-Byzantine Marian devotion in the Holy Land is an open question. Ought we to connect the development of Marian veneration in the fifth century (at the church of the Kathisma between Jerusalem and Bethlehem, then at the church of Mary's Tomb in the Jehoshaphat Valley, and then by 543 at the Nea Basilica near Jerusalem) to the proliferation of these texts that had fuelled the devotion, or may it be the reverse, namely the spread of the written narratives arose from these and other centres of popular devotion?

We merely note the diverse collection of narratives that possibly originated in Syro-Palestine and Egypt, but which had spread throughout Christendom by the tenth century, and we urge the continuing study of these materials.

BIBLIOGRAPHY

Barré, H. (1962), 'L'apport Marial de l'Orient à l'Occident de saint Ambroise à saint Augustin', *Études Mariales* 19, 27–89.

Bovon, B. and P. Geoltrain (1997), *Écrits Apocryphes Chrétienes I* (*Bibliothèque de la Pléiade* 442). Paris: Gallimard.

Cartlidge, D. R. and J. K. Elliott (2001), *Art and the Christian Apocrypha.* London: Routledge.

Clayton, M. (1998), *The Apocryphal Gospels of Mary in Anglo-Saxon England.* Cambridge: Cambridge University Press.

De Strycker, E. (1961), *La Forme la plus Ancienne du Protévangile de Jacques.* Brussels: Société des Bollandistes.

Elliott, J. K. (2005), *The Apocryphal New Testament.* Oxford: Clarendon Press.

—— (2006), *A Synopsis of the Apocryphal Infancy and Nativity Narratives* (*NTTS* 34). Leiden: E. J. Brill.

Erbetta, M. (1983), *Gli Apocrifi del Nuovo Testamento.* 4 volumes. Marietti: Casale Monferrato.

Foskett, M. F. (2002), *A Virgin Conceived: Mary and Classical Representations of Virginity.* Bloomington/Indianapolis: Indiana University Press.

Geerard, M. (1992), *Clavis Apocryphorum Novi Testamenti.* Turnhout: Brepols.

Geoltrain, P. and J.-D. Kaestli (2005), *Écrits Apocryphes Chrétiens II* (*Bibliothèque de la Pléiade* 516). Paris: Gallimard.

Gijsel, J. (1997), *Libri de Nativitate Mariae* (*Corpus Christianorum Series Apocryphorum* 9). Turnhout: Brepols.

Hock, R. F. (1995), *The Infancy Gospels of Jesus* (*The Scholars' Bible* 2). Santa Rosa: Polebridge Press.

Hock, R. F. and D. R. Cartlidge (2001), 'How Mary became the Mother of God', *Bible Review,* January 2001, 13–25.

Jugie, M. (1944), *La Mort et l'Assomption de la Sainte Vierge: Étude Historico-doctrinale* (*Studi-etesti 114*). Vatican City: Bibliotheca Apostolica Vaticana.

Lafontaine-Dosogne, J. (1992), *Iconographie de l'Enfance de la Vierge dans l'Empire Byzantin et en Occident.* 2 volumes. Brussels: Académie royale de Belgique.

McNamara, M. and J.-D. Kaestli (eds) (2001), *Apocrypha Hiberniae I: Evangelia Infantiae.* Turnhout: Brepols.

Mimouni, S. C. (1995), *Dormition et Assomption de Marie: Histoire des traditions anciennes* (*Théologie Historique 98*). Paris: Beauchesne.

Moraldi, L. (1994), *Apocrifi del Nuovo Testamento.* 3 volumes. Turin: UTET.

Schneemelcher, W. (1997), *Neutestamentliche Apokryphen.* 2 volumes. Tübingen: Mohr-Siebeck.

Shoemaker, S. J. (2002), *Ancient Traditions about the Virgin Mary's Dormition and Assumption.* Oxford: Oxford University Press.

Van Esbroeck, M. (1995), *Aux Origines de la Dormition de la Vierge* (*Variorum Collected Studies Series* 472). Aldershot: Ashgate.

Wallis Budge, E. A. (ed.) (1976), *The History of the Blessed Virgin Mary: the Syriac Texts.* New York: AMS Press.

Wenger, A. (1955), *L'Assomption de la Très Sainte Vierge dans la Tradition Byzantin du VIe au Xe Siècle.* Paris: Institut Français d'Études Byzantines.

NOTES

1. One such example is the *Apocalypse of Paul.*
2. Even that is less than ideal, because the use of 'canonical'/'non-canonical' is anachronistic of the second and third centuries.
3. See Hock and Cartlidge 2001: 13–25; Cartlidge and Elliott 2001, esp. ch. 2, 'Mary'; Lafontaine-Dosogne 1992.
4. The most complete MS in Latin is Paris, Bibliothèque Sainte-Geneviève 2787, recently edited by Rita Beyers in McNamara and Kaestli 2001.
5. De Strycker 1961.
6. Hock 1995.
7. Foskett 2002: 160.

8. Jan Gijsel 1997: 32 n. 5 shows that Jacob worked from a résumé by Jean de Mailly based on the *De Nativitate Mariae*. See also *Ibid.*: 17 for references to devotion to Mary from the eighth century onwards.

9. In Bovon and Geoltrain 1997, now published in *Corpus Christianorum Series Apocryphorum* 10, and in a condensed form in *Écrits Apocryphes Chrétiens* I.

10. These psalms were prominent in monastic communities. See the section below on 'Monasticism'.

11. A full version of this text now appears in McNamara and Kaestli 2001: vol. 2, 621–880 = *Corpus Christianorum Series Apocryphorum* 14.

12. McNamara and Kaestli 2001: vol. 2.

13. Details about those are to be seen in Elliott 2005.

14. Barré 1962: 27–89.

15. And cf. Augustine's 'virgo concepit, virgo peperit, virgo permansit' (*Sermon* 51.11).

16. *De Nativitate* 9.5 refers to the birth of Jesus as unique because as Son of God he is 'conceived without sinning' (cf. 9.10 thus applying an immaculate conception to *him* and not to the birth of his mother).

17. See Beyers, in McNamara and Kaestli 2001: 318 n. 4.

18. See Elliott 2006. To the references there we may add the *Ascension of Isaiah* 11.14 and the *Odes of Solomon* 19.8.

19. See Elliott 2006: ch. 4, sections Dx and Dxi.

20. See Gijsel 1997: 8–9.

21. Clayton 1998: esp. 118.

22. Shoemaker 2002.

23. Mimouni 1995.

24. My *The Apocryphal New Testament* (Elliott 2005) includes translations or summaries of twelve such stories of the Assumption from Greek, Latin, Coptic and Syriac, because we are not yet in a position to provide a synoptic presentation of the material, let alone produce a critical edition of the texts of the Assumption:

1. Coptic

A. The Sahidic Coptic *Homily on the Dormition* attributed to Evodius of Rome

B. The *Twentieth Discourse* of Cyril of Jerusalem

C. The *Discourse* of Theodosius of Alexandria

D. A fragment from *The Gospel of the Twelve Apostles*

2. Greek

The *Discourse of John the Divine*

3. Latin

A. The *Narrative of Pseudo-Melito*

B. The *Narrative of Joseph of Arimathaea*

4. Syriac

Various fragments including the *History of the Blessed Virgin Mary*, edited by E. A. Wallis Budge in 1899 (1976 edition)

The Italian collection by Erbetta 1983 is larger – he prints over 25 Assumption narratives. The greatest number of these narratives is found in Geerard 1992, where 64 different texts are listed. Shoemaker 2002 prints English translations of six of the earliest Dormition narratives hitherto untranslated in the Appendices to his monograph:

A. The Ethiopic *Liber Requiei*
B. *Transitus R by John the Theologian and Evangelist*
C. A fifth-century Syriac palimpsest
D. The Ethiopic Six Books
E. The Sahidic Coptic *Homily on the Dormition* attributed to Evodius
F. Jacob of Serug, *Homily on the Dormition*

The recently published collections in *Écrits Apocryphes Chrétiens* (Boron and Geoltrain 1997; Geoltrain and Kaestli 2005) have a French translation by Simon Mimouni of the *Dormition by Pseudo-John the Theologian* in volume I and *Transitus Greek R* in volume 2 (also by Mimouni).

25. This belt is venerated in the Chapel in Prato Cathedral, named Santo Cingolo.
26. *Acta Apostolicae Sedis* 42 (1950: 754).
27. Some of his essays have been gathered together in van Esbroeck 1995. Other influential books on the Dormition stories are: Jugie 1944; Wenger 1955.

5

THE CULT OF THE VIRGIN IN THE FOURTH CENTURY: A FRESH LOOK AT SOME OLD AND NEW SOURCES

STEPHEN SHOEMAKER

Scholars have often maintained that the fourth century knew no Marian veneration. While the writings of the fourth-century Church Fathers bear abundant
witness to Mary's mounting significance in theological and ascetic debates, cultic
veneration of the Virgin is frequently held to be a phenomenon of the fifth
century, consequent to and driven primarily by the events of the Council of
Ephesus.[1] As Richard Price observes in a recent article on the Nestorian controversy, generations of scholars have held a steady confidence that any significant
developments in Marian piety were a consequence and not a cause of the
Council's decision to bestow the title *Theotokos* on Mary. The debates of the third
Council were thus concerned squarely with Christology and free of any influence
from an incipient veneration of the Virgin.[2] Similar views still abide, as evidenced
in a recent article from Averil Cameron, where she writes:

> [D]espite her increasingly important role in doctrinal debates, the personal
> veneration of the Virgin known to later generations was not yet the norm,
> even in the fourth century. It is in practice only after the Council of Ephesus
> and the recognition of her title as Theotokos in AD 431 that we find the real
> development of the cult of the Virgin which was to find expression in the
> sixth century in particular in the establishment of Marian feasts . . . [and]
> stories of her appearances and of miracles performed by her.[3]

While one certainly would not want to underplay the important impetus that
Marian piety received from the decisions of the third Council, recent decades
have seen the emergence of an alternative understanding of the Nestorian controversy, in which Marian devotion is not just an important by-product of the
Council but stands squarely at the centre of its debates.

Kenneth Holum was the first to argue that Marian piety was a dynamic force in
the events of the third Council, identifying Pulcheria as an ardent devotee of the
Virgin Mary who had modelled her own authority after the Virgin and actively
promoted Mary's veneration in Constantinople. According to Holum, when
Nestorius arrived in the imperial capital from Antioch, he was immediately scan-
dalized by what he considered the 'excessive worship and near-deification of
Mary' in the city, bolstered by imperial support.[4] Nestorius quickly moved to
combat these impious errors that had taken root within his new flock, resulting in

a head-on confrontation with Pulcheria that eventually broadened to include related issues in Christology as Cyril of Alexandria seized the opportunity to advance the status of his See. Such a reconstruction of the Nestorian controversy locates Marian piety at the core of the debate and looks on the Council's Christological statements largely as theological adjustments necessary to accommodate the Virgin's veneration. Vasiliki Limberis has taken this theory in some intriguing new directions by exploring further the ways in which Pulcheria (and others) fostered Mary's cult in the early Byzantine capital.[5] Both Holum and Limberis have posed an intriguing argument that Marian piety is not simply a derivation of Ephesian Christology but, as the crux of this debate, devotion to Mary must have been a vibrant element of Christian piety well before Nestorius ever came to Constantinople.

Nevertheless, several scholars have recently called into question the specific emphasis in this hypothesis on Pulcheria's devotion to Mary and her promotion of Marian cult prior to the Council of Ephesus. Price, Cameron, Christine Angelidi, Leena Mari Peltomaa and others have all drawn attention to the lateness and polemical nature of many key sources advancing this view of Pulcheria, and while Kate Cooper has recently proposed that the evidence for Pulcheria's devotion to the Virgin can even withstand such scrutiny, it must be acknowledged that much of the evidence is problematic.[6] Likewise, many of these same scholars follow Cyril Mango in rejecting Pulcheria's identification as the foundress of Constantinople's most important Marian shrines, the churches of Blachernai and Chalkoprateia. Yet Mango's proposal that it was instead the empress Verina who founded these churches is not very convincing, and it seems that Pulcheria still has the more compelling claim of responsibility.[7] Both reports of Verina's involvement with Blachernai, for instance, presuppose that the church was already in existence before her reign, an oddly overlooked point that certainly seems to favour Pulcheria's connection with Blachernai.[8]

While these critiques of Holum's thesis raise important questions that must be addressed, it seems that there is still enough evidence to suggest that Marian piety played an essential role in generating the Nestorian controversy and the Council of Ephesus. Even if it is the case that Pulcheria cannot be linked with the veneration of Mary and the promotion of her cult in the ways that Holum and Limberis suggest, there is considerable evidence indicating that both individual and collective veneration of the Virgin had begun well before the controversies of Ephesus. With or without Pulcheria, it is increasingly clear that cultic devotion to the Virgin was a part of the religious landscape of the eastern Mediterranean world at least fifty years before the Council of Ephesus. Thus it is increasingly difficult, if not impossible, to conceive of the Christological deliberations of Ephesus as sealed off from the broader concerns about Mary generated by her nascent cult. Whether or not Pulcheria and her devotion to the Virgin were important agents at the Council is debatable, but the existence of Marian devotion by the fourth century seems increasingly beyond question, as a number of well-known early witnesses attest.

Perhaps the most famous of these witnesses is the intercessory prayer to the Virgin now identified as an early version of the prayer *Sub tuum praesidium* preserved on small, fragmentary papyrus from Egypt. Although the document's palaeography suggests that it was written sometime around the turn of the fourth century, a strong consensus dates this Marian hymn to the latter part of the fourth century, at which time evidence of prayer to the Virgin first begins to appear in other sources.[9] Other early evidence for a Marian cult comes from the two Cappadocian Gregorys, Gregory of Nyssa and Gregory of Nazianzus. The latter, Gregory of Nazianzus, in his *Oration 24* presents one of the earliest witnesses to such Marian prayer. In this rather peculiar work, a panegyric on 'Cyprian', Gregory freely mixes traditions about Cyprian of Carthage with those of Cyprian of Antioch (in Pisidia), whose feast the oration was presumably intended to commemorate.[10] Cyprian of Antioch was, according to legend, a magician who sought with his spells to seduce a beautiful Christian virgin named Justina. Justina, however, successfully defended herself by calling on her 'husband', Christ, as well as by praying to the Virgin Mary for her aid, since she too was a virgin who had once faced danger.[11] Whether or not a virgin named Justina actually sought the Virgin's assistance and protection through prayer in the early fourth century, as the legend suggests, is really beside the point: the primary significance of this passage lies in its witness to the practice of intercessory prayer to the Virgin among the Nicene Christians of Constantinople by 379, when Gregory delivered this oration.[12] From Gregory's representation of Justina, we may assume that such Marian prayers were fairly common practice in the community that he led, which included, we should note, a number of aristocratic women who were devoted to the cult of the saints and their relics.[13]

At approximately the same time, Gregory of Nyssa records the earliest known account of a Marian apparition, in his panegyric on yet another Gregory, the third-century Gregory Thaumaturgus. This biography, written in the fall of 380, describes Gregory Thaumaturgus's waking vision of the Virgin, in which he received a trinitarian creed from the apostle John at the Virgin's command.[14] Although this story is no guarantee that Gregory Thaumaturgus actually had such an experience, it attests that such appearances of the Virgin Mary were familiar to the Cappadocian Christians in Gregory of Nyssa's flock.[15] In Constantinople, similar experiences were common in Gregory Nazianzen's community, if the fifth-century Church historian Sozomen can be believed. According to Sozomen,

> Gregory of Nazianzen presided over those who maintain the 'consubstantiality' of the Holy Trinity, and assembled them together in a little dwelling, which had been altered into the form of a house of prayer, by those who held the same opinions and had a like form of worship. It subsequently became one of the most conspicuous in the city, and is so now, not only for the beauty and number of its structures, but also for the advantages accruing to it from the visible manifestations of God. For the power of God was there manifested, and was helpful both in waking visions and in dreams, often for the relief of many diseases and for those afflicted by some sudden transmutation in their affairs. The power was accredited to Mary, the Mother of God, the holy virgin, for she does manifest herself in this way. The name of Anastasia was given to this church.[16]

That both Gregorys would describe these phenomena so matter-of-factly suggests that prayers to the Virgin and her apparition were a regular part of the Christian faith in their communities.[17] As Nicholas Constas rightly observes, even though these are the first reports of such phenomena, 'these accounts do not have the air of novelty or innovation', and presumably they reflect already well-established traditions of Marian piety.[18] For whatever reason, those scholars who would maintain a post-Ephesian origin for Marian veneration generally overlook these early witnesses.

Likewise, they ignore strong evidence of early liturgical ceremonies in Mary's honour. By the beginning of the fifth century, both Constantinople and Jerusalem observed annual Marian feasts and, as Walter Ray has argued, the feast of Mary in Jerusalem may be considerably older.[19] Known by the title 'the Memory of Mary', as well as 'the Memory of the Virgin' and 'the Memory of the *Theotokos*', this early feast originally celebrated Mary's divine maternity and her virginity, often observed in close proximity to the feast of the Nativity. The early Dormition traditions and other related sources suggest the possibility of a similar Marian feast in Syria and Egypt by this time, but this remains very uncertain.[20] Although Simon Mimouni posits the existence of such a feast in Egypt by the beginning of the fifth century, even he is willing to acknowledge that the evidence on which his claim rests is somewhat dubious.[21]

In the imperial capital, the feast of the Memory of Mary is first attested in the famous homily on the *Theotokos* by Proclus of Constantinople, a future bishop of Constantinople and one of Nestorius's most ardent opponents.[22] Delivered in 430 at the height of the Nestorian controversy in the presence of Nestorius himself and his main supporters, Proclus responded directly to Nestorius's attacks on Marian piety and in the process 'established the veneration of the *Theotokos* upon theological and exegetical principles which defined the rhetoric and rationale for the cult of the Virgin Mary throughout the Byzantine period'.[23] The occasion for this homily, as Proclus himself informs us, was 'the Virgin's festival', a recently established feast in Mary's honour commemorating her divine maternity and virginity, most likely observed on 26 December (on which date the Eastern Churches still celebrate a similar *Feast of the Theotokos*). As Constas observes in his recent study of Proclus, this new feast of the Virgin had almost certainly been established by one of Nestorius' immediate predecessors as bishop of Constantinople, and for a variety of reasons, Atticus of Constantinople, bishop from 406 to 425, stands out as a likely suspect.[24] In any case, this homily provides evidence that prior to the Council of Ephesus – and more than likely before the arrival of Nestorius – the incipient Marian piety witnessed by Gregory Nazianzen and other late fourth-century sources had found formal expression in the imperial capital through an official, annual feast of the Virgin.

The same is true of Jerusalem, where by approximately the same time a similar commemoration of the Virgin Mary had developed.[25] The Jerusalemite feast of the Memory of Mary, observed on 15 August, is attested by a number of early fifth-century witnesses, including liturgical manuals and homilies for the feast as well as the archaeological remains of the fifth-century church where the feast was observed. The most direct evidence for this annual Marian feast comes from the

Jerusalem Armenian Lectionary, a manual outlining the yearly liturgical celebrations of the Holy City sometime between 417 and 439. Among its many commemorations is a feast of the Memory of Mary, celebrated on 15 August at the third mile from Bethlehem, midway between Jerusalem and Bethlehem.[26] The prescribed lectionary readings for the feast all relate to Christ's birth from Mary, signalling a commemoration of Mary's Divine Maternity similar to the feast of the Virgin in Constantinople witnessed by Proclus. This focus is not at all surprising, since the site itself was strongly connected with the events of the Nativity: according to the second-century *Protevangelium of James*, Christ was not born in the city of Bethlehem but halfway between Jerusalem and Bethlehem in a cave just off the main road, the precise location of this early Marian feast.[27] Although there are some indications that both this location and its feast were earlier connected with the events of the Nativity itself, by the early fifth century the festival had become an annual commemoration of the Virgin Mary.[28]

At the beginning of the fifth century, this site boasted an important church, the church of the *Kathisma*, or 'Seat', of the *Theotokos*, which according to tradition stood on the spot where the Virgin sat to rest briefly before giving birth in the nearby cave. Over the past several decades, two fifth-century churches have been unearthed at this location, and their relations to one another and to the traditions of the *Kathisma* and the Memory of Mary remain somewhat uncertain. The most likely explanation is that the smaller church and its monastery were constructed in the late fourth or early fifth century to serve as the earliest site of this Marian feast, while the larger church, some 300 metres to the south-west at the bottom of the hill, is a more recent construction probably built during the later fifth century to accommodate increasing pilgrimage traffic.[29] In any case, whatever the solution to this liturgical and archaeological puzzle may be, it is quite certain that at least one of these two churches stood on this location by the beginning of the fifth century, housing an altar for the annual observance of Mary's feast.

In addition to these material remains from the nascent cult of the Virgin, several early homilies for the feast of the Memory of Mary also survive from the Jerusalem church. The earliest of these are two homilies in honour of Mary by Hesychius, a priest of Jerusalem during the early fifth century. Hesychius delivered his *Homily 5* to commemorate the Memory of Mary sometime between 431 and 433, and his *Homily 6* was most likely delivered for the same occasion sometime prior to 428.[30] Presumably, both homilies were pronounced in the church of the *Kathisma*, and even if by some chance the shrine was not yet so named, it is safe to assume that Hesychius spoke in one of the two churches standing at the site identified by the *Armenian Lectionary*. In any case, Hesychius' homilies confirm the observance of this Marian feast in Jerusalem by the early fifth century, adding precision to the witness of the *Armenian Lectionary* by establishing the commemoration of the Memory of Mary before 428. A similar homily for this feast delivered by Chrysippus of Jerusalem around the middle of the fifth century bears further witness to the importance of this feast in the liturgical life of Jerusalem during the early fifth century.[31]

It is important to note, however, that Egeria does not mention the Memory of

Mary in her description of Jerusalem's annual liturgical practices, made during her pilgrimage to the Holy City in 383.[32] Yet Egeria's silence offers no assurance that the establishment of this Marian feast postdates her visit, inasmuch as her account does not offer a complete liturgical calendar but focuses only on certain major feasts. Although Egeria rather extensively describes the observances surrounding Epiphany, Lent, Holy Week, Easter and Pentecost, during the period of 'ordinary time' she notes only the dedication feast of the Holy Sepulchre in mid-September. As Walter Ray observes, Egeria 'describes only dominical feasts and . . . does not mention any commemorations of saints', which severely limits the usefulness of her account for understanding liturgical practices outside the Epiphany to Pentecost cycle.[33] Likewise John Baldovin cautions,

> The liturgical data provided by Egeria must be considered carefully in contrast with the A[rmenian] L[ectionary]. Since she does not pretend to give a complete liturgical calendar for Jerusalem but only describes major feasts, one cannot tell how many individual saints were honored by the Christian community in Jerusalem in the late fourth century. On this level, that of a more complete sanctoral calendar, we must overlook differences with the A[rmenian] L[ectionary].[34]

Consequently, Egeria's failure to mention the Memory of Mary does not indicate the absence of this feast from Jerusalem's liturgical calendar in the later fourth century. As Ray, Baldovin and others have observed, it seems likely that many of the sanctoral commemorations described by the *Armenian Lectionary* extend back into the fourth century, and it is certainly possible that the feast of Mary was among these. Nevertheless, only the observance of this feast prior to 428 is certain, as evidenced by the homilies of Hesychius of Jerusalem.

There is, however, considerable evidence for annual liturgical commemorations in the Virgin Mary's honour already during the fourth century, although this evidence has been long overlooked and misinterpreted. In the later fourth century, Epiphanius of Salamis describes a group of Christians, whom he names the Kollyridians, who were already observing regular liturgical celebrations in Mary's honour. While Averil Cameron has recently suggested that 'we should probably leave aside' Epiphanius's reference to this group and their veneration of Mary,[35] doing so would ignore an important witness to the beginnings of Marian piety. Admittedly, it may well be that Epiphanius has invented the existence of a sect named Kollyridians, but the primary issues he addresses in their refutation were real religious phenomena of the late fourth century, as can be determined from other sources. In fact, as will be seen in a moment, a long overlooked source affirms that liturgical ceremonies almost identical with those described by Epiphanius were already being observed in Mary's honour by the later fourth century, if not even earlier.

Writing in the 370s, Epiphanius describes the Kollyridians as a group of women first in Thrace and Scythia and then in Arabia who venerated the Virgin Mary and allowed women to serve as priests, both practices that he forcefully condemns. According to Epiphanius, '[T]hese women prepare a certain carriage with a square seat and spread out fine linens over it on a special day of the year, and they put forth bread and offer it in the name of Mary, and they all partake of the bread.'[36] Epiphanius smears his opponents with the charge that in so doing they have replaced God with Mary, claiming that they 'have done their best and are doing their best, in the grip both of madness and of folly, to substitute her for God'.[37] He further insinuates that their practices amount to pagan goddess worship by drawing comparisons with worship of goddesses Persephone and Thermutis.[38] Epiphanius would no doubt be pleased to learn that his rhetoric continues to persuade many modern readers that his opponents were some sort of Christian goddess worshippers who elevated Mary to be a part of the Godhead.[39] Yet it is by no means clear that this widely held opinion of the Kollyridians represents an accurate understanding of their beliefs and practices. Consideration of Epiphanius' claims about the Kollyridians within the broader frame of his invective against them suggests instead that these rather precocious Christians were simply somewhat ahead of the curve in honouring Mary with cult and veneration, practices that Epiphanius found highly objectionable and tantamount to idolatry.

Epiphanius persistently locates his attack on the Kollyridians' practices within a broader critique of the veneration of the saints. Immediately after introducing the Kollyridians and their 'errors', Epiphanius grounds his response in the context of this larger issue, explaining that '[T]he words, "Some shall depart from sound doctrine, giving heed to fables and doctrines of devils", apply to these people as well. For as the scriptures say, they will be "worshipping the dead" as the dead were given honors in Israel. And the timely glory of the saints, which redounds to God in their lifetimes, has become an error for others, who do not see the truth.'[40] Here the Kollyridian veneration of Mary is joined with the more generic practice of 'worshipping the dead', the saints as Epiphanius clarifies, whose glory 'redounds to God in their lifetimes', and accordingly they are not to be 'worshipped' after their death. Like many other Christian writers of the later fourth century, Epiphanius insists that Mary and the saints may not be venerated but are only to be held in honour.[41] Yet for Epiphanius, unlike some of the others, honouring the saints appears to consist primarily in imitating their examples of Christian excellence, and while he does not explicitly reject any and all cultic ceremonies in honour of the saints, this position seems implied by his rhetoric.

In a particularly revealing passage, Epiphanius counters the Kollyridian veneration of Mary by comparing her directly with several other saints.

Which prophet permitted the veneration [προσκυνεῖεθαι] of a man, let alone a woman? The vessel is choice but a woman, and by nature no different [from others]. Like the bodies of the saints, however, she has been held in honor [τιμᾶ] for her character and understanding. And if I should say anything more in her praise, she is like Elijah, who was a virgin from his mother's womb, he remained so perpetually, and was assumed [ἀναλαμβανόμενος] and has not seen death. She is like John who leaned on the Lord's breast, 'the disciple whom Jesus loved'. She is like St Thecla; and Mary is still more honored than she, because of the providence vouchsafed her. But Elijah is not to be venerated [προσκυνητός], even though he is alive. And John is not to be venerated, even if through his own prayer (or rather, by receiving grace from God) he made his dormition [κοίμησιν] an amazing thing. But neither is Thecla venerated, nor any of the saints. For the age-old error of forgetting the living God and worshipping his creatures will not get the better of me. 'They worshipped and venerated the creature more than the creator', and 'were made fools'. If it is not his will that angels be venerated, how much more the woman born of Ann?[42]

Here as elsewhere in the *Panarion*, Epiphanius appears to disapprove of any cultic veneration offered to Mary or any of the saints, in light of which he strongly condemns the Marian piety of the Kollyridians as idolatrous. Yet nowhere does Epiphanius indicate that the Kollyridians had actually gone so far as identifying Mary with the deity in a way comparable to the trinitarian understanding of her Son's divinity. Instead, he objects to their veneration of the Virgin as being tantamount to 'substituting her for God', and it is quite doubtful that the Kollyridians (or whoever's practices Epiphanius is attacking) understood their actions in this way. To the contrary, it appears that the Kollyridians offered Mary the kind of veneration that was increasingly directed towards Christian saints during the late fourth century, as his comparison seems to suggest.

Presumably, the Kollyridians were no more interested in replacing God with Mary or elevating her to a divine status than were the early devotees of Thecla or John in deifying the objects of their devotion. Epiphanius himself even allows for this possibility, when towards the end of his invective he argues that 'whether these worthless women offer Mary the loaf as though in worship of her, or whether they mean to offer this rotten fruit on her behalf, it is altogether silly and heretical, and demon-inspired insolence and imposture'.[43] Although Epiphanius makes his best effort to trump up the charges against the Kollyridians as idolatrous worship of Mary as a divine goddess, he nonetheless leaves this important hint that the Kollyridians may have understood their actions very differently. Far from replacing God with Mary, these early Christians appear to have been doing little more than honouring Mary with a liturgical ceremony offering loaves of bread on her behalf. To be sure, the actions ascribed to the Kollyridians are in many ways strongly reminiscent of Graeco-Roman goddess worship, but such parallels do not necessarily amount to worship of Mary as a goddess.[44] Innumerable elements of the early Christian faith, and particularly the cult of the saints, strongly resemble aspects of Graeco-Roman religions, and yet they do not entail the rejection of monotheistic worship. In fact, a long overlooked source that is contemporary with Epiphanius, if not perhaps even earlier, confirms that Christians of the fourth century observed precisely such commemorations in Mary's honour, without any indication of having made her into a deity.

The *Six Books* apocryphon, one of the earliest Dormition narratives, directs that a liturgical ceremony almost identical to what Epiphanius ascribes to the Kollyridians should be observed in Mary's honour on three different occasions during the year. Although this text survives in a variety of languages and recensions, the earliest are several Syriac versions whose manuscripts date to the late fifth and sixth centuries.[45] The Greek original from which these derive was most likely already in circulation by the later fourth century, although it may very well be even earlier.[46] The precise dates of the three Marian feasts vary somewhat according to the different early manuscripts, but their approximate times and significance are quite uniform in each version. First there is a feast of Mary two days after the Nativity (celebrated on 24 December or 6 January in the different manuscripts), followed by a second on 15 May and a third on 13 August.[47] Each feast has strong agricultural associations, and none has any connection with Mary's death or any other event from her life, suggesting a very primitive stage in Marian cult before any of the specific occasions in her life came to be memorialized liturgically. Yet the most extraordinary aspect of this brief liturgical handbook from the early Dormition apocrypha is the explicit set of instructions it gives for the celebration of these three feasts:

And the apostles also ordered that any offering offered in the name of my Lady Mary should not remain overnight, but that at midnight of the night immediately preceding her commemoration, it should be kneaded and baked; and in the morning let it go up on the altar whilst the people stand before the altar with psalms of David, and let the New and Old Testaments be read, and the volume of the decease of the blessed one [i.e., the *Six Books* apocryphon]; and let everyone be before the altar in the church, and let the priests make the offering and set forth the censer of incense and kindle the lights, and let the whole service be concerning these offerings; and when the whole service is finished, let everyone take his offerings to his house. And let the priest speak thus: 'In the name of the Father, and of the Son, and of the Holy Spirit, we celebrate the commemoration of my Lady Mary'. Thus let the priest speak three times; and (simultaneously) with the word of the priest who speaks, the Holy Spirit shall come and bless these offerings; and when everyone takes away his offering, and goes to his house, great help and the blessing of the blessed one shall enter his dwelling and establish it for ever.[48]

The similarities between this ritual and Epiphanius' account of the Kollyridians are fairly obvious: on certain days of the year a special bread is prepared and offered to the Virgin, and after a ceremony in her honour (during which the *Six Books* apocryphon is read) the participants take home the consecrated bread and 'all partake of the bread'. These liturgical instructions, combined with the *Six Books* narrative's constant reference to 'veneration' (ܪܚܡܬܐ) offered to Mary, add considerable credibility to Epiphanius' complaints against such practices. While the *Six Books* apocryphon makes no indication of women serving as liturgical leaders, nor is there any direct link with a group named the 'Kollyridians', this early Dormition narrative confirms that by the late fourth century certain groups were regularly venerating the Virgin using a ritual that looks very much like the one Epiphanius attributes to the Kollyridians.

It would appear that this similarity is more than mere coincidence, as Epiphanius himself reveals by establishing several implicit connections between the Kollyridians and the Virgin's Dormition, suggesting a link between his knowledge of these ritual practices and traditions about the end of Mary's life. Epiphanius first addresses the Kollyridians while denouncing the 'Antidicomarianites', an alleged sect that rejected Mary's Perpetual Virginity, discussion of which immediately precedes the Kollyridians. Epiphanius dispenses with the 'Antidicomarianites' by citing in full an earlier writing, his *Letter to Arabia*, in which he rather famously raises the issue of the end of Mary's life for the first time in patristic literature. Although Epiphanius initially considers the subject of Mary's departure from this life while attacking the Antidicomarianites, both the *Letter to Arabia* and the *Panarion* reveal a subtle but striking connection between the Kollyridians and the Virgin's Dormition.

In the *Letter to Arabia*, Epiphanius mulls over several possible endings to Mary's life, but in the end he professes a strict agnosticism and concludes with very deliberate equivocation: 'I am not saying that she remained immortal; but neither am I affirming that she died.'[49] Nevertheless, at the same time, Epiphanius admits to knowing more about the subject than he is willing to disclose: 'For I dare not say, and although I have some ideas, I keep silent.'[50] It is rather puzzling why Epiphanius introduces this topic in his defence of Mary's Perpetual Virginity; its contribution to his argument is minimal at best, and it presents something of a distraction from the larger issue. Clearly there must be some unvoiced reason for so deliberately focusing on the end of Mary's life in the midst of defending her virginity. His sudden return to this theme when first addressing the Kollyridians at the letter's conclusion may hold the key. Here, suddenly and without any explanation, Epiphanius interrupts his discussion of the Kollyridians and reintroduces the topic of the end of Mary's life.

> The holy virgin may have died and been buried — her falling asleep was with honor, her death in purity, her crown in virginity. Or she may have been put to death – as the scripture says, 'And a sword shall pierce through her soul' – her fame is among the martyrs and her body, by which light rose in the world, [rests] amid blessings. Or she remained alive, for God is not incapable of doing whatever he wills. No one knows her end.[51]

The abrupt return to this subject at this point is quite puzzling: Epiphanius gives no reason for it, and he makes no connections whatsoever between the end of Mary's life and either the Kollyridians or their ritual practices. The reader is left wondering why Epiphanius felt compelled to bring the issue up once again in his discussion of the Kollyridians. It would appear that he is deliberately holding something back here, and the clear implication is that there is some sort of unspoken connection between the end of Mary's life and the ritual practices ascribed to the Kollyridians. Otherwise, it is extremely difficult to understand his sudden reintroduction of the topic. This linkage of the end of Mary's life with ritual offerings of bread in her honour certainly suggests Epiphanius' knowledge of the *Six Books* apocryphon, either directly or through awareness of a group that followed its practices and teachings. Yet there is further evidence of this connection in the following section of the *Panarion*, where Epiphanius addresses the Kollyridian heresy more directly and at length.

In denouncing this seventy-ninth heresy, Epiphanius tackles first the issue of women's liturgical leadership, but as he turns to their ritual practices, the theme of Mary's Dormition is once again found to be in the mix, lurking in the background without any clear explanation for its presence. In the passage cited above, where Epiphanius compares Mary to Thecla, Elijah and John, his choices are rather telling. The comparison with Thecla is a rather obvious one, inasmuch as Thecla's popularity in the early Church rivalled Mary's, and indeed Thecla, rather than Mary, stood for centuries as the pre-eminent model for female virgins.[52] Yet it is somewhat surprising to find Epiphanius comparing Mary with an Old Testament prophet and one of the apostles, particularly after he has just excoriated women's liturgical leadership and prophecy. Obviously, these characteristics are not the ones that Epiphanius wants to compare. Instead, he explains that Mary is like Elijah because he was 'a virgin from his mother's womb, he remained so perpetually, and was assumed [ἀναλαμβανμενος] and has not seen death'.[53] Although it has been long overlooked, Epiphanius here unexpectedly departs from the formal agnosticism of the *Letter to Arabia* by declaring Mary's assumption and immortality without any of his previous equivocation. Surely his decision to compare Mary with Elijah in regard to his assumption and immortality, without any further clarification, is telling. While Epiphanius does not address the end of Mary's life as directly here as in the *Letter to Arabia*, he nonetheless again returns to the issue of her Dormition while arguing against the Kollyridian ritual practices.

As he continues to press his case against the veneration of saints in this passage, Epiphanius renews the comparison between Mary and Elijah towards the end, implying that like Mary, 'Elijah is not to be venerated, even though he is alive.'[54] As if to underscore the point, Epiphanius also introduces the tradition of John's miraculous dormition, noting that 'John is not to be venerated, even if through his own prayer (or rather, by receiving grace from God) he made his falling asleep [κοίμησιν] an amazing thing.'[55] Here Epiphanius refers to the various traditions of the apostle John's 'metastasis' that had begun to circulate by this time, many of which include the miraculous removal of his body from the world.[56] The rhetoric in this passage signals even more clearly than in the *Letter to Arabia* a linkage between the Kollyridian ritual practices and traditions about the end of Mary's life. Although Epiphanius does not make the nature of this connection explicit, his arguments leave little question that for some unvoiced reason he felt compelled to join his attack on the Kollyridian ceremonies with the issue of Mary's marvellous departure from this world. Perhaps these opponents justified their veneration of the Virgin through appeal to traditions of the Virgin's miraculous Dormition and Assumption: there is no other clear reason why Epiphanius would introduce the subject as he does.

Epiphanius' rhetorical joining of the Kollyridian bread offerings with the end of Mary's life is particularly important for understanding the early Dormition traditions. His comparison of the Virgin with Elijah clearly affirms what he already hints at in the *Letter to Arabia*: that traditions of the Virgin's Dormition and Assumption were already in circulation prior to the later fourth century, when he first encountered them. Moreover, by repeatedly linking the end of Mary's life with his attack on the Kollyridian liturgical practices, Epiphanius signals a connection between ritual bread offerings in Mary's honour and traditions about her Dormition. This combination points unmistakably towards the *Six Books* apocryphon, which, in the midst of its account of Mary's marvellous departure from the world, enjoins an annual ritual almost identical with that of the Kollyridians. It would appear that Epiphanius's attack on the Kollyridians is directed at least in part against the traditions of the *Six Books* apocryphon, which he knew either directly or through encountering a group that followed its beliefs and practices. The *Six Books* apocryphon is the only known source from the ancient Church actually to prescribe regular, ritual offerings of bread on Mary's behalf, and the fact that these rituals occur in one of the earliest Dormition narratives coincides remarkably with the rhetoric of Epiphanius' invective against the Kollyridians. Surely the striking parallels between the *Six Books* and Epiphanius' Kollyridians are more than just a coincidence.

Epiphanius' account of the Kollyridians is thus not to be set aside, but is an essential witness to Marian veneration in the later fourth century. His apparent knowledge of the *Six Books* apocryphon suggests the existence of this Dormition narrative, at the very least in an early oral form, sometime before 370, the approximate date of the *Letter to Arabia*.[57] The *Six Books* narrative is filled with examples of prayer to the Virgin, instances of Marian intercession, numerous miracles ascribed to her authority, and even Marian apparitions, all of which can readily account for Epiphanius's broad attack on Marian piety in the *Panarion*. Only women's liturgical leadership is lacking from the *Six Books*, although there is nothing that would contradict such a practice. Of course, it may be that Epiphanius has simply thrown this issue in for good measure, or perhaps he has even invented the 'Kollyridians' entirely to address simultaneously the topics of women's liturgical leadership and early Marian devotion. In any case, it seems that the *Six Books* narrative is somewhat older than has previously been thought. Presumably, Epiphanius encountered these traditions sometime before 367 while he was still in Palestine, suggesting that the *Six Books* apocryphon had begun to circulate already by the middle of the fourth century.

Despite the well-earned mistrust that much contemporary scholarship has for Epiphanius' reporting, it would appear that in this particular case he is not completely off the mark. There were in the later fourth century Christians who made liturgical offerings of bread in the Virgin Mary's honour, as the *Six Books* apocryphon attests. Even if we cannot trust every detail in Epiphanius' account of the Kollyridians, together these two sources present a rather solid witness to the celebration of these annual liturgical feasts within the broader context of emergent Marian veneration. Whether an actual sect named 'the Kollyridians' ever existed or not is largely immaterial. The issues that Epiphanius addresses in refuting this group were certainly real phenomena within his broader religious milieu, and thus he presents yet another witness to the practice of Marian cult in the fourth century. Whatever Pulcheria's place in the history books may come to be, there can be no question that cultic veneration of the Virgin Mary had been a part of Christian piety for over half a century before the Council of Ephesus, at least in certain circles, which included, it would seem, Gregory Nazianzen's Constantinople. Consequently, it would be a mistake to isolate once again the Christological debates of the third Council from incipient devotion to the Virgin. Even if Pulcheria may not have been a primary instigator, it is almost certain that popular devotion to the Virgin must have played a central role in the Nestorian controversy and was not merely its by-product.

BIBLIOGRAPHY

Angelidi, C. (1998), *Pulcheria: La Castità al Potere (c. 399–c. 455)* (*Donne d'Oriente e d'Occidente* 5). Milan: Jaca.

Aubineau, M. (1978), *Les homélies festales d'Hésychius de Jérusalem* (*Subsidia Hagiographica* 59). Brussels: Société des Bollandistes.

Avner, R. (2003), 'The Recovery of the Kathisma Church and Its Influence on Octagonal Buildings', in G. C. Bottini, L. D. Segni and D. Chrupcala (eds), *One Land – Many Cultures: Archaeological Studies in Honor of Stanislao Loffreda, OFM* (*Studium Biblicum Franciscanum Collectio major* 41). Jerusalem: Franciscan Printing Press, 173–88.

Baldovin, J. F. (1987), *The Urban Character of Christian Worship: The Origins, Development, and Meaning of Stational Liturgy* (*Orientalia Christiana Analecta* 228). Rome: Pontificium Institutum Studiorum Orientalium.

Bauckham, R. (1998), *The Fate of the Dead: Studies on Jewish and Christian Apocalypses* (*Supplements to Novum Testamentum* 93). Leiden: E. J. Brill.

Benko, S. (1993), *The Virgin Goddess: Studies in the Pagan and Christian Roots of Mariology* (*Studies in the History of Religions* 59). Leiden: E. J. Brill.

Bidez, J. and G. C. Hansen (eds) (1995), *Sozomenus: Kirchengeschichte* (*Griechischen christlichen Schriftsteller der ersten Jahrhunderte, Neue Folge* 4). Berlin: Akademie Verlag.

Cameron, A. (1993), *The Mediterranean World in Late Antiquity, AD 395–600.* London: Routledge.

—— (2000), 'The Early Cult of the Virgin', in M. Vassilaki (ed.), *Mother of God: Representations of the Virgin in Byzantine Art.* Milan: Skira, 3–15.

—— (2004), 'The Cult of the Virgin in Late Antiquity: Religious Development and Myth-Making', in R. N. Swanson (ed.), *The Church and Mary* (*Studies in Church History* 39). Woodbridge: Boydell & Brewer, 1–21.

Capelle, B. (1943), 'La fête de la Vierge à Jérusalem au Ve siècle', *Le Muséon* 56, 1–33.

Carroll, M. P. (1986), *The Cult of the Virgin Mary: Psychological Origins.* Princeton: Princeton University Press.

Constas, N. (1995), 'Weaving the Body of God: Proclus of Constantinople, the Theotokos, and the Loom of the Flesh', *Journal of Early Christian Studies* 3, 169–94.

—— (2003), *Proclus of Constantinople and the Cult of the Virgin in Late Antiquity: Homilies 1–5, Texts and Translations* (Supplements to *Vigiliae Christianae* 66). Leiden: E. J. Brill.

Cooper, K. (1998), 'Contesting the Nativity: Wives, Virgins, and Pulcheria's *imitatio Mariae*', *Scottish Journal of Religious Studies* 19, 31–43.

—— (2004), 'Empress and *Theotokos*: Gender and Patronage in the Christological Controversy', in R. N. Swanson (ed.), *The Church and Mary* (*Studies in Church History* 39). Woodbridge: Boydell & Brewer, 39–51.

Davis, S. J. (2001), *The Cult of Saint Thecla: A Tradition of Women's Piety in Late Antiquity.* Oxford: Oxford University Press.

Devos, P. (1967), 'Le date du voyage d'Égérie', *Analecta Bollandiana* 85, 165–94.

—— (1968), 'Égérie à Bethléem: Le 40ᵉ jour après Pâques à Jérusalem, en 383', *Analecta Bollandiana* 87–108.

Dölger, F. J. (1929), 'Die eigenartige Marienverehrung der Philomarianiten oder Kollyridianer in Arabia', *Antike und Christentum* 1, 1–46.

Förster, H. (1995), 'Zur ältesten Überlieferung der marianischen Antiphon *Sub tuum prae-sidium*', *Biblos: Österreichische Zeitschrift für Buch- und Bibliothekwesen, Dokumentation, Bibliographie, und Bibliophilie* 44, 183–92.

Gambero, L. (1999), *Mary and the Fathers of the Church*. San Francisco: Ignatius Press.

Giamberardini, G. (1969), 'Il "Sub tuum praesidium" e il titolo "Theotokos" nella tra-ditzione egiziana', *Marianum* 31, 324–62.

—— (1975), *Il Culto Mariano in Eggito* (*Pubblicazioni dello Studium Biblicum Franciscanum, Analecta* 6). Jerusalem: Franciscan Printing Press.

Heil, G., J. P. Cavarnos and O. Lendle (eds) (1990), *Gregorii Nysseni Opera*. Leiden: E. J. Brill.

Holl, K. and J. Dummer (eds) (1915, 1980, 1985), *Epiphanius* (*Die griechischen christlichen Schriftsteller der ersten drei Jahrhunderte* 25, 31, 37). Leipzig/Berlin: J. C. Hinrichs/Akademie-Verlag.

Holum, K. G. (1982), *Theodosian Empresses: Women and Imperial Dominion in Late Antiquity*. Berkeley and Los Angeles: University of California Press.

Hunt, A. S., J. d. M. Johnson and C. H. Roberts (1911–52), *Catalogue of the Greek Papyri in the John Rylands Library, Manchester*. Manchester: Manchester University Press.

Johnson, M. E. (2006), 'The Apostolic Tradition', in G. Wainwright, and K. B. Westerfield Tucker (eds), *The Oxford History of Christian Worship*. New York: Oxford University Press, 32–75.

Jouassard, G. (1961), 'Deux chefs de file en théologie mariale dans la seconde moitié du IVème siècle: saint Epiphane et saint Ambroise', *Gregorianum* 42, 6–36.

Jugie, M. (1926), *Homélies Mariales Byzantines II* (Patrologia Orientalis 19.3). Paris: Librairie de Paris/Firmin-Didot et Cie.

—— (1944), *La Mort et l'Assomption de la Sainte Vierge, Étude Historico-doctrinale* (*Studi e testi* 114). Vatican City: Biblioteca Apostolica Vaticana.

Kaestli, J. D. (1983), 'Le rôle des textes bibliques dans la genèse et le développement des légendes apocryphes. Le cas du sort final de l'apôtre Jean', *Augustinianum* 23, 319–36.

Kelly, J. N. D. (1978), *Early Christian Doctrines*. New York: Harper & Row.

Kraemer, R. S. (1992), *Her Share of the Blessings: Women's Religions among Pagans, Jews, and Christians in the Greco-Roman World*. Oxford/New York: Oxford University Press.

Limberis, V. (1994), *Divine Heiress: The Virgin Mary and the Creation of Christian Constantino-ple*. London: Routledge.

Mango, C. (1998), 'The Origins of the Blachernae Shrine at Constantinople', in N. Cambi and E. Marin (eds), *Acta XIII Congressus Internationalis Archaeologicae Christianae: Split – Poreč*. Vatican City: Pontificio Instituto di Archeologia Cristiana, 61–76.

Maraval, P. (2004), *Lieux saints et pèlerinages d'orient: Histoire et géographie des origines à la conquête arabe*. Paris: Les Éditions du Cerf.

McGuckin, J. A. (2001), *St Gregory of Nazianzus: An Intellectual Biography*. New York: SVS Press.

Mimouni, S. C. (1991), 'Genèse et évolution des traditions anciennes sur le sort final de Marie: Étude de la tradition littéraire copte', *Marianum* 42, 69–143.

—— (1992), 'La fête de la dormition de Marie en Syrie à l'époque byzantine', *The Harp* 5, 157–74.

—— (1995), *Dormition et Assomption de Marie: Histoire des traditions anciennes* (*Théologie His-torique* 98). Paris: Beauchesne.

Mossay, J. (ed.) (1981), *Grégoire de Nazianze: Discours 24–26* (*Sources Chrétiennes* 284). Paris: Les Éditions du Cerf.

Peltomaa, L. M. (2001), *The Image of the Virgin Mary in the Akathistos Hymn* (*The Medieval Mediterranean* 35). Leiden: E. J. Brill.

Pétré, H. (ed.) (1971), *Éthérie: Journal de Voyage* (*Sources Chrétiennes* 21). Paris: Éditions du Cerf.

Price, R. M. (2004), 'Marian Piety and the Nestorian Controversy', in R. N. Swanson (ed.), *The Church and Mary* (*Studies in Church History* 39). Woodbridge: Boydell & Brewer, 31–8.

Ray, W. D. (2000) 'August 15 and the Development of the Jerusalem Calendar' (unpublished doctoral dissertation, University of Notre Dame).

Renoux, A. (1971), *Le Codex Arménien Jérusalem 121* (*PO* 35.1, 36.2). Turnhout: Brepols.

Schaff, P. and H. Wace (eds) (1891), *A Select Library of Nicene and Post-Nicene Fathers of the Christian Church: Second Series*. New York: The Christian Literature Company.

Schneemelcher, W. (1992), *New Testament Apocrypha: Writings Relating to the Apostles Apocalypses and Related Subjects*, ed. and trans. R. M. Wilson. Louisville: John Knox Press.

Shoemaker, S. J. (2001), 'The (Re?)Discovery of the Kathisma Church and the Cult of the Virgin in Late Antique Palestine', *Maria: A Journal of Marian Studies* 2, 21–72.

—— (2002), *Ancient Traditions of the Virgin Mary's Dormition and Assumption* (*Oxford Early Christian Studies*) Oxford: Oxford University Press.

—— (2008), 'The Cult of Fashion: The Earliest *Life of the Virgin* and Constantinople's Marian Relics', *Dumbarton Oaks Papers* 62. Forthcoming.

Smith Lewis, A. (1902), *Apocrypha Syriaca* (*Studia Sinaitica* 11). London: C. J. Clay & Sons.

Starowieyski, M. (1990), 'La plus ancienne description d'une mariophane par Grégoire de Nysse', in H. Drobner and C. Klock (eds), *Studien zu Gregor von Nyssa und der christlichen Spätantike*. Leiden: E. J. Brill, 245–53.

Stegmüller, O. (1952), 'Sub tuum praesidium: Bemerkungen zur ältesten Überlieferung', *Zeitschrift für katholische Theologie* 74, 76–82.

Tischendorf, C. (1876), *Evangelia Apocrypha*. Leipzig: H. Mendelssohn.

Triacca, A. M. (1989), '"Sub tuum praesidium": nella "lex orandi" un'anticipata presenza della "lex credendi". La "teotocologia" precede la "mariologia"?', in S. Felici (ed.), *La mariologia nella catechesi dei padri (età prenicena). Convegno di studio e aggiornamento, Facoltà di Lettere cristiane e classiche (Pontificium Istitutum Altioris Latinitatis), Roma, 10–11 marzo 1989* (*Biblioteca di scienze religiose* 95). Rome: LAS, 183–205.

Van Esbroeck, M. (2001), 'Some earlier features in the Life of the Virgin', *Marianum* 63, 297–308.

Verhelst, S. (2001), 'Le 15 août, le 9 av et le kathisme', *Questions liturgiques* 82, 161–91.

Von Campenhausen, H. (1964), *The Virgin Birth in the Theology of the Ancient Church* (*Studies in Historical Theology* 2). London: SCM Press.

Williams, F. (1987, 1994), *The Panarion of Epiphanius of Salamis* (*Nag Hammadi Studies* 35–6). Leiden: E. J. Brill.

Wright, W. (1865), 'The departure of my Lady Mary from this world', *The Journal of Sacred Literature and Biblical Record* 6–7, 417–48; 108–60.

NOTES

1. E.g. von Campenhausen 1964: esp. 7–9; Carroll 1986: xii.
2. Price 2004: 31.
3. Cameron 2000: 5. See also Cameron 1993: 149. In a more recent article, however, Cameron identifies the late fourth and fifth centuries as the formative period of Marian piety, while still pointing to the determinative influence of Ephesus (Cameron 2004: esp. 1–10).
4. Holum 1982: 154.
5. Limberis 1994.
6. Price 2004; Cameron 2004: 9–11; Angelidi 1998; Peltomaa 2001: e.g. 51 n. 10; 57 n. 53; Cooper 1998; Cooper 2004.
7. Mango 1998: 72.
8. I have argued this point in more detail in a forthcoming article: Shoemaker 2008.

9. Hunt *et al.* 1911–52: 3, 47; Stegmüller 1952: 78. See also Giamberardini 1975: 95–7, but see the dissenting opinion of Förster 1995; Giamberardini 1969; Triacca 1989.

10. Mossay 1981: 9–27.

11. Gregory Nazianzus, *Oration 24*, 9–11. *Ibid.*: 54–61; translated by Gambero 1999: 166–7.

12. Mossay 1981: 25; Stegmüller 1952: 78; Peltomaa 2001: 75.

13. McGuckin 2001: 252.

14. Gregory of Nyssa, *Life of Gregory Thaumaturgus*, Heil *et al.* 1990: 16–18.

15. Starowieyski 1990.

16. Sozomen, *Ecclesiastical History* 7.5.1–3. Bidez and Hansen 1995: 306; trans. Schaff and Wace 1891: 378–9.

17. Kelly 1978: 498.

18. Constas 2003: 246.

19. Constas 2003: 31–5, 56–9; Constas 1995: 172–6; Shoemaker 2001; Ray 2000; Johnson 2006: 66.

20. Mimouni 1992: esp. 159–62.

21. Mimouni 1991: 123–33, esp. 127 n. 243; Mimouni 1995: 413–20, esp. 418 n. 20.

22. Proclus of Constantinople, *Homily 1: On the Holy Virgin Theotokos*, Constas 2003: 28–56.

23. Constas 2003: 128.

24. *Ibid.*: 31–5, 56–9; Constas 1995: 172–6.

25. Shoemaker 2001.

26. Renoux 1971: 2.354–7; regarding the date, see 1.166–72.

27. *Protevangelium of James* 17.1.3. Tischendorf 1876: 33; trans. Schneemelcher 1992: 1.433.

28. Ray 2000; Capelle 1943; some rather different speculations on the origin of the feast, also connected with the birth of Christ, are offered in Verhelst 2001.

29. Shoemaker 2002: 81–98; Shoemaker 2001: 23–36. The newly discovered church is well presented by its excavator in Avner 2003.

30. Aubineau 1978: 1.117–205; see also Mimouni 1995: 392–5, esp. in regard to *Homily VI*.

31. Pétré 1971. On the date, see Devos 1967; Devos 1968.

32. Epiphanius, *Panarion* 79.1.7. Holl and Dummer 1985: 3.476.

33. Epiphanius, *Panarion* 78.23.3. *Ibid.*: 3.473; trans. Williams 1987, 1994: 2.618.

34. Baldovin 1987: 94.

35. Cameron 2004: 6–7.

36. Epiphanius, *Panarion* 78.23.6–7. Holl and Dummer 1985: 3.473–4.

37. Epiphanius, *Panarion* 78.23.5. *Ibid.*: 3.473; trans. Williams 1987, 1994: 2.618–19.

38. Epiphanius, *Panarion* 79.5.1–4. *Ibid.*: 3.479–80; trans. Williams 1987, 1994: 2.624–5, slightly modified.

39. Epiphanius, *Panarion* 79.9.3. *Ibid.*: 3.484; trans. Williams 1987, 1994: 2.628.

40. E.g. Jugie 1944: 79–80; Kraemer 1992: 201; Benko 1993: esp. 173, 190; Limberis 1994: 118; Gambero 1999: 122.

41. See the extensive catalogue of parallels in Dölger 1929 and Benko 1993: 173–91.

42. Shoemaker 2002: 46–9. Two early versions of this apocryphon have been published with English translation in Smith Lewis 1902; Wright 1865. Wright's English translation can also be found online at http://www.uoregon.edu/~sshoemak/texts/dormindex.htm.

43. Smith Lewis 1902: ܣܘܡܟ (Syr.); 59–61 (Eng.); Wright 1865: ܝܠܕ (Syr.); 152–3 (Eng.); the fifth-century palimpsest fragments from Sinai also refer to the three feasts, although this particular section is lacking: see Smith Lewis 1902: ܩܠܣܘܗ ; trans. Shoemaker 2002: 371–2. See also Mimouni 1992.

44. Wright 1865: ܡܪܝܡ (Syr.); 153 (Eng.), translation slightly modified. An almost identical version appears in the sixth-century MS Göttingen Syr. 10, fol. 31. The corresponding section is missing from the two fifth-century palimpsests, both of which

are fragmentary, and so we do not know what liturgical instructions may have been present in these manuscripts. The comparable passage from the Göttingen MS is as follows: 'And the apostles ordered that there will be a commemoration of the blessed one in these three months, so that people will be delivered from hard afflictions and a plague of wrath will not come upon the earth and its inhabitants. And the apostles ordered that offerings that have been made to the blessed one should not remain overnight, but in the evening let flour of the finest wheat flour come to the church and be placed before the altar. And the priests will make the offering and set up censers of incense and light the lights. And the entire evening service [Vespers] will concern these offerings. And when the service is finished, let everyone take his offering to his house. Because as soon as the priests pray and say the prayer of my master Mary, the Theotokos, "Come to us and help the people who call upon you," and with the priest's word of blessing, my master Mary comes and blesses these offerings. And as soon as everyone takes his offering and goes to his house, great aid and the blessing of my master Mary will enter his dwelling and sustain it forever.'

45. Epiphanius, *Panarion* 78.11.2–4. Holl and Dummer 1985: 3.462.
46. Epiphanius, *Panarion* 78.11.3. *Ibid.*
47. Shoemaker 2002: 54–7; van Esbroeck 2001; Bauckham 1998: 346–60, esp. 358–60.
48. Epiphanius, *Panarion* 78.23.9. Holl and Dummer 1985: 3.473; trans. Williams 1987, 1994: 2.619.
49. Epiphanius, *Panarion* 79.5.2. *Ibid.*: 3.479.
50. Epiphanius, *Panarion* 79.5.3. *Ibid.*: 3.480.
51. Epiphanius, *Panarion* 79.5.3. *Ibid.*
52. Davis 2001: 4, 21.
53. Epiphanius, *Panarion* 79.5.2. Holl and Dummer 1985: 3.479.
54. Epiphanius, *Panarion* 79.5.3. *Ibid.*: 3.480.
55. Epiphanius, *Panarion* 79.5.3. *Ibid.*
56. Kaestli 1983: esp. 329–30; Schneemelcher 1992: 2.161–3, 204–5.
57. Jouassard 1961: 6.

6

THE *THEOTOKOS* AND THE COUNCIL OF EPHESUS

RICHARD M. PRICE

EARLY USE OF THE *THEOTOKOS* TITLE

It is striking how writers on the cult of Mary tend to skate over the first three or four centuries in the history of the Church. It is an embarrassment for them that the material is so thin. The Virgin is celebrated with devotion and a fertile imagination in the *Protevangelium*, or *Infancy Gospel of James*, which scholars date to the second half of the second century.[1] Several of the pre-Nicene Fathers develop the theme of Mary's perfect response to the divine call at the Annunciation; there was a particular emphasis on her virginity in fourth-century ascetical literature, notably in Athanasius and Ambrose.[2] But none of this is evidence of actual cult, of which the central features are invocation and (in the context of the strongly communal character of early Christian devotion) feast day and festival. An article by Luigi Gambero, 'Patristic Intuitions of Mary's Role as Mediatrix and Advocate: The Invocation of the Faithful for her Help', published in 2001,[3] is typical in trying to draw out of the mention of the Virgin in the pre-Nicene Fathers evidence of a cult of which they make no mention.

The only solid evidence that Gambero adduces for the invocation of Mary is the famous John Rylands papyrus, first published in 1938, that was immediately recognized as containing in only slightly damaged form the earliest known text of the Marian prayer known in Latin as *Sub tuum praesidium*. The restored text runs: 'Under your mercy we take refuge, *Theotokos*. Do not overlook our petitions in adversity, but rescue us from danger, uniquely holy one and uniquely blessed one.'[4] Even though the style of the lettering on the papyrus pointed to a date in the third century, the original editor and most subsequent commentators have preferred a later date on the grounds that both the title *Theotokos* and a prayer of intercession addressed to the Virgin exclude a date prior to the mid-fourth century. How secure is this reasoning?

The title *Theotokos* means 'God-bearer', or the one who gave birth to God, and serves to express simultaneously that Christ is God and yet took on human nature in the womb of the Virgin Mary.[5] When did this title first come into use? The Church historian Socrates, writing in the mid-fifth century, tells us that Origen (d. 254) in his now lost commentary on the Epistle to the Romans 'gave an ample exposition of the sense in which *Theotokos* is used'.[6] Since, however, there is no instance of its use in surviving texts of Origen, it cannot have been in regular use in his day. The earliest undisputed use in an extant text is by Bishop Alexander of Alexandria in 325; only slightly later are the occasional uses of the word in Eusebius of Caesarea and other contemporaries.[7] It is, however, striking that in all these instances the use of the word is incidental: it is not explained or justified, and no weight is placed upon it. The implication is that by the time of the Council of Nicaea in 325 the term was already in standard use. We must also remember that we have so little Greek patristic literature from the second half of the third century that the lack of attestation in this period does not prove that the term was not already in use. It seems reasonable to conclude that it was a novelty requiring explanation in the time of Origen, but had become standard by the end of the third century. Its use on the John Rylands papyrus is not therefore a ground for dating the papyrus later than the third century.

What was the origin of the title *Theotokos*? I am going to argue that the debate over the title during the Nestorian controversy was concerned with its Christological implications and not with the dignity of Mary. But even if it was Christological debate that later brought the title to the fore, I cannot imagine that it was a Christological debate that generated the title in the first place. What theologian, in order to drive home the point that Christ is God, would himself invent the term *Theotokos*? The very character of the word does not belong to prose discourse: it is a poetic neologism that is most likely to have originated in hymnology. The fact that Mary was already being called *Theotokos* early in the fourth century and very possibly a century before that (if Origen indeed discussed the term) is evidence that she was celebrated in hymns at an early date. This is evidence of a cult that must surely have involved the invocation of Mary and a belief in the power and availability of her intercession.

But is this to place the emergence of Marian devotion too early? Stephen Shoemaker in his contribution to this volume provides a full discussion of evidence for Marian devotion from the fifty or sixty years prior to the Council of Ephesus of 431.[8] The evidence he discusses does not bring the emergence of Marian piety to a period earlier than the latter half of the fourth century. If we are to link the papyrus with the flowering of Marian piety that Shoemaker recreates for us so convincingly, we need to date it later than the purely palaeographical evidence would suggest; and indeed most scholars prefer a date in the later part of the fourth century.

But it may be a mistake to link the papyrus to the developments of the late fourth century. It is striking that there is no trace of the *Sub tuum praesidium* prayer in late antique Egypt, or indeed in the Coptic Church at all until Catholic influence in modern times.[9] Some continuity must be supposed, to account for the survival of the prayer at all, but the way in which it fell out of use suggests that it belongs to an earlier, less widespread and less lasting phase in the development of Marian piety. This phase was significant enough to give the *Theotokos* title a place in theological literature from the time of Origen, but prayer to the Virgin does not appear to have became firmly established in Christian piety before the later decades of the fourth century.[10]

In the history of Christian thought and devotion as normally outlined, the *Theotokos* title comes to the fore later still, in the Nestorian controversy of the second quarter of the fifth century. It has often been supposed that the development of Marian devotion received strong impetus from the condemnation of Nestorius, to the extent that one can describe it as more a fruit of Nestorius' defeat than its cause.[11] But have the implications of the Nestorian controversy for the history of Marian piety been rightly estimated? The rest of this paper will attempt to provide an answer.

THE *THEOTOKOS* TITLE IN CHRISTOLOGICAL DEBATE

One notable feature in the use of the *Theotokos* title in the Church Fathers is its citation in Christological contexts, whether to bring out the reality of the human nature of Mary's Son Jesus or to stress the reality of the union between Godhead and manhood in Christ; this can already be claimed of the use of the title by Alexander of Alexandria in 325.[12] Fifth-century debates were anticipated by Apollinarius (d. *c.* 390), who used the title to support his distinctive Christology, where all Christ's experiences, including birth from a human mother, are immediately attributed to God the Word as the sole personal subject, and indeed the sole thinking subject, in Christ.

The title, as is widely known, became the centre of a famous debate that reverberated round much of the Christian world in the second quarter of the fifth century. When in 428 the Syrian monk Nestorius arrived at Constantinople as the newly appointed archbishop, he found the *Theotokos* title being exploited by Arian and Apollinarian heretics to subvert either the full divinity or the full humanity of Christ.[13] He duly criticized the title as a loose use of language, and proposed replacing it with *Christotokos* ('Mother of Christ').[14] His reluctance to call Mary *Theotokos* was widely interpreted, however, to mean that he had doubts about the divinity of her Son.[15] There resulted the celebrated Nestorian controversy, in which Cyril of Alexandria played a major role and the bishops of Syria defended Nestorius with some reservations and attacked Cyril with none. The dispute came to a climax at the Council of Ephesus of 431, at which Nestorius was condemned; within a few years the Syrian bishops had accepted his condemnation.[16] It is manifest from the controversial literature generated by the dispute and from the Acts of Ephesus that the issue was primarily concerned with Christ. In what sense should he be called 'divine'? Are his human experiences, including being formed in Mary's womb with flesh taken from her flesh, to be attributed to the divine Logos as the personal subject who, in some sense, underwent them? Viewed from this perspective, the issue was simply the Christological implications of the title *Theotokos* and not the dignity of the Virgin herself.

A number of recent writers have argued, however, that there had been significant developments in Marian devotion in the city of Constantinople in the period between the fall of John Chrysostom in 404 and Nestorius' arrival on the scene in 428, and that Nestorius' fall was due at least in part to the way in which he offended devotees of the Virgin. A prime role in opposition to Nestorius and in the promotion of Marian piety has been attributed to the empress Pulcheria, who was the unmarried sister of Theodosius II (408–450) and later the spouse of his successor Marcian (450–457).[17] Under critical scrutiny, however, much of the evidence crumbles.[18] The date of the development of intense Marian piety in Constantinople was in fact from the sixth to the eighth centuries; this was the period when Pulcheria became credited at Constantinople with dedicating to the Virgin churches that in fact were built after her time.[19] Moreover, the weight of the evidence suggests that Pulcheria had at first actually supported Nestorius and that she deserted his cause only after the Council of Ephesus; in a letter written after the Council, Epiphanius, an agent of Nestorius' enemy Cyril of Alexandria, laments Pulcheria's lack of zeal for the anti-Nestorian cause, despite the numerous 'blessings' (meaning lavish gifts) that had been showered upon her.[20]

Nevertheless, there is reason to believe that already in the period between the Councils of Ephesus (431) and Chalcedon (451), Pulcheria gained an undeserved reputation as a consistent opponent of Nestorius and that she claimed as a virgin a special relationship with both Christ and his mother.[21] And there is contemporary evidence of a developing Marian cult at Constantinople prior to Ephesus in surviving sermons by Bishop Atticus (406–425) and by Proclus, who was a notable preacher in the city from the time of Atticus and later its bishop (434–446). Proclus's most famous sermon (*Homily 1*) was preached on a feast day of the Virgin in the presence of Nestorius himself.

Only one of Atticus's sermons survives in an uncontaminated version. It contains one short but notable passage relating to the cult of Mary:

> And you, women, who gave birth to Christ and have cast off every stain of sin and have participated in the blessing received by holy Mary, receive in the womb of faith the one who is today born from the Virgin; for holy Mary, having first purified by faith the temple of her womb, then received into this temple the King of the ages.[22]

The sermon on Mary that Proclus preached in Nestorius' presence begins:

> The Virgin's festival, my brethren, summons us today to words of praise, and the present feast has benefits to bestow on those who assemble to keep it. And surely this is right, for its subject is chastity. What we celebrate is the pride of women and the glory of the female, thanks to the one who was at once both mother and virgin . . . Let nature leap for joy, and let women be honoured! Let all humanity dance, and let virgins be glorified![23]

The 'Virgin's festival' referred to here (probably 26 December) was also the occasion for *Homily 5*, which claims that Mary surpassed all the prophets of the Old Testament, for while they simply prophesied the coming of Christ, it was Mary who 'carried him incarnate in her womb':

> Traverse all creation in reflection, O man, and try to see if there is anything greater or even equal to the Holy Virgin *Theotokos* . . . Marvel at the victory of the Virgin, for the one whom all creation praises in fear and trembling she alone admitted ineffably to the bridal chamber [of her womb]. On account of Mary all women are blessed.[24]

The curious language of the bridal chamber reappears in a panegyric of the empress Pulcheria contained in another homily by Proclus:

> Admire the empress's greatness of soul, pouring forth spiritual blessings to all . . . This virgin, after dedicating herself to Christ, depleted and spent riches, by reason of her piety. She made her own soul dead to passions, and admitted the crucified one into the bridal chamber of her soul.[25]

Do these passages amount to a policy of promoting Marian piety, through encouraging the women of Constantinople, and in particular Pulcheria, to take Mary as their model? The answer is yes, but with significant qualifications. It is to be noted that these passages occur in sermons that are uniformly Christological, not Marian, in their prime emphasis, and which have nothing to say about prayer to the Virgin or her powers of intercession. The heart of the message is not that women should focus their devotion on Mary, or pray to her, but that all faithful Christians need to get closer to Christ, while Mary's role is to symbolize in her divine motherhood the goal for all earnest Christians of union with her divine Son.

In all, the evidence for Marian piety in Constantinople during the Nestorian controversy is not to be discounted, but is insufficient to overturn the evidence, from contemporary writers, which shows that the prime cause of Nestorius' unpopularity was not his lack of respect for Mary, but his supposed failure to recognize that Christ was truly divine. In the words of the contemporary historian Socrates, relating to Nestorius' close ally and assistant the presbyter Anastasius:

> This Anastasius, teaching one day in church, said, 'Let no one call Mary *Theotokos*, for Mary was but a human being, and it is impossible that God should be born by a human being.' These words upset all the clergy and laity in the place, for they had long been taught to consider Christ divine and by no means to separate the man of the economy from the Godhead.[26]

THEOTOKOS AT THE COUNCIL OF EPHESUS

Most historians have accepted, even taken for granted, that the issue in the Nestorian controversy was primarily Christological rather than Mariological. It has, however, repeatedly been asserted that Marian devotion received a powerful stimulus from the fact that the Council of Ephesus formally defined that the Virgin is rightly styled *Theotokos*, Mother of God. The frequency of this assertion is odd, since the simple fact, familiar to anyone who has looked at the conciliar acts, is that the council issued no such decree, or indeed any doctrinal definitions. The basis in fact on which this assertion lies is the condemnation of Nestorius at the first session of the council. How important at this session was the question of the titles and dignity of the Virgin?[27]

The session began with a brief account by an Alexandrian notary of the course of the Nestorian controversy to date, after which Nestorius was summoned to attend, to stand trial as a heretic. When he failed to respond to a third summons, the council proceeded to business without him. The Nicene Creed was read out (in its original form) and then the Second Letter of Cyril to Nestorius. This famous and impressive document, which was treated at the Council of Chalcedon of 451 as the most important statement of the Church's faith in Christ after the Nicene Creed, argues for a real union of Godhead and manhood in Christ and the propriety of attributing even his human experiences to God the Word, who as incarnate made them his own. In a few lines at the very end of the letter the *Theotokos* title is defended by reference to the hypostatic union of two natures.[28] It is these few words, as read out at Ephesus, that are cited in one of the best encyclopaedias of Mariology as constituting the council's 'formal sanction' of the *Theotokos* title.[29]

Next, Cyril, who was chairing the session, invited judgement of the letter by the assembled Council Fathers. One hundred and twenty-five bishops in turn, and then the remaining bishops by acclamation, expressed their conviction that it was in complete agreement with the Nicene Creed (in which, of course, the *Theotokos* title does not occur). Only one bishop (Hellanicus of Rhodes) added a reference to Mary as *Theotokos*.[30]

There followed a reading of Nestorius' Second Letter to Cyril.[31] The main contentions of the letter are that, since the Godhead is impassible, the Passion is not to be attributed to it, and that likewise having been born from a woman is a property of Christ's manhood but not of his Godhead. This leads on to the argument that Mary should properly be called not *Theotokos* but *Christotokos* ('Mother of Christ'). The letter concludes by asserting that it is improper to say that God the Word 'appropriated' such human experiences as circumcision and fear of death. The bishops proceeded to declare Nestorius' letter incompatible with the Nicene Creed and therefore heretical. Only one bishop (Acacius of Melitene) spoke at any length and, without mentioning the *Theotokos*, he castigated Nestorius for refusing to attribute the human experiences of Christ to his Godhead.[32] In the episcopal acclamations that followed, the *Theotokos* title did not feature.[33]

There followed the reading of a florilegium of excerpts from orthodox Fathers.[34] The title *Theotokos* occurs in two of them;[35] but it is Christological themes that manifestly determined the choice of passages. Then came a reading of heretical excerpts from Nestorius;[36] of the twenty-five extracts read out, only the first three treat the *Theotokos* title. Then, after the reading of a letter from Bishop Capreolus of Carthage deploring innovation in doctrine, came the formal verdict that declared Nestorius deposed. It made special mention of the letter from Pope Celestine to Nestorius that had been read out earlier in the session and which threatened him with excommunication if he did not correct his teaching 'on Christ our God'; the letter did not allude to the dispute over Mary.[37] The acts of the session then conclude with 197 signatures of bishops (not all present at the session itself) who approved the condemnation and deposition of Nestorius.

In all, the acts of the first session of Ephesus share with other documents relating to the controversy, such as the letters and treatises of Cyril, the characteristic that the issue is presented as a Christological one. The relevance of the

94

Theotokos title is simply that it expresses the truth that Christ, even in his birth and death as man, is God. A document that has been described as marking the opening of the controversy, Cyril's *Letter to the Monks of Egypt*, concludes, 'How can anyone have scruples about calling the holy Virgin the "Mother of God"? Worship him as one and do not divide him into two after the union . . . We have not worshipped a mere man, God forbid, but rather God by nature.'[38] What was seen to be at stake in the controversy was the dignity not of Mary but of Jesus Christ. It is inaccurate and misleading to say that the Council of Ephesus defined or decreed that Mary is the *Theotokos*, the Mother of God. Rather, it adduced the title, which no one queried except Nestorius and his immediate entourage, as evidence that Christ is truly God.

A formal recognition of Mary as *Theotokos* is, however, to be found in a document which, though slightly later in date, has always been associated with the Council of Ephesus, and that is the letter *Laetentur Coeli* sent by Cyril of Alexandria to Bishop John of Antioch in 433 (*Letter 39*), which soon became known as one of the two 'synodical' or 'canonical' letters loosely associated with the council. In this letter Cyril accepted as orthodox an Antiochene Christological statement (known as the 'Formulary of Union' or 'Formula of Reunion') which included the *Theotokos* title:

> We acknowledge our Lord Jesus Christ, the only-begotten Son of God, perfect God and perfect man made up of a rational soul and body, begotten from the Father before the ages in respect of the Godhead and the same on the last day for us and for our salvation from the Virgin Mary in respect of his manhood . . . By virtue of this understanding of the union which involves no merging, we acknowledge the holy Virgin to be *Theotokos*, because God the Word was enfleshed and became man and from the very conception united to himself the temple taken from her.[39]

The Antiochene approval of *Theotokos* was not a concession to Cyril, but simply reflected the fact that Nestorius' criticism of the title had never won the approval of his Syrian allies; John of Antioch had written to Nestorius before the council pointing out that the title was sound and traditional, in response to which a humiliated Nestorius had declared in a sermon preached in December 430 his own acceptance of the title.[40] It was, therefore, the Antiochenes who were responsible for the nearest Ephesus got to 'defining' that Mary is *Theotokos*. And the Antiochenes were happy to accept the title because they appreciated its importance in bringing out the union of Godhead and manhood in Christ. In the words of Theodoret of Cyrrhus, the leading Antiochene theologian of the time:

> If anyone does not call the holy Virgin *Theotokos*, or calls our Lord Jesus Christ a mere man, or separates into two sons the one who is both Only-begotten and Firstborn of all creation, let him lose his hope in Christ.[41]

To say that both Cyril and the Antiochene school approved the *Theotokos* title is not to say that they justified it in quite the same way. For Cyril the rightness of the title followed from the fact that all the human experiences of Christ, including his birth from the Virgin, are to be ascribed to the divine Word as personal subject. But the Antiochenes recognized the humanity of Christ as itself a subject of attribution, and they therefore agreed with Nestorius that it was equally correct to call Mary *Anthropotokos* – 'the Mother of the Man'. In the words of Theodore of Mopsuestia (d. 428), the true father of Antiochene Christology:

> Because they ask, 'Was Mary *Anthropotokos* or *Theotokos*?', let us say both – the former by the nature of the reality, and latter by relation. For she was *Anthropotokos* by nature, because the one in the womb of Mary (and as he also came forth from there) was a man, and she is *Theotokos*, because God was in the man who was born, not circumscribed in him according to nature, but being in him according to a disposition of the will.[42]

What offended Cyril of Alexandria and his allies in such language was not any hint of disrespect towards the Mother of God in calling her also the Mother of the Man. A seemly reverence towards the Virgin was common to both parties in the controversy: Theodoret hailed her as superior to all other women in virtue, as demonstrated by the Father's selection of her to be the mother of his Son.[43] What caused offence was the inadequate expression of the union of divinity and humanity in Christ. The importance of acknowledging the Virgin as *Theotokos* was that it expressed the reality of the incarnation. Mary mattered precisely as the *Theotokos*, the one who gave birth to Christ, God and man. She was not yet a theme in her own right.

Mary and Feminine Weakness

For Cyril's conception of the personal character and dignity of Mary we will do best to turn to his treatment of the familiar biblical stories in his homilies and commentaries. Take, for example, the episode in the synoptic Gospels where Jesus is told that his mother and his brethren wish to see him and he replies, 'My mother and my brethren are those who hear and perform the word of God.'[44] Augustine commented appropriately, 'Mary too is blessed, because she heard the word of God and kept it . . . As Christ's flesh was in the womb of Mary, so his truth was in her mind.'[45] Cyril, in his homilies on the Gospel of Luke, merely observes that Jesus cannot have meant to show disrespect to his mother since 'it was he who had uttered the law through Moses and said, "Honour your father and mother"'.[46] Of special honour to be paid to Mary he says not one word.

Typical of Cyril's fuller treatments of the Virgin is the following passage on the Virgin's role at the foot of the cross according to the Gospel of John (Jn 19.25):

> He introduces as standing by the cross his mother and the other women with her, and it is clear that they were weeping. The female sex is always somewhat tearful and particularly prone to lamentation when it has an abundant cause for the shedding of tears. What is it then that induced the blessed evangelist to go into trivial details and mention the transgression of

96

the women? His reason was to show this – that the Passion in its unexpected-
ness had caused even the mother of the Lord to fall, as it appears, and that
the death on the cross, being extremely bitter, made her depart to some
extent from the thoughts that were fitting, as did also the insults of the Jews
and the mocking of the one who had been hung by the soldiers stationed by
the cross, and the way they dared to divide up his clothes in the very sight of
his mother. For you need not doubt that she admitted into her mind
thoughts of the following kind: 'I gave birth to the one who is mocked on
the tree. Perhaps in saying that he was the true Son of almighty God he was
mistaken. He was apparently in error when he said, "I am the Life." Why was
he crucified? Why was he caught in some way in the snares of the murderers?
Why did he not defeat the plots of his persecutors? Why does he not come
down from the cross, even though he ordered Lazarus to come back to life
and amazed all Judaea with his miracles?'

It is extremely probable that a mere woman, ignorant of the mystery, was
deceived into thoughts of this kind. For we must conceive in all justice that
the nature of the events was sufficient to upset even a sober mind . . . How
then is it surprising if the delicate mind of a mere woman was seduced into
thoughts that exhibit weakness? In saying this we are not guessing blindly, as
someone might think, but proceeding to a surmise on the basis of what is
written about the mother of the Lord. For we remember that the righteous
Symeon, when he took the Lord as an infant into his arms, as it is written,
gave thanks . . . and said to the holy virgin, 'Behold this is for the fall and the
raising of many in Israel, and a sign to be spoken against. And your own soul
a sword shall pierce, so that the thoughts of many hearts will be revealed'
[Lk. 2.34-35]. By 'sword' he meant the sharp onset of grief that cleaves the
mind of a woman and stimulates misguided thoughts . . . [47]

This passage of Cyril's may seem lacking in respect towards the Virgin, but this
would be to judge him by an anachronistic standard. The Virgin *Theotokos* had
indeed an indispensable role in his theology, but it was a more narrowly defined
one than she was to take on later. The Mariology that is revealed to us by the
Nestorian controversy, in both Cyril and his opponents, was firmly Christocentric.
Its aim, as we said above, was to encourage the faithful to receive Christ 'in the
womb of faith', in a spiritual imitation of Mary's giving birth. Her reception of
the divine Word in her womb received great emphasis, both as indispensable for
the incarnation and as a symbol of the reception of Christ into one's soul to
which all Christians are called. This fell short of what may properly be called a
'cult' of Mary; and because her contribution to our salvation was seen to lie in her
physical role in the incarnation of the divine Word, it was not necessary to
suppose her to have been morally and spiritually perfect.

CYRIL OF ALEXANDRIA AND POPULAR PIETY

Nevertheless, Cyril provides us with one significant piece of evidence for the development of a popular Marian piety. For there is one text of Cyril's in which the Virgin genuinely takes centre stage, and that is a sermon that he preached in the cathedral of Ephesus a few days after Nestorius' condemnation. It begins:

> I see the resplendent assembly of all the saints who have eagerly gathered at the invitation of the holy and ever-Virgin Mary the *Theotokos*. My grief has been transformed into joy by the presence of the holy fathers. There has now been fulfilled in our case the sweet words of the psalmodist David, 'See how good and delightful it is for brothers to dwell together in unity.' We hail you, holy mystical Trinity, which has summoned us all to this church of Mary *Theotokos*. We hail you, Mary *Theotokos*, the venerable treasure of all the world, the inextinguishable lamp, the crown of virginity, the sceptre of orthodoxy, the indestructible temple, the container of the Uncontainable, the Mother and Virgin, the source of the one of whom it is said in the holy Gospels, 'Blessed is he who comes in the name of the Lord.'
>
> Hail to the one who contains the Uncontainable in her holy and virginal womb, through whom the holy Trinity is glorified and worshipped in all the world, through whom heaven is glad, through whom angels and archangels rejoice, through whom demons are put to flight, through whom the devil the tempter fell from heaven, through whom the fallen creature is received back into heaven, through whom the whole creation caught in idolatry has come to the knowledge of the truth, through whom holy baptism comes to believers, through whom is the oil of gladness, through whom churches have been founded throughout the world, through whom nations are led to repentance. Why should I say more? Through whom the only-begotten Son of God has shone as a light to those sitting in darkness and in the shadow of death, through whom the prophets spoke, through whom the apostles proclaim salvation to the nations, through whom the dead are raised, through whom kings rule.[48]

For Michael O'Carroll this passage is an 'inspired utterance' that hails Mary as the 'mediatress' through whom are wrought 'all the glories of salvation and sanctification'.[49] But how is it that Mary can be described as the one 'through whom holy baptism comes to believers . . . through whom churches have been founded throughout the world'? Only because all this is the work of Christ, whose work of redemption was initiated by his birth from the Virgin. Mary's essential role was her indispensable contribution to the incarnation; Cyril felt no need at all to expatiate on her holiness or to claim that she possessed unique powers of intercession. It is Christ who remains the unique Advocate on behalf of the human race, while to claim for Mary patronage over her devotees akin to that exercised by other saints would have been to demean rather than exalt her. Cyril's 'high' Mariology did not make him a promoter of the cult of Mary.

This same sermon is described by O'Carroll as 'the most famous Marian sermon of antiquity'. It scarcely deserves this reputation: compared to the sixth-century Marian homilies of Severus of Antioch and others, it is thematically thin and lacks genuine warmth. It remains notable, however, that Cyril, preaching to a popular congregation immediately after Nestorius' deposition, judged it expedient to hymn the praises of the Virgin. It is to be noted that the church where he was preaching, the cathedral of Ephesus, was already dedicated to Mary.[50] He was clearly aware of local devotion to her and played up to it.

Nevertheless, the prominence in Cyril's scriptural homilies and commentaries of a traditional misogyny that treated Mary, and all other women in the Gospels, as types of female weakness raises a question: how could Cyril possibly have written of her in this vein if the cult of the Virgin was already universal? It is manifest that in the age in which Cyril was writing the cult of the Virgin had not developed sufficiently to dictate the reverential and encomiastic attitude towards her that was to be standard in Christian writing and preaching from the beginning of the sixth century.[51]

CONCLUSION

I have argued in support of the traditional view that the Nestorian controversy was Christological not Mariological in its inspiration. I mentioned that another traditional notion has been that Marian piety, though not influential during the controversy, received a powerful spur from the defeat of Nestorius and the definition at the Council of Ephesus that Mary is rightly styled *Theotokos*. Intense Marian piety, it has often been asserted, was not perhaps the cause of the controversy but was certainly its fruit.

We need, however, to reconsider the matter in the light of Ephesus' own agenda. We saw that the council did not define that Mary is *Theotokos*: the appropriateness of the title was not defined by the council, but simply presumed by the Council Fathers, as one among many pieces of evidence that proved Nestorius to be a heretic. It is true that the *Theotokos* title was contained in the 'Formula of Reunion', and that this document, as contained and applauded in a letter of Cyril's, came to be considered one of the 'synodical letters' that expressed the teaching of the council;[52] but in this document too the title received no emphasis. Add to this the evidence presented by Stephen Shoemaker in his essay in this volume for the development of Marian piety in the half-century prior to Ephesus, and we may surely conclude that the importance of the council of Ephesus for this development has been overestimated. Marian piety was already on the increase before Ephesus (even if, as I argued, it was not yet dominant), and its growth was to continue, slowly but surely, in the two centuries that followed the council, achieving its climax (as far as Byzantium was concerned) with the adoption of the Virgin as the patron of the city of Constantinople after the defeat of the Arab and Avar siege of 626.[53]

If we contrast to this the cult of the martyrs, of which there is evidence already in the second century and which had reached extraordinary intensity and popularity by the end of the fourth century, we may surely affirm that the development of the cult of the Virgin in the early centuries of Christian history was belated and gradual. The cult of the martyrs had developed through an extension of a cult of deceased family members that was standard in Graeco-Roman paganism, the obviously novel feature being the fact that the anniversary of a martyr was celebrated not simply by his kin but by the whole Christian community.[54] The Virgin, in contrast, lacked a tomb and relics. The development of her cult had to wait until holy men and women who had not been martyrs began to receive equal veneration, and this was in the latter part of the fourth century.

My particular concern has been to relate this development to the Nestorian controversy, traditionally associated with the formal proclamation of Mary as *Theotokos*, the Mother of God. I have pointed out that the Council of Ephesus made no such proclamation; and a reading of the literature generated by the controversy, particularly the writings of Cyril of Alexandria and the sermons of Proclus, shows that a stress on Mary as the physical bond between the divine Son and the human race did not of itself either constitute or necessarily stimulate Marian cult, involving prayer to the Virgin in view of her unique powers of intercession. The notion that it was the Council of Ephesus of 431 that gave the decisive spur to the cult of the Virgin fails on several counts: it overestimates the importance of Mary's status as *Theotokos* in the Nestorian controversy and at the council of Ephesus, and it fails to see that the expansion of Marian cult that followed the Council was the fruit not of the council itself, but of developments that were already in process before the council was convoked.

BIBLIOGRAPHY

Alvarez Campos, S. (1970–1985), *Corpus Marianum Patristicum*, 8 parts. Burgos: Aldecoa.

Azéma, Y. (ed.) (1964), *Théodoret de Cyr: Correspondance*, Volume 2 (*Sources Chrétiennes* 98). Paris: Éditions du Cerf.

Bardy, G. (1938), 'La doctrine de l'intercession de Marie chez les Pères grecs', *La Vie Spirituelle* 56, Supplément, 1–37.

Barkhuizen, J. H. (trans.) (2001), *Proclus: Homilies on the Life of Christ*. Brisbane: Centre for Early Christian Studies.

Cameron, A. (1978), 'The *Theotokos* in Sixth-century Constantinople: A City Finds its Symbol', *Journal of Theological Studies*, n.s. 29, 79–108.

—— (2004), 'The Cult of the Virgin in Late Antiquity: Religious Development and Myth-Making', in R. N. Swanson (ed.), *The Church and Mary* (*Studies in Church History* 39). Woodbridge: Boydell & Brewer, 1–21.

Carroll, M. P. (1986), *The Cult of the Virgin Mary: Psychological Origins*. Princeton: Princeton University Press.

Chadwick, H. (2001), *The Church in Ancient Society: From Galilee to Gregory the Great*. Oxford: Oxford University Press.

Constas, N. (2003), *Proclus of Constantinople and the Cult of the Virgin in Late Antiquity: Homilies 1–5, Texts and Translations* (Supplements to *Vigiliae Christianae* 66). Leiden: E. J. Brill.

Cooper, K. (1998), 'Contesting the Nativity: Wives, Virgins, and Pulcheria's *imitatio Mariae*', *Scottish Journal of Religious Studies* 19, 31–43.

—— (2004), 'Empress and *Theotokos*: Gender and Patronage in the Christological Controversy', in R. N. Swanson (ed.), *The Church and Mary* (*Studies in Church History* 39). Woodbridge: Boydell & Brewer, 39–51.

Delehaye, H. (1933), *Les Origines du Culte des Martyrs.* 2nd ed. Brussels: Société des Bollandistes.

Elliott, J. K. (1993), *The Apocryphal New Testament.* Oxford: Clarendon Press.

Gambero, L. (2001), 'Patristic Intuitions of Mary's Role as Mediatrix and Advocate: The Invocation of the Faithful for her Help', *Marian Studies* 52, 78–101.

Giamberardini, G. (1975), *Il Culto Mariano in Egitto* (*Pubblicazzione dello Studium Blicum Franciscanum, Analecta* 6). Jerusalem: Franciscan Printing Press.

Grillmeier, A. (1979), *Jesus der Christus im Glauben der Kirche,* Volume 1. Freiburg: Herder.

Günther, O. (ed.) (1895), *Epistulae Imperatorum Pontificum Aliorum, Part 1* (*Corpus Scriptorum Ecclesiasticorum Latinorum* 35). Bonn: Academia Litterarum.

Hansen, G. C. (ed.) (1995), *Socrates: Kirchengeschichte.* Berlin: Akademie Verlag.

Holum, K. G. (1982), *Theodosian Empresses:Women and Imperial Dominion in Late Antiquity.* Berkeley and Los Angeles: University of California Press.

Karweise, S. (1995), 'The Church of Mary and the Temple of Hadrian Olympus', in H. Koester (ed.), *Ephesos: Metropolis of Asia* (*Harvard Theological Studies* 41). Cambridge: Harvard University Press.

Limberis, V. (1994), *Divine Heiress: The Virgin Mary and the Creation of Christian Constantinople.* London: Routledge.

Mansi, J. D. (1901–1927), *Sacrorum Conciliorum Amplissima Collectio.* 53 volumes. Paris & Leipzig: H. Welter.

McGuckin, J. A. (1994), *St Cyril of Alexandria: the Christological Controversy, its History, Theology, and Texts.* Leiden: E. J. Brill.

Migne, J. P. (1857–1866), *Cursus Completus Patrologiae Graecae.* Paris: Éditions Garnier. Referred to in the notes as *PG*.

Nau, F. (trans.) (1919), *Patrologia Orientalis* 13. Paris: Firmin-Didot.

Norris, R. A. (1980), *The Christological Controversy.* Philadelphia: Fortress.

O'Carroll, M. (1982), *Theotokos: A Theological Encyclopedia of the Blessed Virgin Mary.* Wilmington: Michael Glazier.

Parmentier, L. and G. C. Hansen (eds) (2006), *Théodoret de Cyr: Histoire Ecclésiastique,* Volume 1 (*Sources Chrétiennes* 501). Paris: Éditions du Cerf.

Payne Smith, R. (trans.) (1983), *Cyril: Commentary on the Gospel of Luke.* Astoria: Studion.

Price, R. (2004), 'Marian Piety and the Nestorian Controversy', in R. N. Swanson (ed.), *The Church and Mary* (*Studies in Church History* 39). Woodbridge: Boydell & Brewer, 3–8.

—— (2009), *The Acts of the Council of Constantinople of 553.* Liverpool: Liverpool University Press. Forthcoming.

Price, R. and M. Gaddis (2005), *The Acts of the Council of Chalcedon.* 3 volumes. Liverpool: Liverpool University Press.

Roberts, C. H. (1938), *Catalogue of the Greek and Latin Papyri in the John Rylands Library, III: Theological and Literary Texts.* Manchester: John Rylands Library.

Schaff, P. and H. Wace (eds) (1997), *The Nicene and Post-Nicene Fathers* (2nd Series). Grand Rapids: Eerdmans.

Schwartz, E. (ed.) (1927–1932), *Acta Conciliorum Oecumenicorum, I: Concilium Universale Ephesinum (5 vols); II: Concilium Universale Chalcedonense (6 vols).* Berlin: Walter de Gruyter. Referred to in the notes as *ACO*.

Thomson, F. J. (2000), 'The Slavonic translation of the hitherto untraced Greek *Homilia in nativitatem Domini nostri Jesu Christi* by Atticus of Constantinople', *Analecta Bollandiana* 118, 5–36.

Wickham, L. (ed.) (1983), *Cyril of Alexandria: Select Letters.* Oxford: Clarendon Press.

Wright, D. F. (2004), 'From "God-Bearer" to "Mother of God" in the Later Fathers', in R. N. Swanson (ed.), *The Church and Mary* (*Studies in Church History* 39). Woodbridge: Boydell & Brewer, 22–30.

NOTES

1. See Elliott 1993: 48–51.
2. There is an excellent collection of patristic evidence in Bardy 1938: 1–37.
3. Gambero 2001: 78–101.
4. John Rylands *Papyrus 470*, published in Roberts 1938: 46–7. I follow the restoration of the text in Giamberardini 1975: 72–4. The translations in this essay, except where otherwise stated, are my own.
5. The favoured Latin translation was *Dei Genetrix*, from which the standard English rendering 'Mother of God' derives. This disguises the fact that 'Mother of God' (*Mētēr Theou*) was a term that became widely used only much later. See Wright 2004: 22–30.
6. Socrates, *Historia Ecclesiastica* VII. 32.17, in Hansen 1995: 381.
7. See Alvarez Campos 1970–1985: Volume 2, with *Indices*, a separate volume, 85, under 'Theotokos II'.
8. See above. The one detail I would add to his account of Epiphanius's 'Kollyridians' is the reference in Leontius of Byzantium, writing around 540, to 'the bread which the Philomariamites offer in the name of Mary' (*PG* 86A.1364B). This supports the historicity of Epiphanius's group, and also Epiphanius's presentation of them as a special group whose practices were not part of mainstream Christian piety.
9. Giamberardini 1975: 87–92.
10. That the prayer and the early use in literature of the *Theotokos* title belong to Egypt suggest influence from the Egyptian cult of Isis, often represented holding her son Horus in a pose that influenced later Christian iconography of the Virgin and Child.
11. 'All Catholic commentators agree in asserting that Marian devotion increased dramatically after Ephesus' (Carroll 1986: 84). Carroll himself disagrees.
12. In Theodoret, *Historia Ecclesiastica* I. 4.54, in Parmentier and Hansen 2006: 184.
13. See Grillmeier 1979: 647.
14. See the extracts from Nestorius read out at the Council of Ephesus, in Price and Gaddis 2005: 1.324–5.
15. As observed by Socrates, *Historia Ecclesiastica* VII. 32.6, in Hansen 1995.
16. See Chadwick 2001: 526–48.
17. For the supposed role of Pulcheria and development of Marian devotion in Constantinople in her time, see Holum 1982: 130–74; Limberis 1994; Cooper 1998: 31–43; Cooper 2004: 39–51.
18. For a fuller presentation of the argument advanced here, see Price 2004: 31–8.
19. See Cameron 1978: 79–108; Cameron 2004: 1–21.
20. Mansi 1901–1927: 5.987–9.
21. This at least is clear from the pseudepigraphical Count Candidanus and others, *Letter to Cosmas* (Nau 1919: 275–86), a piece of Nestorian propaganda dating in its original form to around 440, even if its account of a confrontation between Nestorius and Pulcheria (treated as a second Herodias) is pure fiction.
22. Thomson 2000: 5–36.
23. *Homily 1.1*, trans. Constas 2003: 137.
24. *Homily 5.2*, trans. *Ibid.*: 261.
25. *Homily 12.1*, trans. Barkhuizen 2001: 168.
26. Socrates, *Historia Ecclesiastica*, VII. 32.2–3. I follow Hansen's edition (1995), which differs somewhat from the inferior text, loosely translated, in Schaff and Wace 1997: 2.170.
27. The acts of this session are to be found in *ACO* 1.1.2, 3–64.
28. Cyril of Alexandria, in Wickham 1983: 8,31–10,4.
29. O'Carroll 1982: 112, 342.
30. *ACO* 1.1.2, 15, 17–18.

31. The full text is in *ACO* 1.1.1, 29–32. There is an English translation in Norris 1980: 135–40. My own translation will appear shortly in Price 2009: Session VI. 13.3–9.
32. *ACO* 1.1.2, 32,14–30. Note too Acacius's account of previous discussions with Nestorius, in which again the *Theotokos* does not feature (*Ibid.*, 38, 13–30). Two bishops did, however, mention the *Theotokos* issue in their verdicts on Nestorius (*Ibid.*, 32, 13; 33, 21).
33. *Ibid.*, 35, 30–36, 7.
34. *Ibid.*, 39–45. Trans. Price and Gaddis 2005: 1.301–9.
35. *Ibid.*, 302, 307.
36. *ACO* 1.1.2, 45–52. Trans. Price and Gaddis 2005: 1.323–33.
37. *ACO* 1.1.2, 36, 12–15; full text in *ACO* 1.2, 7–12. My own translation will appear shortly in Price 2009: Session VI. 15.
38. McGuckin 1994: 245 nn. 1, 261.
39. *ACO* 1.1.4, 17, 9–17.
40. For John's letter (*Epistle 4*) see *ACO* 1.1.1, 93–6, esp. 95, 19–21, and for Nestorius' sermon see *Ibid.*, 1.4, 7, 1–9.
41. *Epistle 83*, in Azéma 1964: 2.218, 16–20.
42. The original Greek text of this passage can most easily be found in Günther 1895: 272, apparatus. The same position was expressed by Theodoret of Cyrrhus, *Epistle 16*, in Azéma 1964: 2.58, 11–25.
43. Pseudo-Justin (= Theodoret), in *PG* 6.1389B.
44. Lk. 8.21. Mt. 12.50 and Mk 3.35 are parallel.
45. *Sermon Denis 25–27* in Alvarez Campos 1970–1985: 3.409.
46. Payne Smith 1983: 182.
47. Cyril, *Commentary on John* 12, in *PG* 74.661B–664A.
48. *ACO* 1.1.2, 102, 14–103, 3. It is to be noted that the other seven homilies of Cyril ascribed to the time of the Council of Ephesus (*PG* 77.981–1009) mention the Virgin either not at all or only in passing.
49. O'Carroll 1982: 113.
50. The acts of the first session of the Council of Ephesus name the cathedral 'the holy church called Mary' (*ACO* 1.1.2, 3). See also Karweise 1995: 311–19.
51. Note especially the Marian sermons of Severus of Antioch delivered in Antioch in the 510s (extracts in Alvarez Campos 1970–85: 4.2, 14–61), which surpass all earlier writing in praise of the Virgin in thematic richness and theological weight.
52. See Price and Gaddis 2005: 2.13–14, 203.
53. See Cameron 2004: 3.
54. See Delehaye 1933, still the best general study of the development of the cult of the martyrs.

7

DID CYRIL OF ALEXANDRIA INVENT MARIOLOGY?

ANTONIA ATANASSOVA

In his fifth-century confrontation with the Nestorians, Cyril of Alexandria did not introduce the term 'Mariology' as a separate category of academic discourse; rather he grappled with whatever ambiguity he found in general theological vocabulary to define Mary's role in salvation history. In the process Cyril became, most likely, the first theologian to stress systematically the interdependence of Christological and Mariological modes of discourse. It is the contention of this paper that he achieved this goal not by inventing a new version of Marian conceptualization, but by tweaking out the implications of existing Christological models and thus helping to formulate Marian discourse as the distinct result of a slow evolutionary process within developing Christology. Not only did he succeed in defending the theology of Mary as necessary, he also contributed to its emerging conceptualization in a way that would assure its successful growth after the Council of Ephesus. In this sense I see his treatment of Marian themes and imagery not as a mere footnote to his Christological perspective, but as an indispensable component of his theological agenda.

Cyril was one of the main participants in the Ephesian controversy as it unfolded against a vast background of scattered Marian references in early Christian culture whose power and challenge lay precisely in their perceived vagueness and generality. In the fifth century, the image of Mary did appear as part of the liturgical, festal and doctrinal idiom of the Church. However, this phenomenon was not without ambiguity, as Cyril's urgent defence of the title *Theotokos* shows. It was his victory at Ephesus, partial as it was, that would become the crucial element in facilitating the development of formal Marian theology as integral to the Christian tradition.

Cyril's contribution to this process is proved by an examination of his correspondence, his five-volume treatise *Against Nestorius*,[1] and homilies which are traditionally dated to the period of the controversy including those delivered at Ephesus (431).[2] This array of texts recreates the essential contours of Cyril's Mariological message as illustrating major propositions in incarnational theology. Moreover, they betray a line of continuity with those works pre-dating Ephesus in which references to Mary and her significance are used to elucidate the particulars of Cyril's theological vision. In the context of his works as a whole, the image of Mary proves to be foundational rather than accidental.

THE CONTROVERSY OVER THE TITLE *THEOTOKOS*

Cyril is best remembered as the defender of Mary's title of *Theotokos*, or God-bearer. We have no certain knowledge of the *Theotokos* origins. Origen was most likely the first to mention the title explicitly and thus promote it as part of Alexandrian theological discourse tradition.[3] It is worth noting that when Athanasius referred to it *c.* 330, he did not question its validity. He used the appellation 'Mary the *Theotokos*' matter-of-factly as if it was a title with which he was well acquainted.[4] At the same time, the title is largely absent from Antiochene theological writings.

In 427 Nestorius, the newly appointed patriarch of Constantinople and a Syrian transplant, wrote to John of Antioch a letter in which he observed that there were people in his See, 'some of which call the holy virgin *Theotokos* and some the mother of the man [Jesus]'.[5] In 428 the issue came up for discussion once again with a group of monks asking Nestorius' opinion regarding the title *Theotokos*.[6] In both cases Nestorius claimed that Mary could not be called the 'Mother of God' because, strictly speaking, God was timeless and eternal. Nestorius offered the solution of calling her the 'Mother of Christ' (*Christotokos*) or, more precisely, 'the mother of the human nature of the incarnate Son'. His suggestion pleased no one. The monks considered his questioning of the rationale of Mary's 'divine motherhood' as detrimental to the definition of Christ's person. If Mary is not the mother of God, then how is the person born of her the Son of God and Saviour? This would also be the way in which Cyril would interpret the incident. The situation implied that the theology of Mary is in need of a decisive formulation.

In his paschal letter of 429, Cyril asserted firmly Mary's position as a God-bearer and her Son as God. As the *Theotokos* debate spread among the monks under his jurisdiction, Cyril also published a formal letter, the *Letter to the Monks of Egypt*. The letter does not mention Nestorius by name, but summarizes the issues which Cyril saw as pertinent to the dispute and refutes the Nestorian proposition of the title *Christotokos*. Cyril enumerated different modes of Christological union (mixture, confusion, alteration, union) and stated his preference for the last one in a way that would not alter its force or conceptual direction later on.[7] Postulating these models reflected directly on Cyril's subsequent development of Marian theology. Nestorius, he would charge in a later text, destroyed 'utterly the mystery of the economy of the flesh by saying that the holy Virgin should not be called *Theotokos*'.[8]

This position should be seen as consistent with Cyril's interpretation of Marian themes in his works pre-dating Ephesus. There Cyril approaches the notion of Christ's birth in a traditional way, not explicitly mentioning Mary as a *Theotokos* but indirectly, I believe, making the usage of the title justifiable in the context of his work as a whole. This approach is visible in his commentary on Isaiah, which reads the prophetic message in Isaiah 7.14 in a fairly conventional way. Here there are two dimensions of the image of Mary that Cyril wanted to underline: the importance of prophecy and the facts of the virginal motherhood. Both of those are related to Cyril's depiction of Christ as God incarnate. Cyril picks on the Jewish insistence of assigning Isaiah 7.14 to Hezekiah rather than to Christ and argues that the 'virginal womb' brings forth the Saviour 'from the power and energy of the Holy Spirit' – a statement which foreshadowed his later and more explicit association of the Son of Mary with the Son of God.[9] Even in this early text, Cyril's Christological vision is consistent with a position that he would defend later on: Christ is God 'both from the womb and before it, or rather before all ages, seeing that he did not lose his own prerogatives on account of the human nature'.[10] If, in those early writings, the title *Theotokos* is used just once,[11] in the course of the Nestorian controversy, Cyril's Mariological argument would become noticeably more articulate and complex.

Nestorius' questioning of the logic of the *Theotokos* title provides a good example of depictions of Mary that would prove questionable and thus provide a precedent for forging an official doctrinal position regarding Mary's role in incarnational theology. Among his most provoking contentions is the limited role he assigns to the Virgin as the mother of Jesus' humanity. His approach to Mariology is further predicated on his understanding of the relationship between human and divine natures in Christ as lacking ontological communication. For Nestorius, God could not be born nor die, as opposed to the human being, Jesus of Nazareth, in which the Son dwelled.[12] Thus a brief detailing of his stance ushers us into the polemical context of early Mariology and outlines the ideas which Cyril would seek to refute.

A fragment found in one of Nestorius' sermons and discussing Mary in light of the radical polarity between Christ's two natures explains the argument which Cyril would endeavour to disprove:

> She is the mother of God because of the Word united with its temple; the mother of God not in the sense of [bearing] the naked divinity onto humanity, but according to the union of the divine word with the temple; truly *Anthropotokos* because of the temple which is co-substantial in nature with the holy virgin.[13]

According to Nestorius, Mary could hardly be considered a *Theotokos*, even in the rhetorical sense of the word, because she was not the source of Christ's 'naked divinity', but purely and primarily related to the human form in which this divinity dwelled, an *Anthropotokos*. The inadmissibility of a mixture of human and divine domains he translated into a depiction of Mary as a habitation or indwelling rather than a birth-giver of God. Another fragment from Nestorius' sermons testifies:

> It is without doubt he who was made by the Holy Spirit (because what is born of her, scripture says, is from the Holy Spirit), whom the Word of God inhabited from the very beginning, not in the sense that the Word of God was born of Mary or had its beginning from her, but in the sense that it was associated inseparably at all times with him who was born of her and who was growing following the course of the months after being formed in the virgin's womb . . . Because God is the creator of time, but is not born in time, he is the creator of the holy Mary, but is not made in her by the spirit.[14]

In Nestorius' description, there is no image of containment of God, rather of the womb of the Virgin as a temporal dwelling in which God stayed.

> A creature did not produce the Creator, rather she gave birth to the human being, the instrument of the Godhead. The Holy Spirit did not create God the Logos . . . Rather, he formed out of the Virgin a temple for God the Logos, a temple in which he dwelt.[15]

Unsurprisingly, this image is reminiscent of traditional depictions of Mary as a tabernacle.[16] From Nestorius' perspective, Mary is also a *Christotokos* because she supplies Christ's body, an entity which he envisions in terms of Scripture-influenced architectural metaphors: 'the body is the temple of the Godhead of the Son, and a temple that is united in a sublime and divine conjunction, in such a way that the nature of the Godhead appropriates the characteristics of this [temple]'.[17] Nestorius stops short of constructing a typological reference to the Virgin laden with the allusion of containment. God himself, Nestorius asserts, could not be contained or circumscribed in the Virgin's womb. For him, the womb of Mary and the tomb are twin images of containment which refer not to God but to the human being with whom God is joined:

> [That] which was formed in the womb is not in itself God . . . That which was buried in the tomb was not in itself God . . . If that were the case, we should manifestly be worshippers of a human being and worshippers of the dead.[18]

Nestorius' language of functionality – not relationality – is dominant in his work, because it preserves the distinction between the two natures, human and divine.

One of its logical consequences is that, from a Nestorian perspective, Mary deserves only peripheral, even if honourable, mention. Mary is associated with the human being who pays the penalty of sin by suffering and dying; she is the mother of the temple in whom God dwelled. Thus her role in theology is limited to her historical persona, shaped as it is by the governing context of Christology. The historical dimension of Nestorius' Mariological vision explains his restraint from praising a woman whose virginal motherhood was a prophetic miracle, but not as praiseworthy or important as the mission of her Son.

It is precisely to this denial of Mary's status in doctrine or devotion that Cyril would react. In 430, as he sought the support of Rome, he sent Pope Celestine a dossier of Nestorian texts with his own commentary attached.[19] One of the main points in it is his appeal to the 'most devout bishops throughout the East and West' and the faith of the Fathers 'in whose writings we always find the Holy Virgin Mary named Mother of God'.[20] In addition, Cyril boasted that the people had thanked him for his defence of the *Theotokos*, but they shut their ears and ran out of the church during one of Nestorius' inflammatory sermons against Mary the Godbearer.[21] He defined orthodoxy as follows: 'Christ is God and . . . the Virgin who bore him is the Mother of God.'[22]

For Cyril, the title *Theotokos* serves a specific purpose by encapsulating the significance of the incarnation as the decisive point in history at which God transforms history from within and, by becoming human, enables human beings to return to him. The vehemence of Cyril's response to Nestorius aims to prove, I believe, that Mariology is not simply a footnote to the Christological question, but its best illustration and summary. That said, Cyril was still struggling with its terminology and was thus liable to misinterpretation. In the context of his overall depiction of the particulars of the incarnational event, Mary would come to play an essential role which goes beyond the purely historical significance of her person.

This is the case because Cyril relied on a Christological conception that emphasized constantly the salvific datum of God's revelation in the flesh. In other words, Cyril's Christology is essentially soteriology guided by the principle of God's condescension or *kenosis*. As a result of the incarnation, Cyril argued, God had bestowed the benefits of his eternal life upon humanity, for in his union with the flesh the Word 'has the power to bring all things to life'.[23] In the context of incarnation and revelation, the Mother of the Word Incarnate occupied a special place: she was the Mother of God 'for she gave birth in the flesh to the Word of God made flesh'.[24] Any account of Cyril's Mariology, then, should start with a consideration of his Christology and move on from there to a more detailed analysis of the significance he assigns to the image of the Virgin.

THE FUSION OF MARIAN AND CHRISTIC THEMES

Cyril's theology of Mary is usually treated within its larger Christological framework as an appendix to the theme of Christic personhood. Studies by Roberto Caro, Arthur Vööbus, and Paul Imhof and Bernhard Lorenz also mention Cyril's Mariological homilies, yet their approach is primarily descriptive.[25] They do not address the thematic structures of Cyril's Mariology. As much as I wish to qualify their argument by underlining the unique significance of the Marian theme in Cyril's work, I see its value in drawing attention to the ways in which the image of Mary is used to complement Christological developments. There are three major principles that could be isolated here as laying out the foundation of Cyril's Christology: (a) the notion of Christic unity, (b) the exposition of Christology as essentially soteriology guided by the principle of God's condescension or *kenosis*, and (c) the theory of exchange of properties between Christ's two natures, human and divine, which enabled Cyril to affirm that it was the divine hypostasis of the Son who had been born in the flesh, suffered and died.

For Cyril, to speak of the impassable God becoming human would have meant to address two particular moments of the scriptural story: the story of the incarnation, or Jesus' birth, and the crucifixion story. To speak of God becoming human is just as important as it is to speak of him suffering and dying on the cross. For Cyril's soteriology, it was essential to affirm that, first of all, it is the Son of God who is born in the flesh, and second, this event of the incarnation opens the door to a complete transformation of humanity, in the course of which human nature starts participating in those life-giving properties of the divine which have been inaccessible to it so far. Already in Cyril's early works, such as his *Commentary on Isaiah*,[26] we see, on the one hand, an emphasis on the soteriological dimension of the incarnation with the central role assigned to the Word, and, on the other, a depiction of the Word as the sole subject of action and experience in the reality of the incarnation, including the birth from a woman. Thus the birth and death of Jesus are the two crucial axes around which Cyril's theopaschite language is built.

In a bold exegetical move, Cyril accomplishes what the Nicene Creed stops short of stating explicitly: identifying the Only-Begotten Son of God with the Lord Jesus Christ. Cyril affirmed that the Son 'was truly born in a God-befitting and ineffable manner from the essence of God the Father, and is to be conceived of in his own hypostasis, yet united in an identity of essence with his Begetter'.[27] The same person who was born of the essence of the Father is also the one who takes on humanity with the fullness of its experiences of generation, suffering and mortality: 'he underwent fleshly birth united from the very womb, making the birth of the flesh his very own. This is what we mean when we say he suffered and rose again'.[28] This conceptualization of Christ emphasizes his oneness – he is the same Son from the Father and born from a woman – at the same time as it takes into account the duality on which this oneness rests: 'Christ conceived of as One out of both, the Godhead and manhood having come together one to another in true union'.[29] As a result of this union of duality and oneness, with Christ, God makes himself a servant without losing his 'dignity', and also remains an object of worship and glorification:

> For he is worshipped with flesh too, as being an object of worship even before it, for He was even yet by Nature God [κατὰ φύσιν Θεός], both before the emptying and when He is said to endure the emptiness, made as we are.[30]

The double-sided formula of *kenosis* and exaltation formed the thrust of Cyril's Christology. He had ample opportunities to test it as the Ephesian controversy provided him with the incentive for examining different Christological models at his disposal (mixture, conjunction, or confusion), mapping out the advantages as well as the weaknesses of each. As he continuously argues, in the incarnation, the union between two realities, human and divine, and their underlying properties is not accidental, docetic, or artificial, but the product of a 'true union, ineffable and surpassing understanding'.[31] He was especially vexed with Nestorius' preference for συνάφεια or conjunction,[32] which, for him, indicated a relative partnership of two separate domains in Christ, God as attached to a human.[33] Cyril insists that the Word creates and owns his humanity in the way each and every one of us owns, directs and uses his or her own body:

> For the body which was united to him was alien [ἕτερος] to him, even though it was born from a woman, but as our own bodies are proper [ἴδιος] to each of us, so in the same way the body of the Only-begotten was proper [ἴδιος] to him and not to anyone else.[34]

Christ is born 'like us' and in this sense the birth from Mary could be called the Son's birth, 'for the Virgin Mother of Christ too bore the Son of God'.[35] Neither reality, human or divine, is compromised in its fullness and authenticity in the union; in the face of Mary's Son they are manifested together in a singular exchange that has no parallel in creation.[36] Mary's humanity is presented as the explicit guarantee of this union:

> It is with reference to this notion of a union without confusion that we proclaim the holy Virgin to be the mother of God, because God the Word was made flesh and became man, and by the act of conception united to Himself the temple that He has received from her.[37]

In this context Cyril charges Nestorius that 'he said the Holy Virgin is not the Mother of God. This is to say distinctly that the Emmanuel, in whom we have hopes of salvation, is not God.'[38] This 'hope of salvation' is the key to Cyril's interpretation of the incarnation. It is only available because, through Mary's birth-giving, the Word becomes man 'like us', and simultaneously 'he is not within the limits that apply to us'. He remains God while seen as a baby 'in swaddling bands', for his deity is 'without quantity or size and accepts no limitations'.[39] Christ took the range of human experiences, Cyril argues, and made them anew: in his birth he destroyed the ancient curse of Eve, on his cross he proved futile the power of the devil, in his resurrection he set all free, and he even won over the heathen with the knowledge of the truth.[40] His enhumanization is meant, in the true Athanasian tradition, to restore human access to God's eternal life: 'For if He has not been made Man, neither did He die for us.'[41]

Cyril's Christology, then, is dynamic and communication-oriented. Within it Cyril saw the element of birth as crucial:

> If he had not been born like us according to the flesh, if he had not partaken of the same elements as we do, he would not have delivered human nature from the fault we incurred in Adam, nor would he have warded off the decay from our bodies . . . human nature, which fell sick through the disobedience of Adam, now became glorious in Christ through his utter obedience.[42]

Cyril disproves the Nestorian conclusion that if we want to do justice to the product of Mary's birth-giving, she should be designated not only as the mother of what is divine (*Theotokos*), but also as a mother of what is human (*Anthropotokos*). If, Cyril suggests, the flesh supplied by Mary is not conceived of as the Word's own, but as the humanity of Christ independent from his divinity, an inadmissible polarity is postulated between the two. Its practical implication is that it destroys the immediacy of God's relation to the world.

This point has become the recent subject of much scholarly conversation. Modern commentators of Antiochian theology such as Paul Gavrilyuk and John O'Keefe have claimed that the debate between the representatives of the Antioch and Alexandrian Christological traditions was concerned primarily with defining the relationship between God and creation.[43] The image of Mary could be seen as the fluid focal point of such a definition. Similarly, Joseph Hallman argues that the way in which the properties of two realms of the Christic being, human and divine, are communicated, or not, is the basis of the split between Cyril and Nestorius. Hallman writes:

> I believe that the differences in Christology are rooted in two different views of the divine being in the incarnation and that this difference of views is related to the acceptance on the one side of the 'communication of idioms' as valid language for the incarnation, and the rejection of this 'communication' on the other side either explicitly or implicitly.[44]

In sum, the Christological differences between the two parties (Nestorian and Cyrilline) are deeply rooted and, in turn, produce diverging valuations of Mary's role in incarnational theology.

CYRIL AT EPHESUS: DEFENDING THE 'DIGNITY OF THE DIVINE BIRTH'

In the records of the Ephesian Council, the title *Theotokos*, or birth-giver of God, showed for the first time a serious Christological analysis attached to its conceptualization. That the *Theotokos* question was integral to the development of any (orthodox) Christological argument is shown by the fact that the bishops' Ephesian evaluation of Nestorius' theology focused on his depiction of Christ as well as his rejection of the *Theotokos*.[45] In the synodical deposition of Nestorius, the denial of the rationale behind the title *Theotokos* is well attested. Various passages in the deposition, culled from Nestorius' writings to illustrate his Christological errors, contain references to Mary. In these texts, the main contours of Nestorius' Mariological position are made clear. He did not subscribe to the identification of God with the Son of Mary, but promoted Mary as the mother of Christ (*Christotokos*).[46] Since, in his interpretation, the title 'Christ' signified the attachment of two natures, the Nestorian Mary gave birth to the manhood (of Christ) conjoined to the divine reality.[47] Mary received God; God came through the Virgin, but was not born of her. For Nestorius, Cyril's notion of generation signified a confusion of the properties of human and divine realities, and predicated of God the characteristics of temporality. According to Nestorius, God was witnessed in the child Jesus, but always as an ontologically separate being, without an interaction or transfer of the characteristics of these two realms, human or divine.[48]

Similarly, at Ephesus, Cyril's rebuttal to this position relied on a fusion of Christological and Mariological themes. During its first day-long session, 'the ecumenical and orthodox synod' read, included in its minutes and confirmed as consistent with Nicaea Cyril's two doctrinal letters to Nestorius.[49] Both documents discussed Mary's integral role in incarnational theology and defend the reasoning behind the *Theotokos*. Their Christological framework postulates that Mary's Son is God who is 'also born of woman in the flesh though owning his existence before the ages and begotten of the Father'.[50] For Cyril, an acknowledgement of Mary as *Theotokos* is indispensable for a true understanding of Christ's mission in the divine economy. This is a carefully nuanced and scripted thesis, for, anticipating the Nestorian objections, Cyril qualifies his message in several different ways: calling Christ God and Mary *Theotokos* does not mean 'that his divine nature originated in the holy Virgin or necessarily required for its own sake a second birth subsequent to that from the Father'.[51] In Cyril's interpretation, the union between God and humanity safeguards against the implication of confessing two Christs, or the adoptionist option in which a man born of the Virgin would have the Logos settle on him. On the contrary, for Cyril the Word makes all human properties, including generation in the flesh, his own. The union between God and humanity is an act of sharing of flesh and blood. This, Cyril affirms, is the 'key to the holy fathers' thinking. [T]his is why they dare to call the holy Virgin "mother of God"',[52] because of the reality of the birth and its feature of a substantial (or hypostatic) union.

Mary's womb is the locus of this substantial unity and a paradoxical illustration of the enhumanization of the impassible deity. Cyril's *Third Letter* argues that Christ 'took flesh of the holy Virgin, making it his own from the womb, and underwent our human birth and came forth as man from a woman'. Simultaneously, Cyril emphasizes the paradoxical nature of the enfleshed Logos: 'even when a baby seen in swaddling clothes at the bosom of the Virgin who bore him, he still filled the whole creation as God'.[53] Furthermore, the theme of Mary's birth-giving is situated in a narrative context where the generation of the divine Word 'according to the flesh' is related to his subsequent suffering and death on the cross.[54] For Cyril, it is essential to map out this continuity between the language of the Son's generation through Mary and the language of God's suffering (theopaschite language), because the theory of communication of properties makes both of those phenomena meaningful and significant.

The best illustration of all these propositions is found in Cyril's *Twelve Anathemas* (or chapters) appended to his *Third Letter*, and the *Explanation of the Twelve Chapters* which he had to provide to the council.[55] The first article on the anathemas list brought up the title *Theotokos*, underlining the importance of this title to the Christian theology of the incarnation: 'If anyone does not confess the Emmanuel to be truly God, and the holy virgin to be Mother of God (for she gave birth in the flesh to the Word of God made flesh), let him be anathema.'[56] In his *Explanation*, Cyril sees the reasoning of the title *Theotokos* as related to the Nicene exposition of the divine economy.[57] As Nicaea postulates, God is made man, Cyril argues, in his unity with the flesh which is done in a manner 'beyond the mind's grasp' and which does not involve mingling, change or confusion in the divine essence. One and the same Son born of the Father is also the person from a virgin 'for the salvation of all'.[58] The purpose of this event is clearly emphasized here as 'economic' (related to the divine economy). The birth which God undergoes in the flesh supplied in Mary's womb is 'not a birth that called him into a beginning of existence, but one intended to deliver us from death and corruption when he became like us'.[59] Because Christ is God, his mother who gives him human existence in truth, not in appearance, is a God-bearer (*Theotokos*).[60] Finally, God's incarnation on behalf of the human race is seen by Cyril as the source of inestimable benefits, rather than as a repudiation of God's impassibility.

By providing the council with a list of scriptural and patristic florilegia, Cyril emphasized that this version of his incarnational theology is consistent with both Scripture and tradition.[61] Two major texts which he brought to the assembly's attention were Athanasius' *Letter to Epictetus* and Gregory of Nazianzus's *Letter to Cledonius*.[62] What is conspicuous about the Athanasian text is its emphasis on the genuine character of Christ's humanity, including its experiential aspect, and portraying Mary as its guarantor. Cyril readily takes on Athanasius' assertion that Mary would be 'superfluous' to the process of the incarnation had she not supplied the physicality of Christ through the process of conception, gestation and birth-giving.[63] Furthermore, both Gregory and Athanasius discussed the role of Mary in a Christological context which had a decidedly anti-Apollinarian flavour. The preference accorded to them by Cyril shows that his own theological position is not as dependent on Apollinarius's Christology as commonly perceived. In this connection Cyril selects authoritative texts that will support his own depiction of Christ as the true Son of God incarnate from the Virgin and truly man as illustrated by the reality of her birth-giving. Thus Cyril's repeated affirmation of Mary's presence ultimately serves to ward off suspicions of docetism and portray Christ as the God who saves.

A consideration of Marian theology in its Ephesian context would not be complete without a look at its liturgical dimension. Cyril's homilies on Mary, presumably delivered at the Great Church of Ephesus, show the novelty of the usage of salutations directed at the Virgin.[64] The salutations or the encomium of Marian praises, particularly prominent in Cyril's *Homily 4*, have an important function: they portray Mary's indispensable role in the incarnation. *Homily 4* begins with a proclamation of the holy Mary as *Theotokos*, or the person through whom God takes visible shape.[65] It continues with a list of salutations addressed to Mary and structured using the phrase 'through her' (δι̇ἡς).[66] The text enumerates the various roles that Mary plays both in incarnational theology and in the life of Christendom: she is the one through whom salvation is made concrete, the Trinity is 'hallowed' (ἡ Τριὰς ἁγιάξεται), and the universality of Christian worship takes place. Mary's presence is the cause of exaltation and angelic joy; she enables a 'fallen creature' to go back to heaven; she brings 'knowledge of truth' (ἐπίγνωσιςἀληθειας), serves as a baptismal font of sanctification, builds the Church, leads missions to the unbelievers and confirms imperial rule. All these images and associations bespeak Mary's unique and exalted status in the divine economy. In addition, they indicate the functions which the Virgin will assume in liturgical parlance. For instance, Mary is repeatedly designated as the one who unites the believers and leads the proclamation of Christian worship. She is also the one who, acting as a mediator between God and humanity, brings people to the faith and endows Christian leaders, emperors included, with the ability to govern. Her veneration is endowed with universal significance, even if it rests on a largely abstract and symbolic depiction of Mary, the virgin mother.

This functional, symbolically perceived side of Marian imagery is once again predicated on the Virgin's connection with Christ. Cyril claims that Christ could not be worshipped as the incarnate God unless his mother is acknowledged as the source of his link to humanity. In turn, Mary's acknowledgement becomes the means for a proclamation of the Christian faith in God as a Saviour. Mary carries the 'sceptre of orthodoxy' (τὸ σκῆπτρον τῆς ὀρθοδοξίας), i.e. the praise directed to her is a praise of the revelation of God in human flesh.[67] Her virginal womb and her birth-giving, the facts of which are explicitly brought up throughout *Homily 4*, transforms her into a 'wondrous thing' (τὸ θαῦμα) which enables humanity to be sanctified.[68]

These Mariological ideas take their impetus from the tradition: notions of Mary as the means for baptism as well as the Second Eve because of whom, as Cyril puts it, 'the devil, seeking to seduce, fell from heaven' are already latent there.[69] However, in Cyril's homilies, these concepts receive a decisive confirmation supplemented by the authority of Ephesus which opens the way for future reconfigurations of the various facets of Marian imagery. Cyril describes Mary as a figure with a unique significance: no other woman could be a mother and a virgin at the same time, the 'crown of virginity' (ὁ στέφανος τῆς παρθενίας) and the 'place of the incircumscribed one' (χωρίον τοῦ ἀχωρήτου).[70]

Particularly noteworthy is Cyril's depiction of Mary as a temple and an enclosure of the 'uncontainable One in your holy virginal womb'.[71] Cyril's attention to Mary's womb is a theological motif that already had some placement in the homiletic tradition: Ephrem the Syrian and Hesychius of Jerusalem had both referred to it.[72] Proclus, another important participant in the Nestorian controversy, had also drawn attention to the life-giving properties of Mary's womb in his *Homily 1*.[73] Yet the notion of Mary's womb as the locus of God's enfleshment, i.e. as a systematically developed theological statement, receives an explicit endorsement only at the Council of Ephesus.[74] This notion is not simply a rhetorical device of praise, but a philosophical idea, connecting a description of the boundless nature of God with the boundaries of creaturely humanity.[75]

In her study of the Akathistos hymn, Leena Mari Peltomaa locates the Ephesian contribution to early Mariology precisely in this notion of χώρα, or 'enclosure' of God linked to Mary's womb.[76] I wish to qualify her supposition further by suggesting that, at Ephesus, the idea of Mary or Mary's womb as a container of the uncontainable God complements and develops in relation to the concept of Mary's motherhood as a whole. In the context of divine motherhood, the notion of enclosed space, i.e. Mary's womb, functions as a crucial detail – nevertheless, a subordinate detail. Mary's motherhood (not simply her womb) is affirmed by the council as the concrete expression of the incarnation and seen by the textual evocation of her conception by the Holy Spirit, her birth-giving and, in addition, the emphasis on the wondrous powers of her womb.[77]

For example, in *Homily 4*, Cyril encourages his audience to marvel at the reality of virginal motherhood in the context of which God appropriates the temple of Mary's body for his own.[78] The frequency of associations with which this image recurs throughout the homily denotes its paramount importance in Cyril's incarnational scheme. Cyril sees the notion of Christ's enclosure, limitation and circumscription in human flesh as laden with paradox, because it concerns the divine person who, by definition, transcends the boundaries of temporal existence. Cyril underscores the divine initiative of enabling this paradox to take place while approaching with awe its mysterious nature.[79] The emphasis he placed on the mystery of the incarnation is not so much a rhetorical flourish, but rather a form of exhortation indicating the proper posture of humanity before God. *How* this paradox of the incarnation becomes reality is a matter of divine dispensation and thus *a priori* not possible to put in human language; yet Mary's womb serves as the embodiment of the concreteness and truthfulness of this reality.

IN THE AFTERMATH OF EPHESUS

After the Council of Ephesus, Cyril embarked on a campaign to transform its doctrine into 'a universally stable reality'.[80] Even if victorious, he had to defend himself against various accusations, especially those of bringing innovations to the Christian faith (in the case of the title *Theotokos*), and propagating simplistic Christological errors such as Apollinarianism or docetism.[81] Especially controversial was the text of the *Twelve Chapters* or anathemas appended to Cyril's *Third Letter to Nestorius*, which did not receive the explicit endorsement of the council.[82]

In responding to his accusers, Cyril's main task was to defend Christ as truly man and truly God. In accomplishing this task, his best theological weapon was the repeated affirmation of Mary's indispensable role in incarnational theology and the orthodox reasoning behind the title *Theotokos*. As his dogmatic *First Letter to Succensus* illustrates, in Cyril's presentation of the economy, the Word is God 'born from the holy virgin according to the flesh, for our sake'.[83] Christ is one, Cyril claims, and thus Mary is the mother of God, not of an inspired man associated with God. Since she 'gave birth to God made flesh and made man, for this reason we also call her the Mother of God'.[84] The body that God takes from Mary is a crucial element in the scheme of the incarnation; God does not fashion his body from his divine nature, but takes it from the Virgin, a notion already familiar from Athanasius's *Letter to Epictetus*.[85] To deny the Logos the properties of his own flesh leads, logically speaking, to the profession of two sons, which for Cyril finds its embodiment in the extreme version of Antiochian theology, represented by Diodore of Tarsus and Nestorius.[86]

The theme of the body as the personal property of the Word and Christ's appropriation of humanity in all its fullness resurfaced in Cyril's letter to Valerian, the bishop of Iconium.[87] Here Cyril repeats the main propositions of his Mariological scheme: he emphasized that Christ is the one Son of God who had taken 'his undefiled body from the Holy Virgin, a body animated rationally'. Christ takes his human body from Mary, but not the 'beginning of his [divine] existence'.[88] It is the fiat of the incarnation that makes the Virgin *Theotokos*. Mary gives birth to the real human body of the one true God. Her birth-giving and the subsequent suffering of Christ on the cross are both crucial points that mark off the reality of God's becoming human:

> If some take away from the only begotten the suffering according to the flesh as ugly and incongruous and improper, let them for the same reasons take away from him also his birth according to the flesh from the Holy Virgin.[89]

These two events – the generation of Christ through Mary and his death – are brought together in the theory of communication of properties. As Cyril sees it, if the birth is nullified, then the Christian mystery is gone, and the 'hope of salvation is henceforward rendered meaningless'.[90] The 'unhappy and loathed' Nestorian suggestion of calling Mary *Anthropotokos* or *Christotokos* fails precisely on this point.[91]

His most detailed exposition on this topic – the unalienable connection between Christology and Mariology – is found in two texts: the *Scholia on the Incarnation*[92] and the treatise *Against those that do not acknowledge Mary to be the Mother of God*.[93] The overarching framework of the *Scholia* is the idea that Christ is truly God who has condescended into true humanity, as Isaiah 7.14 indicates: 'since the holy Virgin was made pregnant by the Holy Spirit she brought forth a son according to the flesh, and thus he was called Emmanuel, for the Incorporeal One was with us through a fleshy generation'.[94] Similarly, in the opening paragraphs of *Quod Maria Sit Deipara*, Cyril stated that God is immutable and undergoes no change in the incarnation: 'ἄνθρωπον μὲν γὰρ τὸν τοῦ Θεοῦ Λόγον ἐπὶ συντελείᾳ τῶν αἰώνων γενόμενον ὁ θεῖος ἡμῖν εὐαγγελίζεται λόγος, οὐκ εἰς ἀνθρώπου μεταβαλόντα φύσιν ἀλλὰ ταύτην εἰς ἑαντοῦ προσλαβόμενον'.[95] In Cyril's presentation, Mary gives birth to the temple united, but not conjoined, to the Word: 'making for itself an indwelling in the temple that was born from the virgin by . . . true union'.[96] The union is realized in a dynamic interrelation of the properties of the two realities, human and divine, for Cyril understands it as 'an economic union whereby the Word endowed the flesh with the radiance of his own glory and divine majesty'.[97] The title *Theotokos* reiterates the facts of the double generation of the Word which underlines the Christic union: the 'incomprehensible manner' of the Son's generation from the Father and the fact that 'for our sake he economically underwent a self-emptying'.[98] The reasoning behind the title justifies such understanding of the divine economy: 'because he assumed from the holy Virgin a body that was truly united to himself, we say that the holy Virgin is *Theotokos*, for she gave birth to it humanly'.[99] Cyril forcefully emphasizes this point: 'she gave birth to God made man', because '[H]e could not have been made man except through birth from a woman'.[100] Cyril finds his scriptural proof texts in correlating Isa. 7.14 and Phil. 2.7: two texts which, in his interpretation, identify Emmanuel, Mary's child, with the Word of God.[101]

For Cyril, Mary's birth-giving is the clearest illustration of the fact that Christ is one. As he summarizes this point:

He underwent a temporal generation and accepted a beginning from the woman so that he could exist like this, but he never set aside his eternal generation from God the Father. He also allowed his flesh to be born according to the laws of his own nature, that is in the manner of a nativity. Nonetheless there was in this very deed something unlike human nature, for he was born of a virgin, and he alone had such an unwed mother.[102]

Cyril comments on Gabriel's greeting to Mary as a proof that God was made man 'born in human fashion from the Virgin'.[103] The Annunciation is a historical moment in which the divine economy is fulfilled. God becomes 'like us' and participates in us physically through the fact of the birth. Cyril refers to the physical aspects of the incarnation – generation, pregnancy and birth-giving – in order to prove that the same divine person participates in both and that the divinity is not lost or transfigured in the act of joining humanity, since 'as God, he is unchangeable'.[104] In turn, the 'natural' (hypostatic) union brings together the impassible God and human suffering: the Word, Cyril states, has a body and a soul, and 'when the flesh suffered, even though he was impassible, he was aware of what was happening within it, and thus, as God, even though he did away with the weakness of the flesh, still he appropriated those weaknesses of his own body'.[105] Thus God participates in all that is human, including suffering, but is not limited by it.[106]

Cyril's position proved to be decisive. Two years after the Ephesian Council, a formula of reunion was finally negotiated between him and his opponents, in large part through imperial intervention. In 433 John of Antioch sent a letter to Alexandria in which he endorsed Cyril's interpretation of the Nicene Creed as orthodox. More specifically, John asserted that, acting in a 'fullness of conviction', and in the 'faith set forth at Nicaea' as 'sufficient for all knowledge of piety', he was prepared to accept the Virgin Mary as *Theotokos* and Cyril's explanation of the 'manner of the incarnation'. John agreed to 'confess one Christ' who was born 'from the Virgin Mary according to his humanity'.[107] Based on this 'understanding of a union without fusion', he acknowledged that the Virgin is the Mother of God because she supplies Christ's own flesh. Hence the praise of Mary is essential for the ecumenical 'confession of faith' and the idea of her divine motherhood is a component in the construction of any authentic Christology.

Cyril's reply was fast and joyful. His letter begins with a quotation from Ps. 95.11, 'Let the heavens be glad and let the earth rejoice', emphasizing the universal need for peace in the Church and perhaps his own personal relief at having the dispute settled.[108] The Mariological theme has a prominent place in this text and is used to elucidate the question of the identity of Christ. Cyril quotes the formula of reunion in which John's admission of the title *Theotokos* served as a way of accepting the Alexandrian explanation of the 'manner of the incarnation of the Only Begotten Son of God'.[109] Yet he also found it necessary to add a few words of instruction and further clarify his version of Mary's elemental role in incarnational theology. Scoffing at his opponents (some of whom were Oriental bishops who possibly felt that the title *Theotokos* was a covert declaration of Apollinarianism), Cyril underscores the significance of his defence of Mary's birth-giving as a critical element of the faith: 'You must surely know that nearly all our struggle on behalf of the faith has been engaged on the insistence that the holy virgin is the Mother of God.'[110] In his previous works related to the controversy, Cyril had already argued that the union enacted through Mary's conception and birth-giving is real in the sense of enabling God to participate in all that is human while remaining God. Now he finds it necessary, once more, to rebuff the accusations of teaching that the 'holy body of Christ had come down from heaven, and was not from the holy virgin'.[111] Cyril refers to the scene of the Annunciation in Lk. 1.30-31 to illustrate his thesis that the Son of God was truly born, lowering himself into human flesh, and did not simply descend from heaven.[112] His praise of Mary, he emphasizes, as the mother of the Word's flesh, is the proof that he rejected docetic depictions of Christ's humanity, while affirming that the divinity is not capable of alteration: 'But if we say that the holy body of Christ, the Saviour of us all, is from heaven and not from her, then how could she possibly be understood as the Mother of God? . . . For he [the Word] ever remains what he is and does not change or undergo alteration.'[113]

In short, the importance of Mary's (symbolic) image, situated at the foreground of Cyril's incarnational scheme, informed the final settlement between the participants in the Ephesian Council. Cyril was cognizant of the fact that Mary's prominent presence in his theology would diffuse the Oriental accusation of Apollinarianism and secure the authentic character of Christ's humanity. He defends Mary's title *Theotokos* as orthodox, not because it makes Mary the origin of Christ's divinity, but because it exemplifies the true character of Christ's person and mission. Cyril describes the Virgin as the person in whom the union between God and humanity takes place and, even more so, becomes a reality whose ultimate goal is salvation.

It should be emphasized that the content of his comments is largely repetitive. As always, Cyril affirms the interdependence of Christological and Mariological modes of discourse. For him, the reasoning behind the title *Theotokos* is Christological but, even more so, refers to the whole context of the incarnation as part of the divine plan of salvation. This theological perspective would be dominant at the Council of Chalcedon (451), even if Cyril died before the convocation of the council.

CONCLUSION

To summarize Cyril's argument in favour of the *Theotokos*, it was (a) composed in response to Nestorius's reductionist theology of Mary, and (b) based on the Christological framework employed by Cyril as an Alexandrian theologian. I proposed that Cyril's Mariology was not simply derivative from his Christology, but an integral part of its structure and message. In Cyril's estimation, one cannot have an orthodox Christology without a consideration of Mary's elemental role in the incarnation.

Cyril's Christological perspective underlines the unity of the divine hypostasis of the Son with his flesh. He argues that the unalienable character of this unity enables human and divine natures to exchange their properties in Christ and thus accomplish the purpose of the divine economy – the restoration and sanctification of all creation in God. In this context, Cyril portrays Mary as a *Theotokos* or God-bearer and describes the Virgin's womb as the locus in which the uncontainable God has voluntarily descended into the limitations of true human existence.[114]

Furthermore, Cyril affirms that Mary's figure is indispensable in theological reflection as well as in the communal life of the Church. The 'holy and most pure Virgin' is to be venerated as *Theotokos*, that is to say, a figure mediating between God and humankind by virtue of her 'divine' motherhood.[115] Veneration finds its truest expression in homiletic delivery as well as in the encouragement of ascetic practices in emulation of Mary's piety and virginity. Cyril's homilies at the Council of Ephesus suggested that the theological and cultic (or homiletic) components of Marian theology should go hand in hand; neither one is intelligible without the other. His understanding of salvation necessitated the application of Marian themes into the praxis of the Church and thus situated Mary prominently in liturgical life and communal practice of devotion.

Finally, if Cyril's work is situated against the larger context of developing Marian Mariological discourse, its impetus and inspirational power are undeniable. Cyril was an active participant in the process by which the theology of Mary was confirmed as an integral part of Christian theology by receiving an explicit and official endorsement at Ephesus. This integration was the result of a heated debate on the conceptualization of Mary's image and its relation to the Church's understanding of Christ's mission and personhood – in sum, a process which was neither easy nor streamlined. The complex chain of events which led to the affirmation of Mary as *Theotokos* at the Council of Ephesus does not allow us to look at the Council as a farce dominated by the Alexandrians and their Christology, nor does it permit us to assume that the theology of Mary has always been present in its mature form within the framework of Christian theology. Instead, in light of the events of 429–431, we have to consider the development of early Mariology as a process of gradual unfolding of theological themes which shows that the Church as a believing community had to clarify the contours of its teaching by (con)testing various theological perspectives and, as a matter of faith and orthodoxy, make a final judgement in selecting one of those as correct. I see Cyril's argument in favour of Mary's significance as the most apt illustration of this process.

BIBLIOGRAPHY

Caro, R. (ed.) (1971–1973), *La Homiletica Griega en el Siglo V*. 3 volumes. Dayton: University of Dayton Press.

Constas, N. (2003), *Proclus of Constantinople and the Cult of the Virgin in Late Antiquity: Homilies 1–5, Texts and Translations* (Supplements to *Vigiliae Christianae* 66). Leiden: E. J. Brill.

Gavrilyuk, P. (2003), 'Theopatheia: Nestorius's Main Charge Against Cyril of Alexandria', *Scottish Journal of Theology* 56.2, 190–207.

Greer, R. (1966), 'The Image of God and the Prosopic Union in Nestorius' "Bazaar of Heracleides"', in R. A. Norris and W. N. Pittenger, *Lux in Lumine*. New York: Seabury Press, 46–61.

Hallman, J. (2002), 'The Communication of Idioms in Theodoret's Commentary on Hebrews', in P. Blowers, A. Christmas, D. Hunter and R. Young (eds), *In Dominico Eloquio: Essays in Patristic Exegesis in Honor of R. L. Wilken*. Grand Rapids: Eerdmans, 369–79.

Imhof, P. and B. Lorenz (1981), *Maria Theotokos bei Cyrill von Alexandrien*. Munich: G. Kaffke.

Loofs, F. (1905), *Nestoriana die Fragmente de Nestorius*. Halle: Niemeyer.

McEnerney, J. (1987), *St Cyril of Alexandria: Letters* (*Fathers of the Church* Volumes 76–7). Washington: Catholic University of America Press.

McGuckin, J. A. (1994), *St Cyril of Alexandria: the Christological Controversy, its History, Theology, and Texts*. Leiden: E. J. Brill.

McKinion, S. (2000), *Words, Imagery, and the Mystery of Christ: a Reconstruction of Cyril of Alexandria's Christology*. Leiden: E. J. Brill.

Migne, J. P. (1857–1866), *Cursus Completus Patrologiae Graecae*. Paris: Éditions Garnier. Referred to in the notes as *PG*.

Nachef, A. (1997), *Mary: Virgin Mother in the Theological Thought of St Basil the Great, St Gregory Nazianzen, & St Gregory of Nyssa*. Dayton: International Marian Research Institute.

Norris, R. (ed.) (1980), *The Christological Controversy*. Philadelphia: Fortress.

O'Keefe, J. (1997), 'Impassible Suffering? Divine Passion and Fifth-Century Christology', *Journal of Theological Studies* 58, 39–60.

Payne Smith, R. (ed.) (1983), *Commentary on the Gospel of St Luke by St Cyril of Alexandria*. Astoria: Studion.

Peltomaa, L. M. (2001), *The Image of the Virgin Mary in the Akathistos Hymn*. Leiden: E. J. Brill.

Pusey, E. (ed.) (1881), *Against Nestorius (Library of the Fathers of the Church 47)*. Oxford: J. Parker.

Quasten, J. (1964), *Patrology*. 4 volumes. Utrecht: Spectrum.

Russell, N. (ed.) (2000), *Cyril of Alexandria*. New York: Routledge.

Schaff, P. and H. Wace (eds) (1997), *The Nicene and Post-Nicene Fathers* (2nd Series). Grand Rapids: Eerdmans.

Schwartz, E. (ed.) (1927–1932), *Acta Conciliorum Oecumenicorum, I: Concilium Universale Ephesinum (5 vols); II: Concilium Universale Chalcedonense (6 vols)*. Berlin: Walter de Gruyter. Referred to in the notes as *ACO*.

Vööbus, A. (1973), *Discoveries of Great Import on the Commentary on Luke by Cyril of Alexandria*. Stockholm: ETSE.

Wickham, L. (ed.) (1983), *Cyril of Alexandria: Select Letters*. Oxford: Clarendon Press.

Young, F. (1983), *From Nicaea to Chalcedon*. Philadelphia: Fortress Press.

NOTES

1. This five-volume treatise was most likely composed in 430 in response to Nestorius' preaching in Constantinople. Current scholarship has shown little interest in the Mariological message of this piece, even though it plays a substantial role in the structuring of the first volume. The English translation is in Pusey 1881. Selected passages are available in modern translation in Russell 2000.

2. See especially the large body of homiletic material structured around the Gospel of Luke which reflects some of the major themes of the controversy. See the English edition (from an extant Syriac translation) in Payne Smith 1983.

3. Socrates, *Ecclesiastical History*, in Schaff and Wace 1997: 2.171.

4. See the *Life of Saint Anthony*, in *Ibid.*: 2.206; also *Discourse III Against the Arians and Discourse*, 2.29. Athanasius' predecessor, bishop Alexander of Alexandria, is also said to have used the title; see Nachef 1997: 17.

5. Loofs 1905: 185; selected fragments available in Latin translation from Marius Mercator, edited in Loofs' volume.

6. Nestorius described the incident in a letter addressed to John of Antioch; Loofs 1905: 183–6.

7. Cyril mentioned wrong depictions of the union as predicated on 'divine favour and good will' or 'outward appearance', or abolishing the difference between natures in his *Second Letter to Nestorius* (Wickham 1983: 7). The three models are also discussed in greater detail as Christological heresies in the later *Scholia on the Incarnation*. Another questionable depiction of the incarnation is the indwelling of Jesus by the Word, because of the connotations of seeing God dwell in Christ as he does in the saints; cf. McKinion 2000: 132.

8. Cyril, *Adversus Nestorium*, in Russell 2000: 135.
9. *Ibid.*: 78–9.
10. *Ibid.*: 80.
11. Wickam 1983: 11. The term *Theotokos* appears in Cyril's *Commentary on Isaiah* IV.4, but the note may have been a gloss.
12. *Reply to Cyril's Second Letter*, trans. McGuckin 1994: 367.
13. Loofs 1905: 302; translation mine.
14. *Ibid.*: 246; Latin translation by Mercator; English translation mine. The same idea is repeated verbatim in a fragment from a sermon, *Ibid.*: 338.
15. *Homily 1*, in Norris 1980: 124–5; same idea is repeated in Loofs 1905: 340.
16. Cf. Lk. 1.35.
17. *Second Letter to Cyril*, in McGuckin 1994: 367.
18. *Homily 1*, in Norris 1980: 130.
19. Cyril's *Letter to Celestine*, in McGuckin 1994: 277.
20. See McEnerney 1987: 1.52.
21. See Russell 2000: 38; McGuckin 1994: 277.
22. McEnerney 1987: 1.62.
23. *Explanation of the Twelve Chapters*, in McGuckin 1994: 292.
24. *Ibid.*: 283.
25. Caro 1971. Also see Vööbus 1973; Imhof and Lorenz 1981.
26. Russell 2000: 71 dates this text to 412–425.
27. *Letter to the Monks*, in McGuckin 1994: 249.
28. See *Second Letter to Nestorius*, in Wickham 1983: 7. This is also how Cyril paraphrases the account of Christ's mission in the Nicene Creed (*Ibid.*: 9).
29. Pusey 1881: 41.
30. *Ibid.*: 73.
31. *Ibid.*: 40–1.
32. This term, common to the Antiochenes, was meant to safeguard the fullness of Jesus' humanity. In the structure of Christic conjunction, Theodore of Mopsuestia and, following him, Nestorius, taught that each nature retains its own *prosopon* or concrete expression in addition to the functional *prosopon* of the Christic union. On this issue see Greer's thoughtful analysis (1966). See also McKinion's discussion of Cyril's reaction to Nestorius in 2000: 86–102.
33. Pusey 1881: 67.
34. Russell 2000: 133.
35. *Ibid.*: 49.
36. Pusey 1881: 113.
37. Payne-Smith 1983: 47.
38. *Letter to Bishop Juvenal*, trans. McEnerney 1987: 1.79.
39. *Ibid.*: 255.
40. *Ibid.*: 53.
41. Pusey 1881: 116.
42. *Ibid.*: 134, 169.
43. See Gavrilyuk 2003: 56.2, 190–207; O'Keefe 1997: 40. O'Keefe claims, '[F]rom this perspective, I think it may be helpful to see the christological controversy less as a debate about terminology and more as a debate about the fullness of God's presence in the world' (*Ibid.*: 41). Francis Young also notes the one-sidedness of portraying the Antiochenes as defenders of Jesus' humanity: see Young 1983: 179–80. A study on the language of God-suffering done by Joseph Hallman supports O'Keefe's and Young's position; see Hallman 2002: 369–79. Hallman's research emphasizes the continuation of the theme of divine immutability as introduced at the Council of Nicaea and carried on to the agenda of Ephesus.

44. Hallman 2002: 370.
45. *ACO* 1.2, 45–64; trans. McGuckin 1994: 369–78.
46. Loofs 1905: 274, 277.
47. *Ibid.*: 248.
48. *Ibid.*: 277, 287.
49. Cyril's *Second and Third Letters to Nestorius*, as they are commonly known; *Epistle 4*, in *PG* 77.44–50; *ACO* 1.1.1, 25–8; and *Epistle 17* in *PG* 77.105–22; *ACO* 1.1, 33–42. The letters are translated in McGuckin 1994: 262–5, 266–75; Wickham 1983: 2–33.
50. *Second Letter to Nestorius*, in Wickham 1983: 7.
51. *Ibid.*
52. *Ibid.*
53. *Third Letter to Nestorius*, in *Ibid.*: 17.
54. *Second Letter to Nestorius*, in *Ibid.*: 7–8.
55. *Explanation of the Twelve Chapters*, in *PG* 76.293–312; trans. McGuckin 1994: 282–93. The original text of the anathemas was so radical and controversial to the Oriental bishops that Cyril was accused of Apollinarianism; for the accusations see *ACO* 1.1.1.7, 33–5.
56. *Ibid.*, trans. McGuckin 1994: 283.
57. *Ibid.*: 283–4.
58. *Ibid.*: 284. This is not a mere rhetorical flourish on Cyril's part, but a definitive theological statement underscoring the divine initiative in the incarnational event.
59. *Ibid.* For Cyril, Christ's birth is one of the blessings he bestows on the human race. See also Wickham 1983: 29 n. 18.
60. *Explanation of the Twelve Chapters*, trans. McGuckin 1994: 284.
61. Florilegia are select, systematically organized passages from patristic writings, usually meant to lend the author's authority to a specific topic of discussion. The official usage of florilegia is unique to Ephesus; we do not have record of a previous council relying on such a technique. It should be noted, however, that Cyril already used the florilegia as means of persuasion in his treatises to the imperial court from 430, especially in his *Address to the Princesses*.
62. Athanasius, *Letter to Epictetus*, *Library of the Fathers of the Church* 45, Pusey 1881: 45–60, trans. McGuckin 1994: 379–89; Gregory of Nazianzus, *Epistle 101*, *PG* 37.176–93, trans. McGuckin 1994: 390–99. Gregory's text declared: 'If anyone does not believe that Saint Mary is the Mother of God (*Theotokos*), he is severed from the Godhead.'
63. Athanasius develops this idea in the context of Luke's Gospel: 'Isaiah prophetically pointed her out when he said: "Behold the Virgin" (Isa. 7.14) and Gabriel was sent to her not simply as a virgin, but as a "virgin betrothed to a man" (Lk. 1.27), so that by the mention of the man who bethrothed her he might demonstrate that Mary was a real human being. This is why Scripture mentions her giving birth, and says: "She wrapped him in swaddling bands" (Lk. 2.7), and that the breasts which he sucked were called blessed (Lk. 11.27), and that a sacrifice was offered because he who was born had "opened the womb" (Lk. 2.23)'; in *Letter to Epictetus*, trans. McGuckin 1994: 383. Notice the image of Mary nursing which Athanasius believes has a scriptural foundation.
64. During the four months spent in Ephesus, Cyril is said to have delivered eight sermons dedicated to Mary. Six of those are preserved in a complete form. See Quasten 1964: 3.123–4.
65. *Homily 4*, *PG* 77.992. The title Μαρία Θεοτόκος is repeated twice in the opening two lines of the homily.
66. *Ibid.* All references to the text follow the translation in Peltomaa 2001: 68–9.
67. *Ibid.*
68. *PG* 77.992.

69. *Ibid.*
70. *PG* 77.994; trans. Peltomaa 2001: 68.
71. *Ibid.*
72. Caro 1971: 1.685; Peltomaa 2001: 70.
73. Proclus refers to Mary's womb several times in the course of the sermon, always as a theological idea which makes the salvific purpose of the incarnation a reality. This is a typical example: 'O womb, in which was drawn up the bond that gives us all liberty! . . . Had the Word not dwelt in a womb, the flesh would never have sat on a throne'; Constas 2003: 139.
74. See Peltomaa 2001: 137.
75. Cf. *Ibid.*: 107: 'To focus the attention on the womb of the Virgin was a characteristic feature of the theological discussion of the time of Ephesus, reflecting the question of how the Incarnation physically took place.'
76. *Ibid.*: 135.
77. For instance, Cyril's dogmatic letters to Nestorius discuss Mary's role in the incarnation not simply in terms of her womb, but as the reality in which the divine Word 'had fleshy birth because he issued from woman for us and for our salvation having united humanity substantially (καθ υπόσταυιν) to himself. The point is that . . . he underwent fleshy birth united from the very womb, making the birth of his flesh his very own'; in *Second Letter to Nestorius*, Wickham 1983: 7.
78. *PG* 77.992. Cf. *Homily 2*, *PG* 77.988, where Cyril refers to Mary as the 'holy *Theotokos*' who gave birth to the one filling all things with his glory.
79. *Homily 4*, *PG* 77.992, trans. Peltomaa 2001: 69: 'The virginal womb, O, wondrous thing! I am struck by the miracle!'
80. McGuckin 1994: 349 n. 1.
81. See Cyril's *Letter to John of Antioch*, *PG* 77.173–82; McGuckin 1944: 344, where both of these charges are mentioned.
82. See *ACO* 1.1, 36; McGuckin 1994: 83.
83. *Letter to Eulogius*, trans. McGuckin 1994: 353.
84. *Ibid.*: 350.
85. *Ibid.*: 354.
86. See Cyril's *First Letter to Succensus, Epistle 45*, *PG* 77.228–37; trans. McGuckin 1994: 352–3. In this text Cyril comments on the 'sickness' of Diodore who 'thought and wrote that he who was born of the line of David from the holy virgin was the one distinct son, and the Word of God the Father was again another and quite distinct son . . . Nestorius became this man's pupil and being rendered dim by his books he also pretends to confess one Christ and Son and Lord, though he too has divided the One and Indivisible into two.'
87. *Epistle 50, ACO* 1.1.3, 90–101.
88. *Ibid.*, trans. McEnerney 1987: 1.213.
89. *Ibid.*: 214.
90. *Ibid.*: 218.
91. *Ibid.*: 227.
92. *Scholia on the Incarnation*, *PG* 75.1369–412; *PG* 48.1005–40 contains a complete Latin translation by Marius Mercator. Only fragments from the Greek text exist (chs 1, 8–11, 13); for a complete list see McGuckin 1994: 294. The references to the text follow McGuckin's translation, *Ibid.*: 294–335.
93. *PG* 76.255–92. See also Quasten 1964: 3.128.
94. *Scholia*, trans. McGuckin 1994: 296.
95. *PG* 76.257. The idea that Christ's divinity is not compromised in the incarnation in interpreted in the context of Jn 1.14: 'and the Word became flesh'.

96. *Scholia*, trans. McGuckin 1994: 319.
97. *Ibid.*: 297, 298; cf. *Quod Maria Sit Deipara, PG* 76.283, where Cyril discusses Elizabeth's greeting to Mary.
98. *Scholia*, trans. McGuckin 1994: 321, 324.
99. *Ibid.*: 321.
100. *Ibid.*: 322.
101. *Ibid.*: 323.
102. *Ibid.*: 318.
103. *Ibid.*: 299.
104. *Ibid.*: 299–300.
105. *Ibid.*: 301.
106. *Ibid.*: 327.
107. See McEnerney 1987: 2.145.
108. *Epistle 39, ACO* 1.1.4, sent in the spring of 433. Trans. McGuckin 1994: 343–8.
109. *Ibid.*: 344.
110. *Ibid.*: 346.
111. *Ibid.*: 345. Cyril is answering an accusation of Apollinarianism.
112. *Ibid.*: 346.
113. *Ibid.*: 346, 347.
114. For example, in his *Third Letter to Nestorius*, Cyril affirms that Christ 'substantially united humanity with himself, and underwent fleshy birth from her womb [ἐπειςὴ καθ' ὑπόςταειν ἑνώσας ἑαυτῷ το ἀνθρώπινον καὶ ἐκ μήτρας αὐτῆς γέννσιν ὑπέμεινε σαρκικήν]. He had not need of temporal birth . . . for his own nature. No, he meant to bless the very origin of our existence, through a woman's giving birth to him united with the flesh, meant too that the curse on the whole race which dispatches our earthly bodies to death should cease' (*Third Letter*, 11, trans. Wickham 1983: 29).
115. *Adversus Nestorium*, in Russell 2000: 132; cf. *Ibid.*: 135: 'the Word came down not into the flesh of any particular person . . . On the contrary, having made his own the body which was from a woman, and having been born from her according to the flesh, he recapitulated human birth in himself.'

8

THE LIFE-BEARING SPRING

MARGARET BARKER

In November 543 CE, a great new church was consecrated in Jerusalem, dedicated to the Holy Mother of God, the Ever Virgin Mary. It was built on the south-eastern slope of the western hill, and was the greatest of all the churches built by the Emperor Justinian, yet it stood for only seventy years. When the Persians invaded Palestine in 614, the Jews rose up against the Christians in the land and tore down their churches.[1] The Patriarch Zechariah and his people were taken into exile in Persia, and the New Church, often called the *Nea*, was never rebuilt. Towards the end of the seventh century, stones from this church were used to build a Muslim palace. Some scholars think that the fury of the Jews was because stones from the Temple Mount had been used to build the New Church.[2] The Temple certainly was a factor in the fate of the *Nea*, but such evidence as survives suggests that the *Nea* was built as a new temple. This was Justinian, who saw himself as Solomon, rebuilding the Temple in Jerusalem.[3]

In 1970 the first remains of the *Nea* were found by Nahman Avigad and his team, a huge structure with a marble floor, and in 1975 parts of the eastern end were uncovered, including a huge vaulted subterranean cistern under the main structure. Procopius, who compiled the official account of Justinian's building works, said that one quarter of the *Nea* was built out over the valley on whose side it stood. This was the part where the priests performed their rites.[4] Archaeologists discovered that the measurements were exactly those of Ezekiel's future temple – 100 cubits wide and 200 cubits long (Ezek. 41.13-14). Procopius says that two huge pillars stood before the main door, presumably the Jachin and Boaz of Solomon's Temple (1 Kgs 7.15-22). There had been no such pillars in the Second Temple, nor in Herod's refurbished 'third' Temple. Justinian was restoring the original Temple. Procopius records the problems they had finding cedar trees large enough for the huge roof; but the roof had to be cedar, like Solomon's Temple (1 Kgs 6.9). Everything known from the ancient sources and recovered by archaeologists points to the fact that this huge church, dedicated to Mary, was constructed as the restored Temple of Solomon, with a water cistern under the sanctuary.

This raises several questions: why should the restored Temple be dedicated to the Holy Mother of God, the Ever Virgin Mary? Why did it need such elaborate plumbing? What did those architects intend to represent by that building?

The dedication of the *Nea* is remembered today as the Feast of the Entry of the

Mother of God into the Temple, as described in the *Infancy Gospel of James* (*Protevangelium*). Mary was depicted as Wisdom – a holy child who lived in the Temple. She was fed by an angel, and she danced there, just as Wisdom had danced before the Lord, according to Prov. 8.30-31. Mary left the Temple when she was no longer a child, and a husband was found for her. Then Mary gave birth to her Son. Revelation 12 tells the same story, but in the form of a vision. A portent appears in heaven, a woman clothed with the sun and crowned with stars. She is about to give birth to her Son, who is immediately caught up to the throne of God, destined to rule all nations (Rev. 12.1-6). Since the Son caught up to the throne of God must be the Messiah, his mother must have been Mary, here depicted as a heavenly being clothed with the sun.

The woman appearing in heaven is set between two affirmations that the kingdom of God is established on earth. The last trumpet sounds and announces the kingdom of God on earth: 'The kingdom of the world has become the kingdom of our Lord and of his Christ and he shall reign for ever and ever' (Rev. 11.15), then the woman is described, then John hears a voice in heaven proclaiming that the salvation and the power and the kingdom of our God and the authority of his Christ have come (12.10). These are all aspects of the one vision; on earth as it is in heaven. The birth of the Christ and the establishing of the kingdom are events in heaven and on earth, as is the battle with evil that ensues. The mother of the Messiah is, therefore a figure both in heaven and on earth.[5]

Origen, in his *Commentary on John*, quoted from the *Prayer of Joseph*, 'an apocryphal text presently in use among the Hebrews'.[6] He was giving evidence for the Jewish belief that important human figures were simultaneously angel beings and humans. Jacob the patriarch had also been Israel, the 'first minister before the face of God, a mighty angel'. So, too, John the Baptist had been both human and angel. The mother of the Messiah would also have been both a human woman and a mighty angel in heaven, and St John's vision of the woman clothed with the sun shows us how the first Christians understood the role of Mary. She was the queen of heaven, crowned with twelve stars, who gave birth to the male child destined for the throne of God. The belief that humans could also be angels on earth accounts for the way the *Infancy Gospel of James* tells the story of Mary. Certain events are described which resonate with the Wisdom traditions – for example, that she danced in the Temple. Mary was Wisdom.

In order to set these visions in context, it is necessary to understand some of the symbolism of the Temple. It represented the creation, visible and invisible, and was divided into two parts by the veil. The holy of holies represented the invisible presence of God at the heart of the creation – outside time and beyond matter. The great hall of the Temple represented the visible world, everything created after the second day in the Genesis account.[7] What concerns us here is the holy of holies, since that is where the woman clothed with the sun appeared. This was the state of the angels, a matter of some controversy, as can be seen from the debates in post-Christian Jewish sources. The angels were created on the second day, or on the fifth, but not, emphatically not, at the beginning. Not on Day One.[8]

There is an enigmatic poem in Proverbs 8 that describes the creation, not as the story is told in Genesis 1, but it assumes that same Temple-based world view. At the beginning of creation, Wisdom was birthed. The verb *qanah* has caused considerable debate – does it mean beget or acquire? – but the other verb used to describe the origin of Wisdom is unambiguously a birth word: *halal*, brought forth. She was begotten not created, and then either 'established' (*nissakti*), or perhaps the word means 'hidden away' (*n^esakkoti*) as in Psalm 139.13b: 'I was hidden in the womb of my mother.' She was brought to birth before the visible world was created; in other words, she existed on Day One, in the holy of holies. This is where Wisdom belonged, and this is why the Woman clothed with the sun appeared in heaven, in the holy of holies.

In the Temple, the holy of holies housed the heavenly throne. Worshippers in the Temple did not distinguish between the actual temple and heaven, and so the psalmist could declare: 'The Lord is in his holy temple, the Lord's throne is in heaven' (Ps. 111.4). When St John saw the heavenly throne, however, it was set by the tree of life, and the river of the water of life flowed from the throne and from the tree. 'He showed me the river of the water of life, bright as crystal, flowing from the throne of God and the Lamb . . . and the tree of life with its twelve kinds of fruit . . . ' Where the tree stood in relation to the river is not clear; the text is obscure, but it seems to say that the river flowed around it or from it (Rev. 22.1-2). However St John may have seen it, the holy of holies had within it the throne, the tree of life and the source of the water of life.

The tree of life was a symbol of Wisdom: 'She is a tree of life to those who lay hold of her; those who hold her fast are called happy' (Prov. 3.18), and happy, in Hebrew *'ašer*, gives a clue as to how this tree of life had been represented in the original Temple. The item known as the *'ašerah* had been the tree of life, the symbol of Wisdom, which had been removed by King Josiah as part of his purge (2 Kgs 23.4-6). The tree had been removed, and replaced, several times. In the reign of King Asa, the *'ašerah* had been removed, along with his mother who had had it installed in the Temple (1 Kgs 15.9-13). The *'ašerah* was linked to the mother of the king and, although her name in Hebrew is *Ma'acha*, in the Greek she is named Ana. Anna was also the name of the mother of Mary – and one wonders if the change was significant. Mary, as we shall see, was also a significant name in the Wisdom tradition.

The tree had been violently removed by Josiah, and Enoch was later to see it in his vision of the mountain of God. This section of *1 Enoch* is the earliest in the collection, and contains ancient material, some of it known to Isaiah. Enoch saw a fragrant tree whose blossoms, leaves and wood never withered, and whose fruit hung in clusters like dates. None would eat the fruit until after the day of judgement, when the Lord came to earth as King. Then the fruit would give life to the chosen ones, and the tree itself would be transplanted to the house of the Lord (*1 Enoch* 24.4–25.6).[9] The return of the tree was a sign of the kingdom, a memory that survives also in rabbinic texts. In the time of the Messiah, they said, the Ark would return to the Temple, together with the fire, the menorah, the Spirit and the cherubim (*Numbers Rabbah* XV.10).[10] The menorah, the seven-branched lamp, was made like a tree and almost certainly, in its original form, represented the tree of life that Josiah had removed. There was a menorah in the Second

Temple, but this cannot have been regarded as the true menorah. Perhaps it had a different shape, or was stood in a different place. Or perhaps it had a different meaning.

The Lady and her tree were controversial and forbidden well into the Christian era. There were elaborate regulations for avoiding the use of trees planted for idolatry or pruned for idolatry, i.e. to make them a special shape, and their branches could not be used in the Tabernacles procession.[11] These prohibitions are linked to objects depicting the sun, the moon and the dragon; anyone finding such an object had to throw it into the Dead Sea. Now the sun, the moon and the dragon are elements in the vision of the woman clothed with the sun, which suggests that what St John saw in his vision was a recognized pattern associated with the idolatrous tree. He saw the Ark and the tree restored to the holy of holies (Rev. 11.19; 22.2), and he heard the risen Lord promise that the faithful would eat again from the tree of life (2.7). This means that the early Christians were in touch with the traditions preserved in *1 Enoch*, and there is reason to believe they knew this actual text.

The book of *1 Enoch* comprises five distinct sections, and fragments from all but one of them have been found among the Dead Sea Scrolls. In other words, there is proof that four sections are pre-Christian. The section not represented is the *Parables* (or *Similitudes*) *of Enoch*, three visions of the holy of holies, which are so similar to early Christian ideas that this section was formerly thought to be a Christian composition. There has been broad agreement among scholars for some time, however, that this section is not Christian, and that it was composed during the last two centuries of the Second Temple period.[12]

In the *Parables*, the holy of holies is the place of the throne and the angels, as we should expect, but there is also frequent reference to water. Righteousness flowed there like water (*1 Enoch* 39.5). There was an inexhaustible fountain of righteousness there, surrounded by fountains of Wisdom, and the thirsty were able to drink from them. Wisdom was poured out like water (49.1), and sinners had 'forsaken the fountain of life' (96.6, not part of the *Parables*).

Similar imagery is found in the Dead Sea Scrolls.[13] The Rule of the Community concludes with this hymn: 'My eyes have gazed on that which is eternal, on wisdom concealed from men, on knowledge and wise design, (hidden) from the souls of men; on a fountain of righteousness and on a storehouse of power, and on a spring of glory (hidden) from the assembly of the flesh' (1QS XI). In the Hymns we read of 'a fountain of knowledge for all men of insight' (1QH II), 'a source of light that becomes an eternal ever-flowing fountain' whose flames consume sinners (1QH XIV), 'trees of life beside a mysterious fountain' where the faithful flourish (1QH XVI), 'my heart shall be open to the everlasting fountain' (1QH XVIII), '[the spring of] eternity, the Well of Glory, and the fountain of knowledge' (1QH XX). The fountain quenches the thirst for Wisdom and all that this implies. The words of Jesus, 'Blessed are they who hunger and thirst for righteousness, for they shall be satisfied' (Mt. 5.6), are one more example; as are the words of the Spirit and the Bride at the end of the book of Revelation: 'Let him who is thirsty come, let him who desires take the water of life without price' (Rev. 22.17).

Water was an important element of the holy of holies. The Lord nourishes his people with the abundance of the Temple, and they drink from the river of his delights – the word is, literally, *Edens*. 'For with thee is the fountain of life, and in thy light do we see light' (Ps. 36.8-9). Jeremiah warned that the people had exchanged their glory for something worthless, they had changed their gods and forsaken the Lord, the fountain of living waters (Jer. 2.12-13). He spoke of the throne and the fountain as though they were together: 'A glorious throne set on high from the beginning is the place of our sanctuary . . . They have forsaken the Lord, the fountain of living water' (17.12-13). Popular proverbs show how this water was understood: 'The teaching of the wise is a fountain of life' (Prov. 13.14); 'The fear of the Lord is a fountain of life' (14.27); and in the time of the Messiah, the whole earth would be filled with this water: 'The earth shall be full of the knowledge of the Lord as the waters cover the sea' (Isa. 11.9; also in Hab. 2.14).

The water which flowed from the holy of holies was wisdom. The Enoch tradition and the Qumran texts make this clear, and it is implied in the Old Testament even when it is not stated explicitly. At some stage, however, wisdom had ceased to flow, and the prophets looked forward to the day when the waters would again come forth from the Temple. The earliest example is Ezekiel's vision of the future Temple, the ideal Temple, free of pollutions, to which the Glory of the Lord could return (Ezek. 43.1-12). Water gushed from this Temple, a great river that flowed into the Dead Sea to sweeten its waters and irrigate the desert. Miraculous trees – clearly trees of life – grew on its banks (43.1-12). Ezekiel had been a priest in the First Temple (1.3), and so the water image must have been part of the Temple as he knew it. Among the later prophets, and especially in the additions to their oracles, water returning to the Temple is part of the future hope for the Temple. 'On that day', they begin, meaning the day when the Lord establishes his kingdom and the true Temple is restored. 'On that day, the mountains shall drip sweet wine and the hills shall flow with milk . . . and a fountain shall come forth from the house of the Lord' (Joel 3.18). 'On that day,' said Zechariah, or perhaps one of his disciples, disillusioned by the Second Temple and the people who had restored it, 'there shall be a fountain opened for the house of David and the inhabitants of Jerusalem to cleanse them from sin and unrighteousness' (Zech. 13.1). 'On that day, living waters shall flow out from Jerusalem, half of them to the eastern sea and half of them to the western sea . . . And the Lord shall become King over all the earth' (14.8–9). The King and the waters would return together.

There is reason to believe that this was controversial, possibly because it became important for Christians. Texts dealing with these ideas were excluded from the Hebrew canon, when it was defined at the end of the first century CE, that is, some 700 years after the destruction of Solomon's Temple. The story of the destruction of the last Temple in 70 CE was told as though it was the story of the first destruction, history repeating itself, and so the restoration of the Scriptures after the disaster was attributed to an 'Ezra', because Ezra had been the hero of the original restoration in the fifth century BCE. The process by which the Scriptures were defined/restored after the destruction of 70 CE is encoded in the story of 'Ezra', who was taken into a trance and told to dictate 94 books, but to make public only 24. In other words, there were 70 books that only the wise were permitted to read: 'For in them is the spring of understanding, the fountain of wisdom and the river of knowledge' (2 Esd. 14.47). Although set in the time immediately after the destruction of the First Temple in 597 BCE, this text actually describes the process of collecting and defining the Hebrew canon after the destruction of the Second Temple. The excluded books gave access to the spring of understanding, the fountain of Wisdom and the river of knowledge. We do not know which these texts were – but clearly some had considered them Scripture, and doubtless continued to do so. They, and the ideas they preserved, must have survived somewhere during the period of the Second Temple. Their existence probably accounts for Jesus' words in the Temple when he had invited people to come to him and drink: 'As the Scripture says "Out of his heart shall flow rivers of living water"' (Jn 7.38). These words are not quoted from the Scriptures we use today, but presumably were in one of the 70 books.[14]

Water and the great tree appear together in the book of Revelation, by the heavenly throne in the holy of holies. They appear together also in the Wisdom of Ben Sira, a Hebrew text composed in Jerusalem about 200 BCE, where they are the symbols of Wisdom. Chapter 24 in its present form is a poem in praise of the law of Moses, but when the rather obvious additions have been removed (e.g. 24.23), the original subject is revealed. This is a poem about Wisdom, a female figure who addresses the angels in heaven, and was enthroned in a pillar of cloud. She had been allocated to Israel – elsewhere this was said to be the role of the Lord (Deut. 32.9) – and she served in the holy tabernacle in Zion (Wisdom belonged in the holy of holies, and the woman clothed with the sun appeared there). She was, in other words, the high priest and guardian of Israel. As a great tree she took root in her people, and she invited them to eat and drink from her. Her teaching flowed forth like water: 'like a canal from a river, like a water channel into a garden . . . I will again pour out teaching like prophecy . . . ' (Sir. 24.30, 33). This was the water that flowed from the holy of holies in St John's vision. Wisdom is not mentioned by name in the vision, but the Bride invites any who are thirsty to drink the water of life (Rev. 22.17).

We know the mother of Jesus as Mary, but her name would have been Miriam, and it is interesting to look at the traditions associated with the other great Lady of that name: Miriam the older sister of Moses and Aaron. Later legend and tradition remembered her as a far more significant figure than just the sister who had watched over the infant Moses and then challenged his authority (Numbers 12), an impertinence for which she was punished with leprosy. Miriam was a woman of the high-priestly house; her brother Aaron was the first high priest. Her younger brother Moses became the law-giver. Miriam herself was remembered as the deliverer in Israel (*Exodus Rabbah* XXVI.1). Aaron became the high priest, Moses the king, and Miriam 'took' Wisdom. She was the grandmother of Bezalel, the man filled with wisdom who built the tabernacle (Exod. 35.30-31), and the ancestress of King David (*Exodus Rabbah* XLVIII.4).[15] Miriam was Wisdom, the older sister of the high priesthood, who has somehow disappeared from biblical story. She was also associated with water. The well in the wilderness was given because of the merit of Miriam, and when she died there was no water for the people (Num. 20.1-2).

What is this story actually telling us? What is encoded in these texts? The memory that during the formative period of Israel's religion, during the Second Temple when the Old Testament as we know it was compiled and, in many cases, actually written, there had been a power struggle between the priesthood, the law and Wisdom. Wisdom, Miriam, had been superseded.[16] This is echoed in other texts: just before the Temple was destroyed in 597 BCE, an enigmatic text in *1 Enoch* says that the priests lost their vision and forsook Wisdom (*1 Enoch* 93.8). Jeremiah was confronted by refugees in Egypt who told him, in no uncertain terms, that Jerusalem had been destroyed because they had abandoned the worship of the queen of heaven, who had protected the city (Jer. 44.16-19). Both these texts refer in different ways to King Josiah's purge. The queen of heaven, Wisdom, had been abandoned, but the biblical text says that Josiah removed and destroyed the Asherah. Enoch saw this tree in his vision, perfumed and glorious, waiting to be replanted in the Temple. Ezekiel, who had been a priest in the First Temple and would have known of the purges that divided his father's generation, also described the departure of the Lady. Those strange visions of wheels within wheels, his attempts to describe the Glory of the Lord leaving the Temple, include not only 'the likeness of the appearance of a human' on the throne (Ezek. 1.26), but also the Spirit of Life, or perhaps 'the Spirit of the Living One', within the 'wheels' – in other words, a female being within the circles of light (10.17). She was leaving the Temple. As she left, the many wings of the Living One made a sound like many waters (1.24). This was the sound of El Shaddai, usually translated 'God Almighty', but most naturally translated 'the deity with breasts'.

The Temple she left was almost certainly not on the Temple Mount. All the imagery of water gushing in the Temple, and the fact that the kings were anointed by the sacred spring, suggests that the First Temple had been built on the eastern hill, the original Zion, over the one natural water source in Jerusalem: the Gihon spring, whose name means 'the gusher' (this spring was later known as the Spring of the Virgin or the Spring of the Lady Mary).[17] By the time Justinian built the New Church, the name Zion had been transferred to the western hill, and so the New Church was built in an exactly similar place, but on the other hill which had no natural spring. A cistern was therefore built under the sanctuary to provide water in the new temple, dedicated to Mary.

Why? Presumably because the original temple had been the house of Wisdom, whose earthly counterpart was Mary. The restored temple was the Church of the Holy Mother of God, the Ever Virgin Mary.

A Jewish Apocalypse written during the short lifetime of the New Church may tell us something about it. The *Book of Zerubbabel* deals with the restoration of the Temple, and reveals that power will be restored to the chosen people 570 years after the destruction of the Temple in 70 CE, i.e. in 640 CE, 26 years after the Persian invasion when the New Church was destroyed. 'Zerubbabel' learned from the archangel Michael about an imminent war against the son of Satan whose mother was a beautiful statue set up in a house of shame. He learned about the mother of the Messiah who would do battle with evil kings. She would hold Aaron's rod of almond that blossomed, and her name would be Hephzibah, the name Isaiah gives to the restored city, the daughter of Zion and the Lord's delight (Isa. 62.1-5). The Jewish Hephzibah was the exact counterpart of the Lady in the book of Revelation who was the mother of the Messiah, and scholars have recognized that her role in protecting the city was that of Mary in Constantinople.[18] The house of shame where the statue stood was probably describing the New Church. There were four altars there (some texts say seven), and people would come from all over the world to worship the statue, to burn incense and to pour libations. The reference to the worship of the queen of heaven in Jeremiah is clear (Jer. 44.19). And at that time, a fountain would come forth from the house of the Lord and water the valley of Shittim. This is a reference to the prophecy in Joel 3.18, but was it simply part of the Jewish hope of restoration? Or was it a reference to the waters in the new temple, the New Church?

It is clear that the imagery of Wisdom was attributed to Mary. These are a few lines from Fr Ephrem's translation of the Akathist Hymn. 'You that surpass the knowledge of the wise, you that pour light on the minds of believers . . . You enlighten the initiates of the trinity . . . You trampled on the error of deception . . . Vessel of the Wisdom of God . . . You show lovers of wisdom to be without wisdom . . . You enlighten many with knowledge . . . She guides all to divine knowledge.' Clearest of all is the association of Wisdom and water: 'You make the enlightenment with many lights to dawn, You make the river with many streams to flow.' The Canon of the Akathist is similar (also in Fr Ephrem's translation): 'Living and ungrudging source' (*zosa kai aphthonos pege*); 'never failing spring of the living water' (*tou zontos hudatos pege akenotos*).[19]

The life-bearing spring is an image with roots in the ancient Temple. Mary as the life-bearing spring is just one example of the many ways in which Mary was recognized and described as the earthly counterpart of the heavenly Wisdom.

BIBLIOGRAPHY

Barker, M. (2000), *The Revelation of Jesus Christ*. Edinburgh: T.&T. Clark.
—— (2003), *The Great High Priest*. London: T.&T. Clark.
—— (2006), 'The New Church', *Sourozh: A Journal of Orthodox Life and Thought*, 103.
—— (2007), *The Hidden Tradition of the Kingdom of God*. London: SPCK.
Ben Dov, M. (1982), *In the Shadow of the Temple. The Discovery of Ancient Jerusalem*. New York/London: Harper & Row.
Charlesworth, J. H. (1983), *Old Testament Pseudepigrapha*, Volume 1. London: Darton Longman & Todd.
Conybeare, F. (1910), 'Antiochus Strategos. Account of the sack of Jerusalem in AD 614', *English Historical Review* 25, 502–16.
Danby, H. (trans.) (1989, orig. 1933), *The Mishnah*. Oxford: Oxford University Press.
Dewing, H. B., and G. Downey (1914–1940), *Procopius: On Buildings (Loeb Classical Library)*. 7 volumes. Cambridge: Harvard University Press.
Freedman, H. (trans.) (1939), *The Midrash: Genesis*, Volume 1. London: Soncino Press.
Ginzberg, L. (1907), *Legends of the Jews*, Volume 1. Philadelphia: Jewish Publication Society of America.
Heine, R. E. (1989), *Fathers of the Church* 80. Washington: Catholic University of America.

Himmelfarb, M. (1990), 'Sefer Zerubbabel', in D. Stern and M. J. Mirsky, *Jewish Fantasies*. New Haven/London: Yale University Press, 67–90.

Lehrman, S. M. (trans.) (1939), *Exodus Rabbah*. London: Soncino Press.

Migne, J. P. (1857–1866), *Cursus Completus Patrologiae Graecae*. Paris: Éditions Garnier. Referred to in the notes as *PG*.

Slotki, J. J. (trans.) (1961, orig. 1939), *Midrash Rabbah*. 5 volumes. London: Soncino Press.

Smith, G. A. (1907), *Jerusalem*, Volume 1. London: Hodder and Stoughton.

Suter, D. W. (1981), 'Weighed in the Balance. The Similitudes of Enoch in Recent Discussion', *Religious Studies Review* 7, 217–21.

Vermes, G. (1997), *The Complete Dead Sea Scrolls* in English. London: Penguin.

NOTES

1. Conybeare 1910: 502–16.
2. Ben Dov 1982: 241.
3. I set out the evidence for this in Barker 2006.
4. Procopius, *Buildings* V.vi, in Dewing and Downey 1914–40.
5. For detail see my book, Barker 2000: 200–11. The version of the Bible used here is *The Common Bible*, London: Collins, 1973.
6. Origen, *Commentary on John* II.31, in *PG* 14, trans. Heine 1989.
7. The tabernacle/temple as a microcosm of the creation is widely known in Jewish and Christian texts. For Jewish material, see Ginzberg 1907. For an introduction to the Christian tradition, see my Barker 2000: 17–20, and in more detail, my book Barker 2003, chs 7 and 8.
8. For example, the emphatic statements in Genesis Rabbah 1.3 that the angels might have been created on the second day or the fifth, but not on the first. Text in Freedman 1939.
9. Translation in Charlesworth 1983.
10. Translation in Slotki 1961.
11. *Aboda Zara* 3, in Danby 1989.
12. See Suter 1981: 217–21.
13. The version used here is Vermes 1997.
14. There are many indications that the early Church knew 'lost' scriptures; see my book, Barker 2003, ch. 12.
15. Lehrman 1939.
16. For detail, see my book, Barker 2007: 57–61.
17. Smith 1907.
18. Suggested by Himmelfarb 1990: 69. This article includes an English translation of the *Book of Zerubbabel*. Hebrew text in *Revue des Études Juifs* 68 (1914), 144.
19. Fr Ephrem's translation can be found at www.anastasis.org.uk/akathist.htm.

9

CANDLEMAS: A FESTIVAL OF ROMAN ORIGIN

ALISTAIR MACGREGOR

This article first appeared in two consecutive issues of the Ushaw Library Bulletin and Liturgical Review *8 (April 1999) and 9 (August 1999), and was reproduced in* Maria: A Journal of Marian Studies *2.1, 26–45 (August 2001).*

THE LITURGICAL EVIDENCE

The feast of the Presentation of the Lord, formerly of the Purification of the Blessed Virgin Mary and popularly known as Candlemas, is first referred to at Rome in a decree of Sergius I, who was Pope from 687 to 701.

> He decreed that on the [feast] days of the Annunciation of the Lord, the Assumption and Nativity of Saint Mary, Mother of God and ever virgin, and on the day of St Simeon which the Greeks call Hypopante, a procession [literally 'a procession with a sung litany'] should go from St Hadrian's Church and that the people should meet at the basilica of Santa Maria Maggiore.[1]

A number of observations may at once be made. (1) Although the feast we now call Candlemas is referred to by non-Marian titles, St Simeon and the Encounter, the fact that it is listed with the three other Marian feasts leaves us in little doubt that this festival also was celebrated in honour of Mary. (2) Chronologically the festival is out of sequence within the year; it should come first. (3) All four festivals were to have the same format – in other words, they were to be standardized. After a gathering at the church of Sant' Adriano in the Roman Forum, a papal procession would make its way from that church to Santa Maria Maggiore, the church that was dedicated to Our Lady and completed about the year 440 during the reign of Pope Sixtus III. (4) By the end of the seventh century, all four Marian feasts had been established in Rome.

This papal procession at Candlemas, which is first attested in the decree just referred to, started in the early hours of the morning at the church of Sant' Adriano in the Forum and moved to Santa Maria Maggiore, where pontifical High Mass was then sung. This Mass was one of the 89 stational Masses at which the Pope presided during the year in the City of Rome.[2] By the seventh century, three of the stational Masses at which the Pope presided had come to be preceded by a procession from another church.[3]

On each of these three days, the Pope and his court would assemble at the first church, where the gathering for this non-eucharistic preliminary ceremony was known as the *collecta*. Here the Pope would utter what is known as the *oratio ad collectam*, or 'the prayer at the gathering', and then a procession would form and make its way to the church or basilica where the stational Mass was to be held. Now, there is considerable uncertainty as to the purpose and origin of the *collecta* and the procession that preceded each of those three stational Masses to which we have just referred. Geoffrey Willis, in his chapter on Roman stational liturgy, states that the addition of a *collecta* to a stational Mass gave the observance of the day a greater solemnity.[4] This claim may well be true of subsequent centuries, but it is difficult to see why these three days should have been honoured at this time above all the other festivals.

We know that the procession on Greater Rogation Day followed the same route on the same day as that taken during the pagan festival of Robigalia; and the ceremonies involving the two shorter processions between Sant' Anastasia and Santa Sabina (on Ash Wednesday) and between Santi Cosma e Damiano and San Caesaro (1 November) may well have their origins in former pre-Christian religious rites. Of the four Marian processions, supposedly ordered by Pope Sergius, the Church has never been in doubt – at least not until recent times – that the one held on 2 February had pagan antecedents.

There is evidence to suggest that the four Marian festivals had been established in Rome before the pontificate of Sergius I,[5] and we have noted that he was responsible for standardizing the ceremonial. Evidence for these four feasts after the time of Sergius can be found in the tenth-century *Pontificale Romano-Germanicum* (hereafter *PRG*).[6] In spite of the fact that it was compiled in northern Germany, but in common with other similar contemporary or earlier documents, the *Ordines Romani*, this pontifical not only records the liturgy of papal Rome, but attests the papal liturgical practices of that city for several centuries prior to its being compiled, a feature of Roman liturgical books that could still be observed as late as the 1960s, when the Roman Missal continued to record the location of the stational Masses that ceased to be celebrated as stational Masses in the fourteenth century. In this tenth-century pontifical there are detailed accounts of two Marian feasts, the Purification and the Assumption. The latter does not concern us immediately. However, the earliest description of what actually happened at the Feast of the Purification of the Blessed Virgin Mary is to be found in the late eighth-century *Ordo Romanus* 20 which, like the tenth-century *PRG*, records the papal liturgy of Rome of a previous age.

1. On that day, just as dawn is breaking all the people proceed from every deaconry or from every titled parish chanting the litany or singing antiphons, and they all in their respective groups carry lighted wax candles in their hands, and enter the church of Sant' Adriano the Martyr, and wait for the Pope.
2. In the meantime the Pope enters the sacristy and puts on black vestments, and the deacons likewise put on black chasubles.
3. Then all [the people] enter in front of the Pope and receive from him a wax candle each.

4. When this is done, the choir begins the antiphon *Exsurge, domine, adiuva nos.* And at the end of the verse, the Pope leaves the sacristy with the deacons to his right and to his left; and the Pope nods to the choir that they should sing the *Gloria* [*Patri*].

5. Then he [the Pope] goes up in front of the altar and bows in prayer until the choir begins the repeat of the antiphon. He rises from prayer, and greets the altar, as do the deacons on either side of him.

6. At the end of the antiphon, the choir does not say the *Kyrie eleison*; but the Pope, standing in front of the altar, says 'The Lord be with you' followed by 'Let us pray'. The deacon says 'Let us kneel'; and after a little while he says 'Rise'.[7] Then the Pope utters the prayer formula.

7. Meanwhile seven crosses are brought out and carried by the cross-bearers walking among the people . . . [8]

The first thing to note is that this ceremony begins just before dawn. The people gather in Sant' Adriano and wait for the arrival of the Pope. The Pope arrives and vests along with his deacons in the former *secretarium senatus* (afterwards the church of Santa Martina), which then functioned as the sacristy to Sant' Adriano. Then there is a distribution of candles (*Section 3*). In *Section 4*, the choir begins to sing the antiphon *Exsurge, domine*, and the Pope enters the church from the sacristy. In *Section 5*, the Pope goes to the altar for private prayer; after which (*Section 6*) he stands in front of the altar; and, after his invitation to prayer and the instructions of the deacon, he utters the *oratio ad collecta*, the prayer formula for the gathering. After this the procession is formed and heads for Santa Maria Maggiore for Mass.

Previous writers and scholars have cited these first six subsections and commented on some of the more prominent features of this description. It is a little surprising, however, that no one, as far as I am aware, has noticed the difficulty in the rubrics and that the passage, as it stands, is disjointed. It is usually cited as early evidence, if not the earliest documentary evidence, for the distribution (as opposed to the blessing) of candles at Candlemas; but as far as I am aware, no one has ever asked the question: If all the members of the congregation have entered Sant' Adriano ahead of the Pope, already carrying candles (*Section 1*), why should they then have to enter the church once more, presumably having gone outside again, to receive what would appear to be a second candle (*Section 3*)? D. R. Dendy, apparently unaware of the difficulty, states that all the members of the congregation went into the vestry, and the distribution of candles took place there.[9] A more plausible way to resolve this difficulty with the text as it stands is to assume that the word 'all' (*omnes*) in *Section 3* refers to the deacons, who would already be in the sacristy possibly without candles, and that the Pope hands a candle to each of them after entering the church. This is perhaps not an unreasonable conclusion. However, it ought to be pointed out that the slightly later *Ordo Romanus* 15 elaborates the word 'all' by listing the clergy and the religious of Rome, men, women, infants, old people and many visitors.[10]

Perhaps the simplest way to account for this inconsistency is to realize that the document records two different stages in the development of the ceremonial that surrounds this festival. *Sections 3* and *5* are, in my view, later additions to the text. We have just observed that *Section 3* refers to what appears to be a second entry into church on the part of the congregation after the distribution of a possible second candle. If we now remove this section from the text, we find that *Section 4* follows on smoothly from *Section 2* so that *his expletis* ('When this is done') will now refer to the vesting, and the exit from the sacristy now balances the entry into that room. *Section 3*, therefore, would appear to be an addition inserted into the rubrics to update a development in the ceremonial; and it relates to a change in ceremonial whereby the people, instead of entering the church of Sant' Adriano already holding their own lighted candles, now enter the church empty-handed and later receive their candles from the Pope himself, a feature of the ceremony mentioned in *Ordo Romanus* 15 and by Bede in his *De Temporum Ratione*, written *c.* 725.[11] What appears to have happened is this: whereas the people formerly took their own candles already lit, candles supplied by the church are now distributed by the Pope to members of the congregation (and we know from [admittedly] much later evidence that the cost of the wax for the candles was borne by St Peter's).[12] The copyist of *Ordo Romanus* 20 has recorded this development; but either he has failed to notice the inconsistency with *Section 1*, or he has deliberately left the wording of *Section 1* as it stands. If the latter, we may have an instance of one of Paul Bradshaw's liturgical principles – in fact Principle 8.[13] This states that sometimes a rubric or liturgical direction is retained in the text of a service book even though it no longer applies to the ceremony to which it relates; but that it continues to be copied out of respect for tradition and the inherited text. We have already made mention of the continued recording of the medieval stational church in twentieth-century Tridentine missals.

When we come to examine *Section 5*, we find that this section also may be removed, not because it records an awkward addition to the text, but because it appears to be an expansion or elaboration of the information contained in *Section 4*. In fact, *Section 5* may be inserted without affecting the sense of *Section 4*. Therefore, *Sections 1–6* as they stand would appear to be an updated version of an older set of directions.

THE PAGAN PRECEDENT

We can now tentatively reconstruct the growth and development of the ceremonial that took place on the Feast of the Purification. It is my belief that a feast of our Lord, known as 'St Simeon' or 'The Encounter', was introduced into Rome in the sixth or seventh century, and a stational Mass was celebrated on 2 February, the fortieth day after Christmas, in Santa Maria Maggiore. This church was the scene of other important stational Masses in the Roman liturgical year, for instance, the first Sunday of Advent, two of the Masses of Christmas Day, and Easter Day. Also on 2 February, a candlelit procession in honour of the Virgin Mary took place in the early hours of the morning. Previously part of a pagan ritual, it was at that time unconnected with St Simeon's Day and existed as a Marian event in its own right.[14] When the procession became Christianized is unknown. After *c.* 630, when the old Roman senate house, the *Curia*, was converted into a church to receive the relics of the Bithynian martyr St Hadrian, whose feast day was 8 September, that church became a focus for the worship of the Virgin Mary whose nativity was celebrated on the same day. It is possible that a *collecta* was instituted at Sant' Adriano to celebrate this Marian festival and followed by a procession to Santa Maria Maggiore. Bernard Botte has shown that the institution of the four Marian feasts took place during the course of the seventh century. He argues convincingly that prior to this institution the Assumption (*natale*) of Mary had been celebrated in Rome on 1 January.[15]

Then between 630 and the pontificate of Pope Sergius, it was decided that the pre-dawn procession held in February in honour of Our Lady should also begin at Sant' Adriano; and, almost certainly during this period, the nocturnal procession on 15 August, which was a feature of the Feast of the Assumption, became diverted to take in Sant' Adriano before it reached the great basilica of Santa Maria Maggiore.[16] For a time the participants in the procession continued to provide and carry their own candles; but subsequently – possibly during the pontificate of Sergius, possibly later – the Church came to provide the candles, which were handed to each member of the congregation by the Pope himself outside Sant' Adriano, prior to the start of the *collecta* inside the building. The later testimony of *PRG*, already referred to, reveals a highly developed ceremony in which the candles were blessed by a number of prayer formulas, aspersed with holy water and honoured with incense, and then carried along with the banners and relics through the dark streets of Rome to Santa Maria Maggiore. The blessing in addition to the distribution of the candles shows that by the tenth century the Church had taken complete control of the entire ceremony.

Now what of the origin of this candlelit procession on the second day of February? Apart from the views of a few modern scholars, the Church has never doubted that this feature of the festival was inherited from its pre-Christian forebears. In comparatively modern times, Caesar Baronius was the originator of the theory that Candlemas was the Christianization of the *Lupercalia*, the pagan Roman festival held in honour of the god Pan; and even today this theory is trotted out from time to time. It is based on a combination of two basic facts: (1) Candlemas is of pagan origin, and (2) the *Lupercalia* took place in February (actually on the 15th). However, it is Bede who is the earliest writer to record the pre-Christian origins of the procession, and subsequent medieval accounts seem to be based, by and large, on his account.

He [Numa] dedicated the second [month] to Februus, that is, Pluto who was regarded as the lord of lustrations, and it was necessary to purify the city in that month in which he decreed that obligations should be paid to the shades of the dead. Christianity turned to its advantage this custom of lustration, when in the same month on the day of St Mary the whole people, together with the priests and ministers, singing melodious hymns processed from church to church and through the congenial places of the city. And they all carried in their hands lighted candles which the Pope had given to them. With the increase in popularity of this custom, he taught them to perform this activity as well on the rest of the festivals of the same blessed mother and perpetual virgin – not as part of the quinquennial purification of an earthly dominion, but as an annual (and perpetual) reminder of the heavenly kingdom.[17]

Bede clearly links the Christian festival with the quinquennial lustration, or act of purification, held on the *Campus Martius*, the Field of Mars in the north-west of Rome; but he wrongly mentions Pluto instead of Mars. Durandus of Mende, writing at the end of the thirteenth century, identifies Februa, not Februus, as the mother of Mars, as though to correct Bede.[18]

Pope Innocent III, however, writing a century earlier, records an alternative tradition which sees the origin of the candlelit procession in a ceremony commemorating the search of the goddess Ceres for her lost daughter Proserpina (*Sermo XII: In Purificatione*):

> Why is it that we carry lighted candles at this festival? . . . For the pagans dedicated the month of February to the Underworld because they erroneously believed that Proserpina had been snatched away by Pluto at the beginning of that month. Because they believed that her mother Ceres searched for her all night throughout Sicily with torches lit on Etna, at the beginning of the month they traversed the city [of Rome] during the night in commemoration of this event. For this reason that festival was called Amburbale 'going around the city'. Now since the holy fathers were unable to eradicate this custom completely, they decided that they should carry their lighted candles in honour of the Virgin Mary; so that what was formerly done in honour of Ceres and Proserpina is now done in praise of the Virgin Mary. For this reason we also carry lighted candles at the Purification of the Virgin, so that purified through grace, we may be worthy of attending the wedding banquet with burning lamps like the wise virgins.[19]

Although he does not actually describe the festival as an annual event, he does refer to a circumambulation of the city of Rome, a fact also mentioned by Bede, but not in so many words. What are we, therefore, to make of this evidence?

First we can identify some of the features from these accounts about which we can be reasonably confident. The procession took place in February. It involved the carrying of candles. The participants moved about the city. This much is self-evident, and already known from our examination of *Ordo Romanus* 20. If we now return to that document and compare the description it contains with the accounts of Bede and Innocent, we can see that the *Ordo* contains both additional and corroborating details:

1. The procession takes place at night [*Section 1*]. This could be inferred from the accounts of Bede and Innocent, though Bede does not actually mention this fact.
2. The procession moves between and therefore visits two churches, i.e. Sant' Adriano and Santa Maria Maggiore. It would appear very likely that the participants processed from their *parish* churches – acting as

feeder churches – since they arrive at Sant' Adriano already singing [*Section 1*]. This bears out Bede's statement that they moved from church to church.

3. Again, the mention of singing corroborates Bede's reference to 'melodious songs'.

4. The listing of all the priests, monks, city population, and a large number of visitors to Rome in the slightly later *Ordo Romanus* 15 confirms Bede's mention of 'the whole people, together with the priests and ministers'.[20]

So far so good as regards the evidence of Bede, but with the proviso that Bede implies that the Christian festival was an adaptation of an existing pagan one. It is interesting to note that Bede also uses the phrase 'the day of St Mary', whereas according to Sergius's decree it is 'St Simeon's Day'. But what about Pope Innocent, who attributes the origin of Candlemas not to a purificatory lustration, but to a pagan commemoration of the Ceres and Proserpina myth? In support of this theory I can offer the following evidence.

Firstly, the evidence of classical literature. We know from classical writers that Ceres's fruitless search for her daughter Proserpina was followed by a period of withdrawal which was caused by her anger and deep mourning. The search was re-enacted at Rome with a nocturnal procession through the city, involving torches, singing and the participation of women.[21]

Secondly, the evidence of language. According to the poet Ovid, and indeed Innocent himself, Ceres searched for Proserpina with the aid of torches.[22] These are a satisfactory means of illumination for a nocturnal procession, and Ovid mentions the fact that torches were distributed to the participants in the rites of Ceres.[23] Yet it is difficult to see why torches were replaced by wax candles in view of the fact that candles are eminently unsuitable for an out-of-doors procession through the streets of Rome in the middle of winter. However, it is not difficult to see why this substitution should have taken place in view of the similarity between the Latin word for wax candle, *cereus*, and the Latin name of the goddess *Ceres*. And it is worth bearing in mind that the nocturnal procession on the Feast of the Assumption in August was illuminated by street lamps attached to the walls of the houses, rather than by hand-held candles.[24] A perhaps more questionable instance of linguistic evidence is to be found in the Proper Preface of the Eucharistic Prayer in the eighth-century Gelasian sacramentaries, and concerns the verb *rapere*, 'snatch, abduct'.

Because through the mystery of the Word Incarnate the light of your brightness has shone before the eyes of our minds, so that, while we recognise God visibly, *we may be swept away* through him *by love* of things invisible.[25]

This verb is always used with the notion of speed and often violent motion, and it is found only on extremely rare occasions within a liturgical context. In this Preface it is used in conjunction with the noun *amor*, 'love'. Given that according to mythology Proserpina was forcibly abducted by Pluto, who was consumed with passion for her, it is not beyond the wildest stretch of the imagination to see in the Latin phrase *amore rapiamur*, 'we may be swept away by love', an echo of a long-lost formula or the subconscious inclusion of a phrase which alludes to the pagan origin of the ceremony.

Thirdly, there is the evidence of topography. A further possible link between the Christian procession of Candlemas and the ceremony held in honour of Ceres and Proserpina relates to the content of that pagan ceremony. The mythographers inform us that Pluto emerged from the underworld to abduct Proserpina, and that Ceres, her mother, then started to look for her daughter during the night. The site of the original abduction was thought to be in Sicily; but with the spread of the cult of Ceres from that island the site was transposed in a number of different versions of the myth to other locations, including Rome. It is significant that within less than 100 yards of the church of Sant' Adriano is a depression in the centre of the Roman Forum, known in classical times as the *Lacus Curtius*, which was believed to be one of the entrances to the underworld.[26] It is just possible, therefore, that this procession in honour of Our Lady formerly started from this point.

Lastly, there is the evidence of the ceremony itself as recorded in the surviving descriptions; and here we are on somewhat firmer ground. Two facts require comment. The first is that the Christian ceremony of the *collecta* and procession took place in the dark – in fact as dawn was breaking. In view of the evidence of pagan Roman writers, there is no reason to doubt that the commemoration of the goddess Ceres's search for Proserpina also took place at night.[27] The second item of evidence concerns the adjective 'black' in *Section 2* of the rubrics of *Ordo Romanus* 20.

Now black vestments are also mentioned in the description of Candlemas in the tenth-century *PRG*; but we have no further evidence for liturgical colours at this festival until the thirteenth-century Pontifical of Durandus. This document appears to record the use of either black or violet;[28] but the fourteenth-century *Ordo Romanus* 14 mentions only violet, and the fact that vestments of this colour are worn for the distribution of the candles and the procession, and are changed to white for the celebration of Mass in Santa Maria Maggiore.[29] This twofold use of colour survived in the Roman rite until 1970, when the reformers of the 1960s, opting for liturgical 'slickness', directed that white should be used throughout the whole ceremony.

The use of black, and later violet, vestments, together with the act of contrition at the *collecta* and the fact that in subsequent centuries the Pope walked barefoot to Santa Maria Maggiore – these are seen as unequivocal indications that the first part of Candlemas had a penitential mood and direction; and this has often per- plexed commentators.[30] For apart from the prediction of suffering in Simeon's second prophecy in the Gospel for the day, the themes of this festival – purifica- tion, encounter and presentation – do not suggest penitence; and Candlemas never falls in Lent, 4 February being the earliest date Ash Wednesday can occur. And yet, from the earliest surviving account of Candlemas in *Ordo Romanus* 20, it is clear that the festival has a penitential aspect. Fortunately, the tenth-century pontifical *PRG* provides a clue which may explain how the festival came to acquire this mood of penitence. After the words 'the deacon says "Let us kneel"', this pontifical adds the proviso 'if it occurs after Sexagesima'.[31] Now there can be little doubt that the pontifical, which is describing the same ceremony as that found in *Ordo Romanus* 20, is actually recording an older tradition with the inclusion of these words 'if it occurs after Sexagesima'. And the clear inference is that if this ceremony on 2 February, with its gathering in the dark, its *collecta* in Sant' Adriano and its procession to Santa Maria Maggiore, is held before Sexagesima Sunday, the words indicating contrition – 'Let us kneel' – are not used; and that the ceremony does not have a penitential aspect or mood. In order to understand the significance of the mention of Sexagesima, it is necessary to comment on the period that preceded Lent in Rome in the seventh century.

In Rome during the sixth century there was a movement to extend the penitential season of Lent by incorporating the three Sundays that precede Ash Wednesday. This pre-Lent period was achieved over a period of time. By *c.* 520, Quinquagesima Sunday and the two days following had been included in this extended Lent. By *c.* 560 it had been extended to include Sexagesima Sunday; and by 590, the year that Gregory the Great became Pope, it had taken in Septuagesima Sunday also.[32] (This 17-day period of penitence and preparation for Lent survived within the Roman Church until Vatican II).

Now, I have suggested that at one point in the development of the Roman liturgy, the *collecta* on 2 February was not regarded as having a penitential mood if it fell before Sexagesima, which was at one stage, as we have observed, the start of pre-Lent. It is therefore not unreasonable to believe that before the time when pre-Lent began to emerge *c.* 520, a penitential mood was not a characteristic of this feast day since Ash Wednesday always falls after 2 February. Similarly, it is not difficult to see why Candlemas came to be permanently regarded as having a penitential mood when pre-Lent was put back to include Septuagesima, since nearly half the number of times Candlemas occurs fall after Septuagesima – and, of course, this festival was already characterized by the wearing of sombre vestments. What is significant about the rubric relating to the fall of Candlemas after Sexagesima is that it suggests that the candlelit gathering and procession were incorporated into the liturgy of the day at some point after the incorporation of Sexagesima into pre-Lent, but before the inclusion of Septuagesima – in other words, sometime between *c.* 560 and 590. If we then accept that when the candlelit procession was incorporated into the liturgy of St Simeon's Day on 2 February it already possessed a Marian orientation, and if we accept that the incorporation took place in the sixth century, this would make Candlemas the oldest Marian feast in Rome.[33]

If we then accept that the primitive Candlemas acquired its penitential mood largely as a result of its close proximity to or its occurrence in the preparatory season of pre-Lent, what is the origin of the candlelit procession and the seemingly incongruous black vestments? Modern commentators have either ignored or overlooked the change in the Middle Ages from black to violet in the colour of the liturgical vestments, and have understandably regarded without distinction both colours as an indication of the penitential aspect of Candlemas.[34] They have also overlooked, or in some cases dismissed as fanciful, the possibility that the candlelit procession through the streets of Rome might be the Christianized descendant of the ceremony commemorating the search of the goddess Ceres for her daughter Proserpina. Now it will be recalled that, because of her failure to find her daughter, Ceres in her anger and distress withdrew into a form of mourning with the result that the earth's vegetation withered and died – a state recalling the very depth of winter and suggested by the month of February. It is my belief that the use of black vestments is derived from a pagan Roman ceremony in which the mourning of Ceres, the sense of loss at the supposed death of Proserpina and the association with the underworld were all conveyed and symbolized by the wearing of garments of this colour.[35]

To sum up: (1) In the sixth century the Roman Church celebrated two separate liturgical solemnities on 2 February. The first was a pre-dawn candlelit procession in honour of the Virgin Mary. It was the Christianization of a pagan religious ceremony involving the Roman goddess Ceres, which retained a number of features that had characterized the pagan ceremony, such as the time of year and the time of day, the use of candles and the colour black, the visitation of a number of different locations, the singing, the presence of women, and above all the commemoration of a female deity.[36] The other solemnity was a feast day commemorating the presentation of Jesus in the Temple, known as St Simeon's Day, or The Encounter, and held on the fortieth day after Christmas.

(2) Sometime during the second half of the sixth century, the two liturgical occasions were joined together. Unlike Greater Rogation Day (the former pagan *Robigalia*) and the Feast of St Mark, which were both celebrated on 25 April but which, having little in common, were never welded into a single celebration, the fusion of the two solemnities on 2 February was facilitated by the prominence of the Virgin Mary in the Gospel for St Simeon's Day. However, the two aspects of the liturgy, the purification and the presentation, were never successfully united and remained in tension with each other, until they were again separated in 1969. This was partly because the Marian-orientated procession did not have its origins in the concept of purification, but mainly because the ceremony became dominated by the use of hand-held candles, which in later centuries were believed to possess protective properties. We must also remember that, even though two of the stational Masses of Christmas Day were celebrated in Santa Maria Maggiore, that festival never became a Marian feast; and it is very likely that the Presentation would never have become a Marian feast had there not been a Marian liturgical observation on the same day.

(3) The intrusion of the theme of purification into the Marian-orientated candlelit procession resulted in wild and erroneous theories as to its origin. Ancient Rome had a number of public rituals involving cleansing and purification, called 'lustrations'. It is not difficult to see how the communal cleansing of land and buildings became confused with the personal ritual purification of the human body; and how the blurring of that distinction between public and personal cleansing, assisted by the equating of the two Latin nouns *lustratio* (with its dual notion of cleansing and procession) and *purificatio*, in turn reinforced the concept of purification in the liturgy of Candlemas.

(4) The feast of Candlemas acquired its penitential mood mainly because of its proximity to the season of Lent, but partly, as I have tried to show, because of the use of sombre vestments, inherited from a pre-Christian ritual that re-enacted the myth of Ceres, Proserpina and Pluto.

APPENDIX: THE ROUTE OF THE PROCESSION

In the foregoing article I mentioned briefly the two references in the documentary sources to the route which the Candlemas procession took through the streets of Rome:[37] (1) in Bede's eighth-century account of the origin of the festival, and (2) in the description of the ceremonial as contained in the twelfth-century *Ordo Romanus* 11. Two considerations should be constantly borne in mind when evaluating the evidence of both these sources. Firstly, at least 400 years separates the two accounts. Secondly, during this period the topography of the city of Rome underwent some change through the collapse and destruction of buildings which caused the inevitable rise in the level of the city and the disappearance of certain streets.

Ordo Romanus 20

This late eighth-century document gives no indication as to the itinerary or the places visited.[38] It does, however, record that the procession started from the church of Sant' Adriano, the former Roman senate house (*Curia*), and that the sacristy to this church was the *secretarium senatus*, an annex to the Curia which had previously functioned as an office and committee room. It was subsequently upgraded into a church to receive the relics of St Martina, still attached to the senate house, but was replaced in 1640 by the detached baroque church dedicated to SS Luca e Martina.

The Evidence of Bede

Referring to the route, Bede states:

All the people, together with the priests and ministers, singing modulated hymns, *move from church to church and through the suitable places of the city . . .*[39]

The evidence is disappointingly meagre. We can tentatively guess that more than two churches were visited during the procession, and leave it at that. The other phrase, *per congrua urbis loca* ('through the suitable places of the city'), tells us little more. I was wrong previously to have translated *congrua* as 'congenial'. Either 'suitable' or 'appropriate' seem better renderings. The former could refer to the practicalities involved in organizing the procession and imply that narrow or badly maintained streets were avoided. Alternatively, 'appropriate' or 'fitting' might suggest that certain locations of dubious reputation, which were considered in need of some kind of sanctification, were deliberately included for a visit along the route. However, whatever churches and sites were visited, it is probably safe to conclude that the route remained the same from year to year, in the same way that starting and finishing points were fixed and the content of the liturgy for the festival was unchanging.

147

The Evidence of Ordo Romanus 11

The twelfth-century *Ordo Romanus* 11 is the earliest document to record the itinerary of the Candlemas procession.

> The Pope . . . proceeds unshod in front of the Arch of Nerva, and enters Trajan's Forum. Leaving by way of the Arch of Aurea and entering the vaulted colonnade, he proceeds directly past the House of Eudoxia; and crossing the House of Orpheus by way of the stone, he makes his way past the titular church of Santa Prassede to the basilica of Santa Maria Maggiore.[40]

The *collecta* having finished at the church of Sant' Adriano, the procession set out in a northerly direction along an ancient road, which formerly led to the Asylum (with the Capitoline Hill on its left), towards Trajan's Forum. The 'Arch of Nerva' must be a mistake for the Arch of Septimius Severus: an arch commemorating the former emperor is unknown, while the structure built in honour of Severus stands only a few yards from the entrance to Sant' Adriano.

After a distance of about a quarter of a mile the procession entered Trajan's Forum, one of the wonders of the ancient Roman world, described by the historian Ammianus Marcellinus as a 'construction unique under the heavens . . . and never again to be imitated by mortal men'.[41]

It then crossed and left that forum through the *arcum Aureae*. Assuming that the second word in the Latin phrase is genitive singular, then the nominative is otherwise unknown. One possibility is that the word is a corruption of Aurelii and that the Arch of Marcus Aurelius stood at some distance to the north along the via del Corso not far from the church of San Lorenzo in Lucina.[42] If *Aureae* is not a corruption, it is much more likely that the phrase is a nickname for the main entrance to Trajan's Forum – a magnificent arch on its eastern side – which provided access into the Forum of Augustus. This 'marketplace' in turn stood next to the smaller area called Nerva's Forum, or the *forum transitorium*.[43] It is to this last-mentioned forum that the phrase *portico absidata*, 'vaulted colonnade', refers. Portions of this colonnade remain.

A superficial reading of the Latin text would suggest that the procession moved straightaway to the titular church of Eudoxia, later to be renamed San Pietro in Vincoli; but the preposition *iuxta*, 'near to', and the mention of the two locations immediately after the reference to this church tell us that the procession did not visit this church, but made a considerable detour back into the Roman Forum whence it had started.

The first element in the phrase 'crossing the House of Orpheus by way of the stone' presents difficulties; but 'by way of the stone' can be explained satisfactorily if the *silex*, 'stone', mentioned here is to be identified with the *silex* described in a later section of the same *Ordo Romanus* 11. For we learn that the *silex* was situated 'where Simon Magus fell'.[44] Now according to tradition (and to one version of it), Simon of Acts 8.9-24 met St Peter on the via Sacra in Rome and challenged the apostle to a competition of levitation. Simon succeeded in flying for a time, but as a result of St Peter's prayers he crashed to the ground after only a short flight. The impression of the apostle's knees was left in the stone on which he had knelt, and this stone was subsequently removed to the nearby church of Santa Maria Antiqua and later transferred to the church of Santa Francesa Romana (formerly Santa Maria Nova), where it remains to this day.[45] If my identification of the *silex* is correct, then the procession would have visited the Roman Forum (again), possibly entering it near Constantine's Basilica or the church of SS Cosma e Damiano.[46]

The next named point of the itinerary is the House of Orpheus, which is otherwise unknown. After leaving the Roman Forum, the procession headed for the church of Santa Prassede first in a south-easterly direction towards the Colosseum, before turning north-east for Santa Prassede. Unless both the name and the true location of the 'House of Orpheus' have been lost to posterity, two possibilities exist that may explain this otherwise unknown building. (1) The procession would have passed close to or even on top of the ruins of Nero's Golden House, the *Domus Aurea*.[47] Since the remains of this palace were always subterranean at any stage in the history of the Candlemas procession, and since the name of Orpheus is associated with the subterranean regions of the underworld, the House of Orpheus may be none other than the Golden House.[48] (2) The Baths of Trajan were subsequently built partly on top of the remains of the Golden House in that part of Rome known as the *Mons Oppius*, the Oppian Hill. Is it just possible that in the course of time *Oppius* has been corrupted into *Orpheus*, helped by the suggestion given in (1)? From the House of Orpheus the procession made its way past Santa Prassede to the basilica of Santa Maria Maggiore where the stational Mass was to take place.

It remains now to consider whether the route of the papal procession outlined in the twelfth-century *Ordo Romanus* 11 was the same as that in the seventh century. As I pointed out at the beginning of this article, the topography of Rome had changed somewhat over the intervening centuries as a result of warfare and earthquakes. On the other hand, if the route in the seventh century followed an itinerary inherited from pagan Roman religion, there appears to be no reason why it should have changed in subsequent centuries; for it followed an unusual course, one which was unrelated to the liturgical practices of Rome in the High Middle Ages. Add to this the general tendency of liturgical ceremonial to be very conservative, certainly in bygone centuries. Two facts may be adduced in favour of the theory that the procession on 2 February was the successor to the pagan Roman practice of 'beating the bounds', viz. a circumambulation of the city walls of Rome. Firstly, we saw that the procession, after leaving Sant' Adriano, moved inexplicably north into Trajan's Forum. This area lay next to the old Servian Wall of Rome. Secondly, the procession ended at Santa Maria Maggiore after passing the church of Santa Prassede. Both these buildings stood in very close proximity to that same wall.

BIBLIOGRAPHY

Andrieu, M. (1940), *Le Pontifical Romain au Moyen-Age* III. Vatican: Bibliotheca Apostolica Vaticana.

—— (1951), *Les Ordines Romani du Haut Moyen Age* III. Louvain: Spicilegium Sacrum Lovaniense.

Beard, M., J. North and S. Price (eds) (1998), *Religions of Rome I: A History*. Cambridge: Cambridge University Press.

Botte, B. (1933), 'La première fête mariale de la liturgie romaine', *Ephemerides Liturgicae* 47, 425–30.

Boyle, A. J. and R. Woodward (eds) (2000), *Ovid: Fasti*. London: Penguin.

Bradshaw, P. (1992), *The Search for the Origins of Christian Worship*. London: SPCK.

Dendy, D. R. (1959), *The Use of Lights in Christian Worship* (*Alcuin Club Collection* 41). London: SPCK.

Deshusses, J. (1971), *Le Sacramentaire Grégorien*. Fribourg: Spicilegium Friburgense.

Duchesne, L. (ed.) (1886), *Le Liber Pontificalis*. Paris: Ernest Thorin.

Dumas, A. and J. Deshusses (eds) (1981), *Liber Sacramentorum Gellonensis* (*Corpus Christianorum: Series Latina* 159). Turnholt: Brepols.

Fortescue, A. (1918), *The Ceremonies of the Roman Rite Described*. London: Burns & Oates.

Foster, B. O. (trans.) (1924), *Livy: History of Rome – Volume 3* (*Loeb Classical Library* 172). Cambridge: Harvard University Press.

Hall, J. B. (ed.) (2004), *Claudian: De Raptu Proserpinae* (*Cambridge Classical Texts and Commentaries* 11). Cambridge: Cambridge University Press.

Hänggi, A. and A. Schönherr (eds) (1970), *Sacramentarium Rhenaugiense*. Freiburg: Universitätsverlag.

Heiming, O. (ed.) (1984), *Liber Sacramentorum Augustodunensis* (*Corpus Christianorum: Series Latina* 159B). Turnholt: Brepols.

Huelsen, C. (1906), *The Roman Forum*, trans. J. B. Carter. Rome: Loescher.

Lanciani, R. (1897), *The Ruins and Excavations of Ancient Rome*. London: Macmillan.

—— (1901), *New Tales of Old Rome*. Boston: Houghton & Mifflin.

Martimort, A. G. (ed.) (1986), *The Church at Prayer* IV, trans. M. J. O'Connell. London: Geoffrey Chapman.

Migne, J. P. (1844–1865), *Cursus Completus Patrologiae Latina*. Paris: J. P. Migne. Referred to in the notes as *PL*.

Platner, S. B. (1904), *The Topography and Monuments of Ancient Rome*. Boston: Allyn & Bacon.

Rolfe, J. C. (trans.) (1935–1939), *Ammianus Marcellinus: History Volume 1* (*Loeb Classical Library* 300). Cambridge: Harvard University Press.

Seyffert, O. (1899), *A Dictionary of Classical Antiquities*. London: Sonnenschein.

Stevenson, K. W. (1988), 'The Origins and Development of Candlemas', *Ephemerides Liturgica* 102, 316–46.

Vogel, C. and R. Elze (eds) (1963), *Le Pontifical Romano-Germanique du Dixième Siècle* II. Vatican: Bibliotheca Apostolica Vaticana.

Willis, G. G. (1994), *A History of Early Roman Liturgy* (*Henry Bradshaw Society, Subsidia* 1). London: Boydell Press.

NOTES

1. Constituit autem ut diebus Adnuntiationis Domini, Dormitionis et Nativitatis sanctae Dei genetricis semperque virginis Mariae, ac sancti Symeonis, quod Ypapanti Greci appellant, letania exeat a sancto Hadriano et ad sanctam Mariam populus occurrat (Duchesne 1886: 1.376).

2. The system of the stational Masses was one of the ways in which the Church of Rome

expressed its unity. Each year the Pope would say Mass in each of the four great Roman basilicas and in each of the 25 *tituli* churches (i.e. the greater parish churches of the City of Rome). The church in which each Mass was celebrated was known in Latin as a *statio*. For an account of the growth and development of the system of Roman stational Masses, see Willis 1994: 71.

3. On Ash Wednesday, Greater Rogation (25 April) and St Caesarius (1 November).

4. Willis 1994: 71.

5. Martimort 1986: 133–5.

6. Vogel and Elze 1963.

7. The act of kneeling just before prayer was an act that signified contrition and penitence.

8. From Andrieu 1951: 235–6:

   1 Ipsa autem die, aurora ascendente, procedunt omnes de universas diaconias sive de titulus cum letania vel antiphonas psallendo et cerea accensa portantes omnes in minibus per turmas suas et veniunt in ecclesia sancti Adriani martyris et expectant pontificem.

   2 Interim ingreditur pontifex sacrario et induit se vestimentis nigris et diaconi similiter planitas induunt nigras.

   3 Deinde intrant omnes ante pontificem et accipiunt ab eo singular cerea.

   4 His expletis, inchoat scola antiphonam *Exsurge, domine, adiuva nos*. Et dicto versu, egreditur pontifex de sacrario cum diaconibus dextra levaque et annuit pontifex scola ut dicatur *Gloria*.

   5 Deinde ascendens ante altare, inclinans se ad orationem usquedum inchoat scola versum ad repetendum, surgit ab oratione, salutat altare et diaconi hinc et inde.

   6 Ipsa antiphona expleta, non dicit scola *Kyrieleison*, sed pontifex stans ante altare dicit: *Dominus vobiscum*, deinde *Oremus*, et diaconus: *Flectamus genua*; et, facto intervallo, dicit iterum: *Levate*; et dat pontifex orationem.

   7 Interim egrediuntur cruces VII, portantur a stauroforo permixti cum populo . . .

9. Dendy 1959: 178.

10. Andrieu 1951: 113, 79.

11. *Ibid.*; *PL* 90.351D.

12. *Ordo Romanus* XII (Cardinal Cenci), in *PL* 78.1068B.

13. Bradshaw 1992: 75.

14. While the *oratio ad collectam* (in the Gregorian Sacramentary) may contain echoes of the Candlemas procession, the prayers of the Mass set for 2 February contain little to suggest that the feast is a Marian one (Deshusses 1971: 123–4). Even in Sergius's Decree, the link between St Mary and St Simeon is not overt.

15. Botte 1933: 425–30.

16. According to Vogel and Elze 1963: 2.138, the procession started at the basilica of St John Lateran, where in the chapel of St Laurence the *acheiropoieton* picture of Christ was kept, and ended at Santa Maria Maggiore. This involved a considerable detour from the original route, since the procession had to move through the Roman Forum in order to reach Sant' Adriano.

17. Secundum [mensem Numa] decavit Februo, id est, plutoni, qui lustrationum potens credebatur, lustrarique eo mense civitatem necesse erat, quo statuit ut iura diis manibus solverentur. Sed hanc lustrandi conseutudinem bene mutavit Christiana religio, cum in mense eodem die sanctae Mariae plebs universa, cum sacerdotibus ac ministris, hymnis modulatae vocis per ecclesias, perque congrua urbis loca, procedit, datosque a pontifice cuncti cereos in manibus gestant ardentes, et augescente bona consuetudine, id ipsum in ceteris quoque eiusdem beatae matris et perpetuae virginis festivitatibus agere didicit, non utique in lustrationem terrestis imperii quinquennem, sed in perennem regni coelestis memoriam (*De Temporum Ratione*, in *PL* 90.351C–D).

18. *Rationale Divinorum Officiorum* (Antwerp, 1614), fo. 526.
19. Quid est autem quod in hoc festo cereos portamus accensos . . . Gentiles enim Februarium mensem inferis dedicaverunt, eo quod sicut ipsi putabant, sed errabant, in principio ejus mensis Proserpina rapta fuerat a Plutone; quam quia mater ejus Ceres facibis accensis (in Aethna tota nocte per Siciliam quaesisse credebatur, ipsi ad commemorationem ipsius) in principio mensis urbem do nocte lustrabant. Unde festum illud appelabatur Amburbale. Cum autem sancti Patres consuetudinem istam non possunt penitus exstirpare, constituerunt, ut in honore beatae Virginis Mariae cereos portarent accensos et sic quod prius fiebat ad honorem Cereris, modo fit ad honorem Virginis; et quod prius fiebat ad honorem Proserpinae, modo fit ad laudem Mariae. Ob hoc quoque in Purificatione Virginis cereos accensos portamus, ut purificati per gratiam, cum accensis lampadibus quasi prudentes virgines ad nuptias ingredi mereamur (*PL* 217.510A–B).
20. The mention of large numbers of visitors (*copiosa multitude*) in Rome in February is interesting (*Ordo Romanus* 15.79).
21. Mary Beard *et al.* 1998: 70.
22. Ovid, *Fasti* 3.786, in Boyle and Woodward 2000; and Claudian, *De Raptu Proserpinae* 3.370–403, in Hall 2004.
23. Huic Cereris sacris nunc quoque taeda datur' (*Fasti* 4.494).
24. Vogel and Elze 1963: 2.138.'
25. Quia per incarnati verbi mysterium nova mentis nostrae oculis lux tuae claritatis infulsit, ut dum visibiliter deum cognoscimus per hunc invisibilium *amore rapiamur* (Dumas and Deshusses 1981:24; Heiming 1984: 26; Hänggi and Schönherr 1970: 94).
26. Huelsen 1906: 33. See also Livy's *History of Rome*, book 7, chapter 6, in Foster 1924.
27. Ovid, *Fasti* 3.786, in Boyle and Woodward 2000; and Claudian, *De Raptu Proserpinae* 3.370–403, in Hall 2004.
28. Andrieu 1940: 658–9.
29. *Ordo Romanus* XIV (Peter Amelius), in *PL* 78.1198C–D.
30. For the best modern discussion of the tensions and difficulties associated with this feast, see Stevenson 1988: 316–46.
31. Si tamen infra sexagesima evenerit (Vogel and Elze 1963: 2.6).
32. Willis 1994: 82.
33. If Bede is to be believed, this would be the earliest Marian feast to use Sant' Adriano as a starting point for the procession. However, in a future article, 'The Marian Feasts at Rome in the Seventh Century', I will argue that Bede may have been mistaken.
34. Durandus' Pontifical shows that the use of black and violet was not uniform throughout the Latin Church in the thirteenth century, but that both colours signified penitence (Andrieu 1940: 658–9). For modern writers, see e.g. Stevenson 1988: 339; Fortescue 1918: 257.
35. For the wearing of dark clothing at Roman funerals, see Seyffert 1899. For a reconstruction of the itinerary which the procession followed, see the Appendix above.
36. The time of year and the fact that it was held at daybreak militate against the view that the ceremonial was part of a purifactory rite.
37. The late eighth-century *Ordo Romanus* 20, while it mentions the churches of Sant' Adriano and Santa Maria Maggiore, gives no indication of the route which the procession took.
38. Andrieu 1951: 236.
39. Plebs universa, cum sacerdotibus ac ministris, hymnis modulatae vocis *per ecclesias, perque congrua urbis loca, procedit* . . . (*De Tempore Rationum*, in *PL* 90.351C, my emphasis).
40. Pontifex . . . procedens discalceatus ante arcum Nervae, intrat per forum Trajani; et exiens arcum Aureae in porticu absidata ascendit per directum (*Aliter* domum) juxta

Eudoxiam, et transiens per silicem domum Orphei, ascendit per titulum sanctae Praxedis usque ad sanctam Mariam Majorem (*PL* 78.1037A).

41. Ammianus Marcellinus, *History* 16.10.15, in Rolfe 1935–1939.
42. It was demolished in 1662.
43. So-called because it acted as a passageway to the Esquiline Hill.
44. *PL* 78.1046: ubi cedidit Simon Magus.
45. Lanciani 1897: 91; 1901: 89.
46. Blocks of volcanic lava (*silex*), quarried from the nearby Alban Hills, were used to pave the streets of Rome. See Platner 1904: 23; Ammianus Marcellinus, *History* 14.6.16, in Rolfe 1935–1939.
47. It may be significant that we have already encountered an *arcus Aureae*.
48. Those who visit this monument will be only too aware of the eeriness of the cavernous subterranean rooms of this quasi-netherworld.

10

Pope John VII's Devotion to Mary:
Papal Images of Mary from the Fifth to
the Early Eighth Centuries

Eileen Rubery

INTRODUCTION

It is almost impossible to imagine a cult without images. They are frequently an inseparable part of the process of worship and are usually one of the vehicles through which communication with the focus of the cult takes place. Images may also be seen to be the conduit for the divine response, which can lead to them gaining a reputation for being miraculous. Iconic images of Mary were rare in the third and fourth centuries. This lends support to the proposition that the cult of Mary had not then developed significantly. Mary was only portrayed then in imagery where her presence was necessary to *Christ*'s story. Most frequently this was in representations of the Adoration of the Magi (Figure 1). Her presence in such scenes cannot be taken to reflect any particular devotional focus on her.

Figure 1: Adoration of the Magi from a fourth-century sarcophagus in the Vatican Museums, Rome. From Bosio 1632: 95.

Iconic images of Mary began to appear in the fifth century, and included a group of images commissioned by or closely associated with the papacy that make an excellent group within which to trace the development of her imagery in Rome. Following his conversion to Christianity, Constantine made significant donations to the popes so that they could build and decorate new churches. From this time onwards, if the evidence of the *Liber Pontificalis*, or 'Book of the Popes', reflects in any way papal priorities, the popes saw building and decorating the major churches of Rome as one of their major responsibilities.[1]

This paper considers the images of Mary commissioned by the popes that have survived in Rome up to 707, when Pope John VII (705–707) died (Table 1). It explores the origins of these images and traces the development of the iconography of her cult in Rome. It opens with a consideration of the mosaic panel commissioned by Pope John VII in old St Peter's Basilica, in which the Pope styles himself 'Servant of the Mother of God' and so unequivocally demonstrates the existence, by the beginning of the eighth century, of the cult of Mary in Rome. The paper then moves back in time to pick up the development of Marian imagery from where Geri Parlby left it (in Chapter 3 above), in the catacombs. It traces the development of the image of Mary in Rome forward to John VII's mosaic image of Mary again. This image is then reassessed in the context of these

Table 1: Key Images of Mary in Rome up to 707[1]

Date of image and original site	Pope	Description of image(s)	Technical details of image
1. 432–440 Santa Maria Maggiore	Sixtus III (432–440)	Triumphal arch mosaics of the Life of Christ[2]	Mosaic on triumphal arch of main apse: Annunciation and Adoration of the Magi (Fig. 3).
2. ? before 600:[3] ? Santa Maria Antiqua	?	*Madonna di San Luca:* icon (fragments)[4]	Base is two fragments embedded in wooden frame in the medieval period. Encaustic paint applied directly to canvas.[5] (Figure 12) Head measures 53cm x 41cm.[6]
3. 550–600: Santa Maria Antiqua[7]	?	'Palimpsest' Madonna, enthroned with Christ-child and two angels	Palimpsest fresco on right side of the triumphal arch of the main apse. (Figure 6)
4. ?? before 584: Santa Maria Maggiore	?? Gregory I (590–604)[8]	Madonna and Child icon (now called *Salus Populi Romani*)[9]	? encaustic or tempera. Cypress-wood base 117cm x 79cm.[10] (Figure 9)
5. 609: Santa Maria ad Martyres (Pantheon)[11]	Boniface IV (608–615)	Frontal posed Mary, standing with gold hands, halo and frontal Christ-child	Poplar wood with encaustic painting. Present dimensions 1.00m x 0.475m. Estimated original size 2.0m x 0.85m.[12] (Figure 11)

Table 1: continued

Date of image and original site	Pope	Description of image(s)	Technical details of image
6. 640–642 San Venantius Chapel (Lateran Baptistery)[13]	John IV (640–642)	Orant Mary between saints under giant figure of Christ[14]	Main apse mosaic in chapel built for relics of saints (Figure 14).
7. 706: Oratory of John VII in St Peter's[15]	John VII (705–707)	Maria Regina; Orant Mary in centre of life of Christ above altar	Mosaic removed from St Peter's in 17th century. Orant Mary now in San Marco, Florence (Figure 2, central panel, and Figure 7)
8. 706: Oratory of John VII, in St Peter's[16]	John VII (705 –707)	Fragment of Adoration of the Magi from Life of Christ	Mosaic removed from St Peter's in 17th century. Fragment of Adoration of the Magi now in Santa Maria in Cosmedin, Rome. (Figure 2: top right-hand narrative panel)
9. 705–707 Santa Maria in Trastevere[17]	? John VII (705–707)	*Madonna della Clemenza*: Mary crowned with Christ-child, angels and papal patron	Poplar board 164cm x 116cm including the frame; 153cm x 105cm minus frame. Text on the frame:[18] IMAGO QUAE PER SE FACTA EST.[19] (Figure 13)
10. Santa Maria in Tempuli.[20]	?8th century	*Madonna Avvocata*	Encaustic on poplar wood 71.5cm x 42.5cm. Gold paint (8th century or earlier) on hands and on cross on shoulder.[21] (Figure 16: note additional gold hands and a gold cross have been added to this image.)

1 The images are listed in approximate chronological order, but note that the dates for some of these images are contested.
2 Cecchelli 1956.
3 Belting 1996: 127 suggests c. 550.
4 Krautheimer 1959: Vol. 2; Cellini 1950. This image is now in the sacristy at the church of Santa Francesca Romana.
5 Belting 1996: 124.
6 *Ibid.*: 72, 124.
7 Krautheimer 1959: 2.249–267; Gruneisen 1911.
8 Markus 1997: 98 (possibly obtained during his sojourn in Constantinople before he was Pope).
9 Wolf 1990.
10 Belting 1996: 69; Bertelli 1961b: 98 n. 22.
11 Bertelli 1961a.
12 *Ibid.*
13 Davis 2000: 68.
14 Oakeshott 1967: 150.
15 Nordhagen 1965.
16 *Ibid.*
17 Bertelli 1961b.
18 *Ibid.*: 16.
19 'An image that was made by itself.' That is, it was not made by human hands.
20 Belting 1996: 314–15; Koudelka 1961. Originally at Tempuli near the Caracalla baths. Moved in the thirteenth century to San Sisto and then in 1575 to SS Domenico e Sisto (an old copy is still to be found there). In 1931 it was moved to the convent of Santa Maria del Rosario in Monte Mario.
21 Belting 1996: 315

earlier images. In this way this paper seeks to demonstrate how, by the beginning of the eighth century, four main sources of Marian imagery (Tables 2a–d) had combined and given rise to four of the main types of Roman image of Mary that continued to be found in Rome from the eighth century onwards.

THE ORATORY OF POPÉ JOHN VII (FIGURE 2)

On 21 March 706 the first oratory dedicated to the Virgin Mary in old St Peter's Basilica was consecrated (Figure 2).[2] Over the altar, seven mosaic panels containing scenes from the 'Life of Christ' surrounded an arresting mosaic of an orant, crowned Mary to whom, on her left, an obsequious Pope John VII, with a square halo (indicating that he was still alive) presented a model of the oratory. Three mosaic inscriptions stated that John, unworthy bishop and servant of the Mother of God, had dedicated the oratory to her:

BEATÆ DEI GENITRICIS SERVVS (to the right of Mary);

+IOHANNES INDIGNVS EPISCOPVS FECIT (below Mary);

DOMVS *SCÆ* DEI GENITRICIS MARIAE (over the altar).[3]

When John died he was buried in front of the altar, and his epitaph said:

Here Pope John erected for himself a tomb, and ordered that he be laid under the feet of the Lady, placing his soul under the protection of the holy mother, the unwedded virgin and parent, who brought forth God.

Previous squalor removed, he brought together splendour from all parts, so that posterity might be amazed by the lavishness, not with eagerness for ostentation . . . but with pious fervour for the mother of God. Not sparing riches, he distributed whatever he had that was precious in your service holy mother . . .[4]

God is referred to in this section of the epitaph almost *en passant*; his presence is entirely contingent on Mary 'the unwedded virgin who brought forth God'. John places his soul 'under the protection of the holy mother'. In the mosaic Mary stands alone; there is no Christ-child. This mosaic and epitaph therefore provide clear evidence of the presence of a Marian cult in Rome, supported by the papacy, by the eighth century. This paper will explore the origins of this iconography, and will outline the paths whereby the 'typical' images of Mary in Rome from the eighth century onwards may have arisen. It will show that as Marian imagery developed, it borrowed elements of the imagery of Roman empresses, aristocratic women (including virgins, matrons and mothers), female saints and orants. These elements were combined into the iconography of Mary. By re-isolating them, it is possible to gain some idea of the characteristics that contemporary Christians felt were important in the emerging cult of Mary.

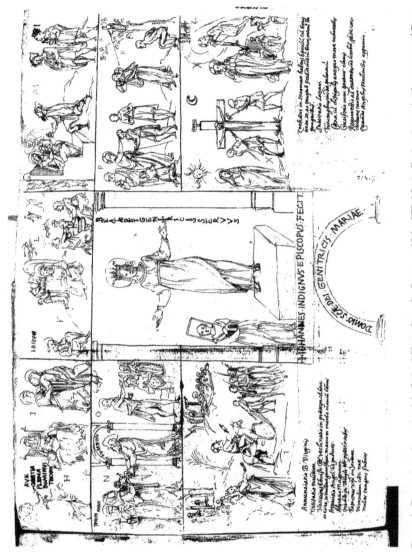

Figure 2: Engraving of mosaic of the Life of Christ from the Oratory of John VII. Maria Regina image in the centre and Pope John VII with a square halo to her right presenting a model of the Oratory to her. This central scene is surrounded by seven panels depicting the life of Christ. Three inscriptions are around the central figure of Mary and over the apsidal arch. From Grimaldi, Descrizione *(1621, Vat Lat 11988: Folios 70v–71r). © Bibliotheca Apostolica Vaticana (Vaticano).*

THE EARLIEST CHURCHES DEDICATED TO MARY IN ROME AND THE EARLIEST IMAGES OF MARY ASSOCIATED WITH THEM (TABLE 1)[5]

In the next two sections the ten surviving images listed in Table 1, that form the basis of the development of imagery of Mary in Rome up to the time of Pope John VII, are briefly discussed and their key points identified. This first section traces the development of images of Mary in the first four churches dedicated to Mary in Rome from the 430s onwards, while the next section considers three additional images of Mary in three churches not dedicated to her.

A. Santa Maria Maggiore: The Triumphal Arch Mosaics (Pope Sixtus III, 432–440: Figures 3, 4 and 5b; Table 1.1)

The first church in Rome dedicated to Mary, now called Santa Maria Maggiore, was on the Esquiline. The words XYSTVS EPISCOPVS PLEBI DEI inscribed over the centre of the surviving triumphal arch mosaics confirm that the mosaic decorations of the apse were commissioned by Pope Sixtus III (432–440).[6] The iconography of the fifth-century mosaics on the triumphal arch have puzzled many art historians and there is no consensus as to their meaning.[7] Nevertheless, certain aspects are clear enough to make these mosaics the right place to start when considering the earliest images of Mary in Rome.

On the left in the top register, a seated Mary spins the temple veil from red thread in a basket to her right. She is surrounded by three angels (Figures 3 and 4a). Above her, a dove approaches on the left and the angel Gabriel, with hand raised to indicate speech, on her right. Mary wears a golden *palla*; her hair is in a bun on the top of her head, surrounded by gems, further gems are placed on her forehead and by each ear.[8] A white shawl is loosely caught over her arms, while her collar and belt buckle are also dotted with pearls and gems. In the register below, in what is clearly an Adoration of the Magi, a diminutive but composed Christ, toga-ed, holding a scroll and sporting a halo with a cross at its centre, sits on an imperial *synthronon*; four angels stand behind the throne. A woman sits either side of the Christ-child: on his right, she resembles Mary in the scene above (Figures 3 and 4a and b); on his left she wears a veil or *maphorion* over her golden dress (Figures 3 and 4a and c).

Which of the two women in the Magi scene is meant to be Mary? So far no entirely satisfactory answer has been found, but the solution may lie in the doctrinal disputes over the precise relationship between Christ's human and divine nature that were current in the fifth century. The issue of the nature of Christ was discussed at the Council of Ephesus in 431 and finally settled, as far as the papacy was concerned, at the Council of Chalcedon in 451, when the solution outlined by Pope Leo the Great (440–461) in his *Epistola Dogmatica* prevailed.[9] According to Leo, Christ's two natures – the human and the divine – existed in Christ in such a way that each remained separate and acted according to its own qualities and characteristics yet was also combined. One of the consequences of this conclusion, that Mary had contained God in her womb and so was Mother of God (*Theotokos*), not

Figure 3: Line drawing of top two registers of the left side of the fifth-century triumphal arch mosaic at the Basilica of Santa Maria Maggiore, Rome, showing the Annunciation to Mary in the top register, left, and (probably) the Annunciation to Joseph at top register right; and the Adoration of the Magi in the second register with the 'Ever Virgin' image of Mary to the left of the enthroned Christ-child and the 'Mother of God' image of Mary to the right. For a coloured photo of this mosaic, see Cecchelli 1961: Table 49. Line drawing © E. Rubery.

Figure 4: Comparison of the three female figures (probably of Mary) from the triumphal arch at Santa Maria Maggiore. (a) Figure in gold from Annunciation scene; (b) figure in gold from Adoration of Magi scene; (c) figure in blue with gold dress underneath from Adoration of Magi scene. For a coloured photo of these mosaic figures see Cecchelli 1961: Table 49. Line drawings © E. Rubery.

just Mother of Christ *Christotokos*), was agreed at the Council of Ephesus in 431: 'If anyone will not confess that the Emmanuel is very God and that therefore the Holy Virgin is the Mother of God (Θεοτόκος) . . . let him be anathema.'[10]

From around this period Mary is frequently addressed by the double title of 'Ever Virgin, Mother of God'. Proclus, Patriarch of Constantinople, for example, uses the dual term in the first of his three famous orations on the Virgin, delivered at the Virginity Festival organized by Empress Pulcheria in 428–429: ' . . . we now call Mary Virgin, *Theotokos*, She is the unstained treasure of Virginity'.[11]

If the puzzling imagery in Santa Maria Maggiore is considered within the context of these names for Mary, then at the time of the Annunciation, Mary is clearly a virgin, and the way she is depicted in the Annunciation section of the mosaic resembles that of Sant' Agnese, a popular virgin martyr saint in early Rome, when she is depicted on fourth-century Roman gold glass (Figures 4a and 5c). The hairstyle, with its pearl decorations etc., is very similar. Even more similar to the Santa Maria Maggiore figure are the 22 virgin saints who process up the nave at Sant' Apollinare Nuovo in Ravenna towards an enthroned Mary (Figures 4a and 5a). This mosaic was made shortly after Emperor Justinian the Great regained Ravenna in the 540s.[12]

The same costume is worn by the figure to Christ's right in the Magi scene in the second register (Figures 3 and 5b), which therefore must represent the 'Ever Virgin' Mary, the Virgin notwithstanding having given birth to the enthroned Christ in the centre.

Figure 5: Comparison of figure in gold from the Adoration of the Magi scene with two images of Virgin Saints: (a) One of the Virgin saints from the procession of Virgin Saints in the nave at Sant' Apollinare Nuovo in Ravenna; (b) figure in gold from Adoration of Magi scene from triumphal arch at Santa Maria Maggiore; (c) gold glass image of Sant' Agnese from Catacomb of Pamphilus. Fourth Century. For colour images, see (a) Bovini 1957: Plate 20; (b) Cecchelli 1961: Table 49; (c) Elsner 1998: Figure 159. Line drawings © E. Rubery.

Figure 6: Line drawing reconstruction of the Madonna and child with angels from the palimpsest wall on the right side of the triumphal arch of the apse at Santa Maria Antiqua in the Roman Forum: reconstruction draws on various images in Gruneisen 1911; Wilpert 1917; Romanelli and Nordhagen 1964: Plate 15; and Bertelli 1961b. Line A-A represents the approximate position of the edge of the new apse that destroyed the angel on the left. Line drawing © E. Rubery.

Figure 7: Line drawing from the Mosaic of Sant' Agnese in the apse of Sant' Agnese Fuori le Mura, Rome, commissioned by Pope Honorius I (625–38). For a colour image of this mosaic, see Oakeshott 1967: Plate XVI. Line drawing © E. Rubery.

The figure on the left of Christ, although also dressed in gold, wears a *maphorion* over her dress, indicating that she is a wife and mother (Figures 3 and 4c). She holds in her left hand the *mappa* or senatorial handkerchief which indicated that, by accepting the incarnation, she initiated the salvation of the human race. This figure is therefore clearly the 'Mother of God'. The two aspects of Mary are depicted by two separate figures either side of the incarnate figure of Christ. His diminutive figure combines his human nature, as evidenced by the presence of his Mother, with his divine nature, as evidenced by the continued virginity of his Mother who contained his divinity without losing her virginity. This composition can therefore be seen as a unique exposition of the two states of Mary, the two natures of Christ and how they were combined into one being – Christ.

As Cyril, Patriarch of Alexandria (412–444) and one of the key players at Chalcedon in relation to agreeing the doctrine on the natures of Christ, said in one of his many texts on the *Theotokos*:

> For Jesus . . . the same Logos, having come into the blessed Virgin herself, took himself his own temple from the essence of the Virgin. He went forth from her as a man and was seen to be a man externally, though internally he existed truly as God. Therefore after his birth he preserved the virginity of his Mother, although this is not true of any of the saints . . . Therefore it is right and just that the blessed one should be called Theotokos and Virgin Mother.[13]

The high profile enjoyed by female saints in Rome up to the seventh century is not always appreciated, but is clear from both the nave procession at Sant' Apollinare in Ravenna, mentioned above, and from the mosaic in the apse at Sant' Agnese Fuori le Mura (*c.* 625), where Agnes stands alone in the centre in even more pearl-bedecked clothes than she wears in the gold glass image of her already described. Here she is wearing a gemmed tiara (Figure 7).[14] Like the Santa Maria Maggiore virgin, Agnes also carries a white shawl (Figures 5a, b, c and 7).

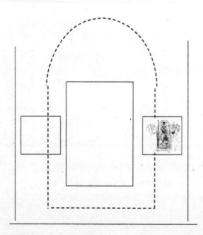

Figure 8: Original position of the fresco of the palimpsest Madonna on the right side of the triumphal arch of the apsidal wall. The central rectangle outlines the original niche, which left additional space at either side so that the angel on Mary's right hand side was accommodated. This angel was destroyed when the later larger arched apse (dashed outline) was created. On the left is shown the probable position of a second composition, perhaps of Christ with angels. Reconstruction developed from a variety of sources, including Bertelli 1961b; and Wilpert 1917: Figures 21 and 22. Line drawing © E. Rubery.

This mosaic of Sant' Agnese is clearly closely related to surviving fragments of a fresco (usually dated to 550–600) of Mary enthroned with the Christ-child and flanked by two angels, on the right side of the apsidal arch in the papal church of Santa Maria Antiqua (Figures 6 and 8).[15] Here Mary's tiara is a little more elaborate, and she has additional bands of decoration linking the front and back panels of her tabard on either side, but the encrusted overgarments worn by both women are clearly related. In this fresco, created a century later than the Santa Maria Maggiore mosaics, the two aspects of Mary are combined so that, in contrast to her appearance in catacomb 'Magi' images, where she always wears a *maphorion* (Figure 1), here she is dressed as a virgin, but holds Christ as the Mother of God and a *mappa* as the initiator of salvation (Figure 6).

B. Santa Maria Maggiore: The *Salus Populi Romani* Icon (??Pope Gregory I, 590–604: Figure 9; Table 1.4)

Santa Maria Maggiore also contains an early icon of Mary wearing a *maphorion* with gemmed cuffs to her *stola*, or undergarment, and holding Christ on her left arm (Figure 9).[16] Reputed to have been painted by 'St Luke and the angels', that is, to be an *acheiropyta*, such 'miraculous' icons became substitutes for the relics needed to dedicate the altar of a church but, of course, not available for Marian churches once Mary's bodily Assumption was generally accepted.

The provenance of this image is not known, though it has been suggested that it might have been acquired by Pope Gregory the Great (590–604) while he was papal *apocrisarius* in Constantinople in 584, before himself becoming Pope. It was painted in either encaustic or tempera and has not been restored so that several layers of paint overlie the original, making dating difficult.[17] The composition does have some features in common with surviving copies of the famous *Hodegitria* image, also allegedly painted by St Luke, which legend said had been acquired by Empress Pulcheria (414–453) from the Holy Land. This *Hodegitria* image is now lost, but it was widely copied in the East and many copies of it survive, including a depiction of it being venerated in a thirteenth- to fourteenth-century icon, now in the British Museum (Figure 10).[18]

Both the *Salus Populi Romani* and the *Hodegitria* images mark a step change in the way the Mother of God and the Christ-child are represented. Whilst catacomb images and the sixth-century 'palimpsest' Mary at Santa Maria Antiqua (Figures 1 and 6) depict Christ, as a symbol of the incarnation, facing away from Mary and towards the Magi, these two later images show Mary and Christ interacting with each other as Mother and Child.[19] They therefore reflect the greater interest in Mary as Mother as opposed to her being simply the receptacle for the incarnation. It is Pope Sergius I's (687–701) *vita* that first records the procession in Rome on the feast of the Assumption of Mary on 14/15 August, while Pope Gregory III's (731–741) *vita* is the first to record the donation of an image of Mary to Santa Maria Maggiore.[20]

In this Roman version of the *Hodegitria*, Mary is dressed in a *maphorion* edged with gold, with folds highlighted in gold. She looks out at the viewer, not at the Christ-child, while he looks at her. Her hands overlap (right over left) in front of

Figure 9: Salus Populi Romani *icon of Mary with Christ from Santa Maria Maggiore, Rome, sixth/seventh century (?). For a colour image, see Pietrangeli 1988: 125. Foto © Bibliotheca Hertziana – Max-Planck-Institut für Kunstgeschichte, Rom.*

Figure 10: Detail from the upper register of the icon of 'The Triumph of Ortho-doxy', showing an image of the Hodegitria *icon of Mary with the Christ-child being displayed for venera-tion. The* Hodegitria *icon was kept in Constantinople and widely reproduced. This 'Triumph of Orthodoxy' icon is probably from the thirteenth or fourteenth century and is now in the British Museum, London. For a colour reproduc-tion of the icon, see Cormack 2000: Figure 13. Photograph © British Museum.*

166

the child's lap, and she holds a senatorial *mappa* in her left hand. A similar pose is found in a fresco of Mary and the Christ-child on a column at Santa Maria Antiqua.[21] In contrast, in the *Hodegitria* icon (Figure 10), Mary points to the child with her right hand, identifying him as 'the Way' (which is what *Hodegitria* means). These differences make it possible that the *Salus Populi Romani* could have been a Roman composition reflecting the Roman interpretation of the developing cult of Mary, rather than an Eastern import.

C. Santa Maria ad Martyres: The Pantheon Madonna Icon (Pope Boniface IV, 608–15: Figure 11; Table 1.5)

The second church known to be dedicated to Mary in Rome is the church of the 'Ever Virgin Santa Maria ad Martyres', which Emperor Phocas (602–610) permitted Pope Boniface IV (608–615) to establish in the pagan Pantheon in 609.[22] A large fragment of an icon of Mary and the Christ-child survives in this church, which might have been donated by the emperor for the dedication service.[23] No doubt originally a rectangular icon, this was converted into a silhouette figure at an unknown date. Bertelli has suggested that originally it was full length, and he calculates that this would have made it around two metres high. However, the raw

Figure 11: Icon of the Madonna and Child from the Pantheon (Santa Maria ad Martyres), AD 609. For a colour image, see Belting 1996: plate opposite 264. Foto ©: Bibliotheca Hertziana – Max-Planck-Institut für Kunstgeschichte, Rom.

lower edge does not necessarily indicate that there has been a reduction in the height of the icon, since processional icons were usually fixed into a support via the lower edge, which often therefore appears damaged or unfinished (see the *Madonna della Clemenza*, Figure 13a, for such an example). The image might always have been half-length, like the *Salus Populi Romani* from Santa Maria Maggiore (Figure 9). Whilst similar to the *Salus Populi Romani* icon in wearing a *maphorion*, here Mary faces directly to the front, and both she and the Christ-child stare at the viewer. The only evidence of maternal closeness is the slight turning of the Christ-child towards her, and the fact that by enclosing the child within both arms she does bring him into close contact with her body. Mary has gold hands, a common attribute of miraculous icons; and it is not possible to see what clothes she is wearing under her *maphorion*. Mary's frontally directed big, soulful, penetrating eyes echo those of the Fayyum mummy portraits from fourth-century Egypt, and the icon was painted in encaustic, as were these portraits. It is at present kept in the Chapel of the Canons in the Pantheon.

D. Santa Maria Antiqua: The 'Palimpsest' Madonna (?550–600: Figures 6 and 8; Table 1.3)

The third Marian church established in Rome is first mentioned in the *vita* of John VII: 'He adorned with painting the basilica of the holy mother of God which is called Antiqua . . .'[24] The text suggests this church had been in existence for some time and it may have been established before Santa Maria ad Martyres, possibly as early as 550–600.[25] The lower arms of the walls of the triumphal arch of the main apse (Figure 8) have been frescoed many times and sections of each layer are still visible on the right side, best seen in Wilpert's retouched photograph, Plate 133.[26] Although only fragments of the image survive, the 'Palimpsest' fresco of Mary with the Christ-child (Figure 6) on the right side, already mentioned in connection with the Sant' Agnese mosaic (Figure 7), still clearly depicts her dressed as a Roman virgin saint. It may be contemporary with the consecration of the church, which is in a second-century building in the Forum at the foot of the Palatine Hill. Here Mary wears a two-tiered gemmed tiara with a fine veil falling behind her shoulders. Mary presents the Christ-child as a symbol, as in the 'Magi' image on the sarcophagus (Figure 1). She holds a *mappa* and wears a highly decorated tabard-like garment over her blue skirt. Originally she may have been flanked by two angels, but the central square niche in the wall was widened at a later date to form an arched apse, resulting in the loss of the left part (to the left of the line 'A–A' in Figure 6). There may have been a matching panel on the left arm of the triumphal arch depicting Christ flanked by angels (Figure 8). If so, the arrangement was iconographically similar to that of the mosaic panels at Sant' Apollinare Nuovo in Ravenna, where the nave ends near the apse with enthroned images of Christ and Mary. These were probably executed for Theodoric the Great (493–526) by Roman mosaicists.[27] However, at Sant' Apollinare, Mary wears a *maphorion*, not a tiara, and is flanked by four, not two, angels.[28]

E. Santa Maria Antiqua ?: The Madonna di San Luca (? 4th–6th century: Figure 12; Table 1.2)

Although this church was probably dedicated around 550–600, that is, later than Santa Maria Maggiore, it is called Antiqua. One possible explanation for this is that it possessed an ancient image of Mary that was older than the church and so already revered.[29] The church was damaged by an earthquake in the 850s and abandoned, its function and probably its most valuable possessions, possibly including this ancient icon, being transferred to a nearby, newly built church, Santa Maria Nova, now called Santa Francesca Romana, between 847 and 855.[30] At the time of Pope Honorius III (1216–1227), a fire was recorded in this church, which probably destroyed most of the icon. The pilgrim's guide *Mirabilia Urbis Romae* of 1375 describes how, in a miracle, the faces of the Mother and Child 'painted by St Luke' had survived a fire and could still be seen in the church.[31] Two fragments, probably from this Madonna di San Luca, can now be seen in the sacristy at Sta Francesca Romana. They were rediscovered in the 1950s under a later Marian icon (Figure 12).[32] They are painted directly onto linen in encaustic, a technique used for Egyptian mummy paintings from the first two centuries CE; in contrast, later encaustic images are usually painted directly onto the wood.[33] If the provenance of these icon fragments is correct, then this image could be the earliest Marian icon in Rome. However, it has to be accepted that the original image need not even have been of Mary; it could have been simply a mother and child, later considered to be Mary and the Christ-child. Because only the faces of the two figures survive, no comment on Mary's costume is possible; it is not even

Figure 12: Madonna di San Luca icon fragment from the sacristy of Santa Francesca Romana (previously called Santa Maria Nova), Rome. For a colour image, see Belting 1996: Plate I. Foto © Biblioteheca Hertziana – Max-Planck-Institut für Kunstgeschichte, Rom.

clear that she wears a *maphorion*. There is one further interesting aspect to this image: Mary faces to the left and so, unusually, the child is seated on her right arm. Whatever its origin, it is a hauntingly beautiful image and, based on the size of the face, would have been a large icon.

F. Santa Maria in Trastevere: The *Madonna della Clemenza* Icon (? Pope John VII, 705–707: Figure 13; Table 1.9)

The fourth church dedicated to Mary in Rome was Santa Maria in Trastevere, built at the site of the third-century Oratory to St Callistus. The earliest reference to a Marian church here is in Pope Hadrian I's *vita* (772–795), which refers to 'God's holy Mother's church in Trastevere'.[34] No information on the original apse or triumphal arch decoration survives, but the church contains a large icon that has been attributed to John VII and is now known as the *Madonna della Clemenza*.[35]

Clearly the costume and head of Mary in this image are closely related to those of the orant Mary from the mosaic in John VII's oratory. Her crown is very similar, with horizontal rows of pearls, pinnacles and a central cross, her collar and shoulder pads have the same arrangements of gems and pearls and both women have long pendulia depending from the lower rim of their crown (Figures 13b and 17).

However, here Mary does not stand alone; instead, like the fresco at Santa Maria Antiqua, she is flanked by two angels carrying staffs (Figure 13a). However, as at the oratory at St Peter's, there is a patron, this time kneeling on Mary's left, though all that clearly remains of him is his eye (just below and to the left of the two rows of pearls on the diagonal transverse edge of Mary's costume), the corner of his *pallium* and the negative shadow of the curve of his back (Figure 13c). As at Santa Maria Antiqua, Mary is frontally posed with a frontal, 'symbolic' Christ-child on her knees. Although Mary is clearly sitting (the throne is unmistakeable), the arrangements at her lap and around the Christ-child are perplexing, as her clothes seem to balloon up to provide a lap for the Christ-child. Furthermore, the ratio of her head to her 'seated' height is 6.5:1, comparable to that of the standing Mary in Pope John's oratory mosaic (6.1:1). In contrast, the ratios of head to height of the seated figures of Mary in the mosaics at Santa Maria Maggiore or the fresco at Santa Maria Antiqua range from 5.0 to 5.5:1. These proportions suggest the *Clemenza* icon originally depicted a standing figure that resembled the standing figure of Mary in the mosaic in Pope John's oratory (Figure 2). Possibly it was 'converted' to a seated figure holding the Christ-child by overpainting. One even wonders whether the addition of the Christ-child, throne and angels might all have been inserted at a later date. Further careful examination of the way additional layers of paint were added to this image might help clarify how the present image was arrived at.

The cross Mary carries in her right hand *is* a later painted addition, and it has been suggested that originally a metallic cross was present. Both this icon and the mosaic in Pope John VII's oratory dress Mary in an imperial purple *palla* (turned to brown by time in the icon) over a tunic. This fits with her elaborate pinnacled 'imperial' crown with its pearl pendulia. Overall this icon now has a somewhat militant and defensive aura.

(a) Icon of Madonna dells Clemenza *from Santa Maria in Trastevere, Rome. For a colour image, see Belting 1996: Plate II.*

(b) detail of head and shoulders showing the imperial crown and gemmed collar and shoulder pads;

c) detail of kneeling Pope at right side of image.

Figure 13: (Foto © Bibliotheca Hertziana – Max-Planck-Institut für Kunstgeschichte, Rom.)

Along three sides of the original frame is inscribed a text including on the left frame the words DS QYOD IPSE FACTYS EST, suggesting this was also an *acheiropyta*.[36] Finally this image, uniquely, shows clear signs of intense use as a cult image, with particular loss of paint around the feet of both Mary and the Christ-child, presumably from kissing and washing activities. However, given its long sojourn in the church, the date of this damage and so of this cult activity must remain uncertain.

OTHER KEY IMAGES RELEVANT TO THE DEVELOPMENT OF MARIAN ICONOGRAPHY IN ROME[37]

Three early relevant images of Mary are found in churches *not* dedicated to Mary and also need to be considered. The images at San Venantius and St Peter's were commissioned by popes, while the patron for the Madonna Avvocata is not known.

G. The Chapel of St Venantius in the Lateran Baptistery: The Apse Mosaic (Pope John IV, 640–642, and Pope Theodore I, 642–649: Figure 14; Table 1.6)

The lower register of this apse mosaic, commissioned by John IV, contains an orant figure wearing a *maphorion* flanked by the apostles Peter and Paul and other saints. The upper register contains a bust of Christ blessing, flanked by two angels. Although not named, the orant is usually presumed to be the Mother of God.[38] The relics of Dalmatian saints, including St Venantius (Bishop of Duvno), were translated to Rome and the Lateran complex by John IV because pagans

Figure 14: Engraving of part of the left side of the apse mosaic from the chapel of St Venantius, Lateran Baptistery, Rome, showing Mary as an orant in the centre beneath the bust of Christ, and part of the procession of saints to her right. Commissioned by Popes John IV (640–642) and Theodore I (642–649). For a black-and-white image of the apse, see Oakeshott 1967: Figure 99. From Rouhault de Fleury 1877.

Figure 15: Fresco of the child Nonnosa (whose tomb this is) between her father and mother in the hypogeum of Teotecno in the catacombs of San Gennaro, Naples, c. sixth century. Foto © Bibliotheca Hertziana – Max-Planck-Institut für Kunstgeschichte, Rom.

were desecrating their tombs.[39] In the apsidal conch Mary acts as intercessor, leading the procession of saints either side of her towards Christ.[40] This is the earliest image of an orant Mary without the Christ-child in Rome, and so marks an important stage in the development of Marian iconography. Here Mary has taken over orant imagery from funerary art in the catacombs. Such imagery focuses on the need for intercession for the souls of the dead. Such activity had previously been the provenance of saints and members of the defunct's family, as can be seen in the fresco of the Teotecno family in the catacombs in Naples, where the dead child is flanked by her parents and all have adopted the orant pose (Figure 15).

H. San Sisto Vecchio: The *Madonna Avvocata* (? 8th century: Figure 16; Table 1.10)

The *Madonna Avvocata*, now in Santa Maria del Rosario on the Monte Mario, but originally in the Monasterio Tempuli and then in Ssn Sisto Vecchio by the Baths of Caracalla, became, according to Belting, the most popular image of Mary in Rome in the thirteenth century.[41] It generated a large number of replicas, including images at Santa Maria in Aracoeli and San Gregorio Nazianzeno in Campo

173

Marzio.[42] Like the image at St Venantius, Mary wears a *maphorion* and is without the Christ-child. The catacombs contain many orant women, some of whom look very like Mary in this image, but who are, from the accompanying inscriptions, clearly neither Mary nor saints but simply married women. A good example of such an image is the sixth-century fresco in the hypogeum of the Teotecno family in the catacombs of San Gennaro in Naples (Figure 15).[43] The inscriptions in that fresco make it clear that the figure wearing a *maphorion* on the left is the mother, Ilaritas, of the young girl, Nonnosa, herself dressed as an elite virgin (and so resembling the gold glass image of Sant' Agnese, Figure 5c). The posture of the hands of Ilaritas (Figure 15) is strongly reminiscent of the pose of the *Madonna Avvocata*.

I. St Peter's, Oratory of John VII: The Central Image of Mary in the Mosaic of the Life of Christ (Pope John VII: Figures 2 and 17; Table 1.7)

Returning to the mosaic from the oratory in St Peter's, it is clear that a number of these earlier images could have contributed to the development of this highly original composition. The orant images in the catacombs, the apse at St Venantius and the icon at Santa Maria del Rosario all have features in common with this standing orant Mary. These features are consistent with the intended function of the oratory, as evidenced by John VII's epitaph, quoted above, as the burial place for John VII's body. In such a site there would be a need for prayers to be said for the deceased; and who better to convey those prayers to Christ than the Mother of God herself?

Figure 16: Madonna del Rosario *icon, now in the monastery church of Santa Maria del Rosario on the Monte Mario, originally from the church of San Sisto Vecchiao, near the Baths of Caracalla. Note that the metallic golden hands and cross are later additions. For a colour image, see Belting 1996: Plate V. Foto © Bibliotheca Hertziana – Max-Planck-Institut für Kunstgeschichte, Rom.*

However, her costume and her crown have no link with death and the hereafter. This costume needs to be explored in more depth to establish its origins and hence its meaning. As in the mosaic at Santa Maria Maggiore, here Mary wears a tunic under a *palla*. As in the icon at Santa Maria in Trastevere, but unlike in the mosaics at Santa Maria Maggiore, here Mary's *palla* is of imperial purple, not aristocratic gold.[44] Here Mary is no longer equated with a Virgin saint, but is raised to imperial status. This is further emphasized by the second striking feature of this image of Mary, her imposing, gemmed and multi-pinnacled crown with long pendulia of pearls. Such a crown is of a different order of significance from the tiaras and gems of the earlier images of female saints above (Figures 5, 6 and 7).

This aspect of the mosaic is also clearly closely related to the crown worn by the *Madonna della Clemenza* at Santa Maria in Trastevere (Figure 13a and b). The most relevant and well-known depiction of such a crown that has survived is that worn by Empress Theodora (500–548) in the panel in the presbytery of the Palatine chapel at San Vitale in Ravenna (Figures 18 and 19a). The imperial administration of the West was established in Ravenna following the reconquest of Italy by Justinian the Great in the 540s. This mosaic was inserted into the presbytery around 545.[45] Theodora's crown and those of Mary in the oratory mosaic and in the *Clemenza* icon possess many similarities (Fig 13a and b, 17, 18 and 19). All have deep,

Figure 17: Mosaic fragment of Mary as Orant Empress, originally from the oratory of Pope John VII (705–707), now in the Ricci Chapel at Basilica San Marco, Florence. For a colour reproduction, see Verzone 1967: 172. Photograph © E. Rubery.

Figure 18: Line drawing of Empress Theodora from the mosaic panel in the sanctuary at San Vitale, Ravenna, c. 540. For a colour reproduction of the entire mosaic panel, see Cormack 2000: Figure 34. Line drawing © E. Rubery.

Figure 19: Line drawings of the heads and shoulders of the Empress Theodora from Ravenna and the orant Maria Regina from Rome/Florence for comparison of crowns. Line drawing © E. Rubery.

gemmed bases, decorated with horizontal rows of pearls and gemstones. The upper border of each base supports several pinnacles, the central one being rather more prominent than the lateral ones. Depending from the lower margin of the bases are long pearl pendulia. The three heads are each enclosed in enormous haloes whose circle is completed by the gemmed collar worn over their outer garment. Though all wear imperial purple, Theodora is not wearing a *palla*, but, beneath her collar, an imperial *chlamys* fixed at her shoulder by a large gemmed buckle. This difference probably reflects the intended function of the mosaic panel in the church in Ravenna, not any lesser status of Mary compared with the empress. Mary is in an oratory interceding on behalf of the soul of the Pope (after his death), or (at Trastevere) interceding for those venerating her icon, while Theodora is participating in a public imperial ceremony.

It is even possible to propose the possible nature of this ceremony. An earlier image of this particularly elaborate style of crown in imperial imagery can be found on a few coins of Empress Licinia Eudoxia (422–462), daughter of the Eastern Emperor Theodosius II and wife of the Western Emperor Valentinian III (Figure 20). These were issued by the mints of Rome and Ravenna, probably at the time Eudoxia was elevated to Augusta by Valentinian in 439.[46] These coins are particularly striking because, in the fifth century, profile images of imperial figures wearing a laurel wreath were the norm.[47] Licinia Eudoxia is depicted frontally, wearing formal imperial dress, including an elaborate crown, pendulia and a *chlamys*. Her crown has the characteristic series of horizontal rows of precious jewels along its base, six pinnacles arising from its upper edge with pendulia from the lower. It resembles Theodora's and Mary's in both crowned versions, in bearing a central cross, though Mary's and Theodora's crosses sit on top of their central pinnacle while Licinia's arises directly from the top edge of the base, between the pinnacles.

No coins of the first Empress Theodora have survived, probably because she did not provide an heir for the Empire. But if this coin marked the coronation of Eudoxia as Augusta of the West, then the panel depicting Theodora wearing the same type of crown could mark the elevation of Theodora to Augusta of the West,

Figure 20: Coin of Empress Licinia Eudoxia (422–462), wife of Western Emperor Valentinian III, showing her wearing a pinnacled crown with pendulia similar to that of Theodora in the panel at Ravenna. Possibly issued to mark her coronation as Augusta in 439 (Grierson and Mays 1992: Coin 870). Obverse: Gold solidus: 4.49g: 21mm. Issued at Ravenna: Inscription: LICINAEVDO XIAPFAVG. Bust: facing and wearing a crown with pinnacles, central cross and pendulia. © Dumbarton Oaks, Byzantine Collection, Washington DC.

following its reconquest. The corresponding panel of Justinian would then represent his accession as Augustus of the West. While there is no evidence that the imperial couple ever visited the West, a service in the Palatine Chapel to mark the new political situation and so their new status, possibly even with proxies standing in for them, is plausible, and could have been followed by the creation of mosaic panels to mark the event and emphasize the significance of the ceremony.

A later similar mosaic panel at Sant' Apollinare in Classe commemorated an actual imperial visit to Ravenna by Constantine IV (668–685) and his son (and later emperor) Justinian, to confer a *priviligia* on the city at the end of the seventh century.[48] Knowledge of the original meaning of these panels therefore probably persisted for the 150-plus years up to the beginning of the eighth century. Furthermore, Pope John was in dialogue with that emperor, Justinian II (685–695), over the Acts of the Quinisext Council convened by Justinian II in 686/7. Justinian II was very anxious to get papal endorsement for the Acts and had sent them to John with a request that he convene a Council in Rome and let him know which Acts were acceptable to the papacy.[49] If the suggested function of the Theodora panel is correct, then by depicting Mary wearing this type of crown, John VII was not only identifying Mary as an imperial figure, but also invoking her coronation as Augusta or Empress. Can one go as far as suggesting that John is not seeing her here as *Maria Regina* (a term often used to describe this image), but more as *Maria Augusta*?

There is another intriguing feature about the oratory image. In the apse at St Venantius, Mary intercedes directly with Christ, who is situated above her in the same apse. But in St Peter's there is no proximate image of Christ. Within the oratory itself the only images of Christ above Mary's outstretched arms are in the narrative scenes of the Nativity and the Adoration of the Magi (Figure 2). In the Nativity, Christ appears twice, once in the background, in the crib with the midwife Salome stretching out her arm to him to be healed, and again bottom right, where he is being bathed by the two midwives. In the Magi scene he is on the left, but facing to the right and apparently much more interested in the gold offered by the first Magus than in his mother below. Therefore Mary's prayers here were probably not directed at an image of Christ, but rather directly to his divine but unseen form, as was the case for orants in the catacombs, who were frequently depicted without any obvious intercessor above. One should resist the temptation to read the absence of Christ as a sign of even greater importance becoming attached to Mary and her cult at this time, given the convention with respect to orants extant in the catacombs.

J. St Peter's, Oratory of John VII: The Adoration of the Magi Narrative Scene in the Mosaic of the Life of Christ (Pope John VII: Figure 2, top right; Table 1.8)

Finally, before leaving this mosaic, it is important to note that the iconography of the Adoration of the Magi scene in this mosaic has returned to the iconography found in the catacombs (Figures 1 and 2, top right narrative scene). The puzzling Sant Maria Maggiore iconography of two women and an independent Christ-figure (Figure 3) was not used here (or indeed anywhere else subsequently). It appears unique to Santa Maria Maggiore.

ANALYSIS OF THE DEVELOPMENT OF EARLY PAPAL IMAGERY OF MARY IN ROME

There are only ten images of Mary linked to the papacy in Rome in the fifth to early eighth centuries (Table 1). Most previous attempts to link these images together coherently have failed. But if these images are seen in the context of the four types of female imagery present in Rome in the third to fifth centuries, then a coherent relationship between them emerges and generates four key eighth-century types of Marian image. Table 2 provides a schematic summary of the links that the rest of the paper will describe. These types can also be seen to relate to the key religious and political concerns of this period, and a further section will explore these issues.

Tables 2a–d each start with one of the four original types of female image discussed in the previous two sections. It is noteworthy that only one of these types was specific to Mary. These are:

(a) Mary, Mother of God;
(b) The Virgin saint;
(c) The Empress;
(d) The Orant woman.

The rest of this section will consider how these four sources contributed to the development, by the eighth century, of four key types of image of Mary:

- The Mother of God;
- The *Hodegitria* type;
- The *Madonna Avvocata*;
- The *Maria Regina*.[50]

(a) Mary, Mother of God (Table 2a)

In the catacomb image (Figure 1), and in the Adoration of the Magi scene in John VII's oratory (Figure 2, top right), Mary presents the Christ-child to the Magi as a symbol of the incarnation, not a son. Mary could be portrayed frontally (as in the image from the crypt of the Madonna from the catacombs of St Peter and San Marcellinus in Table 2a),[51] or in profile in Magi images, but she always wears a *maphorion* and is seated. In the earliest Magi scenes the number of Magi can vary between two and four, eventually settling at three. The image itself persists into the eighth century and beyond and can be seen in the top left scene in the engraving of the mosaic in Figure 2 and in the fragment of that mosaic still preserved at Santa Maria in Cosmedin.[52] Without the Magi, it becomes the proto-type for all enthroned images of Mary with the Christ-child, whether she is alone or flanked by angels, saints, and/or patrons. This iconography can be seen in the

179

Table 2a: Mary,, Mother of God

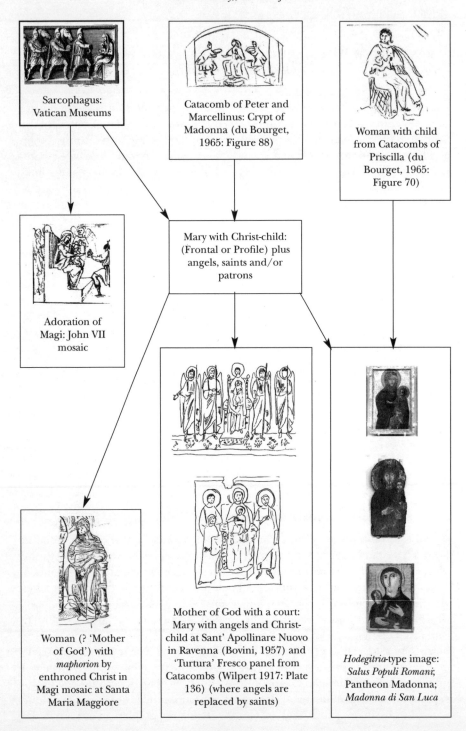

Sarcophagus:
Vatican Museums

Catacomb of Peter and
Marcellinus: Crypt of
Madonna (du Bourget,
1965: Figure 88)

Woman with child
from Catacombs of
Priscilla (du
Bourget, 1965:
Figure 70)

Adoration of
Magi: John VII
mosaic

Mary with Christ-child:
(Frontal or Profile) plus
angels, saints and/or
patrons

Woman (? 'Mother
of God') with
maphorion by
enthroned Christ in
Magi mosaic at Santa
Maria Maggiore

Mother of God with a court:
Mary with angels and Christ-
child at Sant' Apollinare Nuovo
in Ravenna (Bovini, 1957) and
'Turtura' Fresco panel from
Catacombs (Wilpert 1917: Plate
136) (where angels are
replaced by saints)

Hodegitria-type image:
Salus Populi Romani;
Pantheon Madonna;
Madonna di San Luca

Table 2b: The Virgin Saint

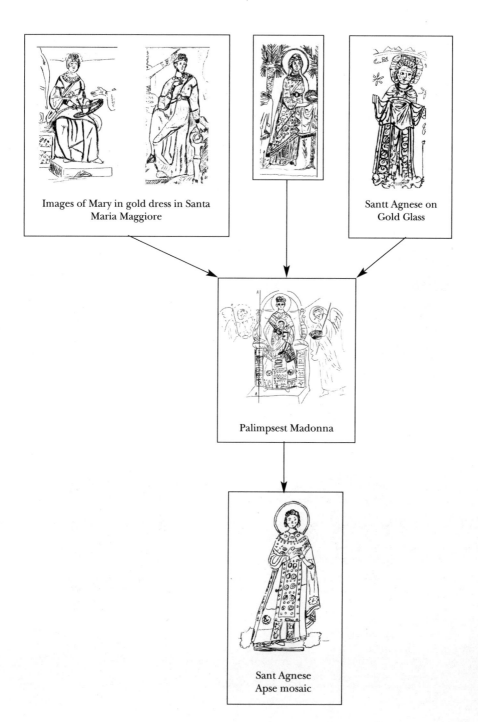

Images of Mary in gold dress in Santa
Maria Maggiore

Santt Agnese on
Gold Glass

Palimpsest Madonna

Sant Agnese
Apse mosaic

Table 2c: The Empress

Coin of Licinia
Eudoxia

Theodora from San Vitale,
Navenna

Mosaic from Oratory
of John VII

Icon of *Madonna della
Clemenza*

Maria Regina

Table 2d: The Orant woman

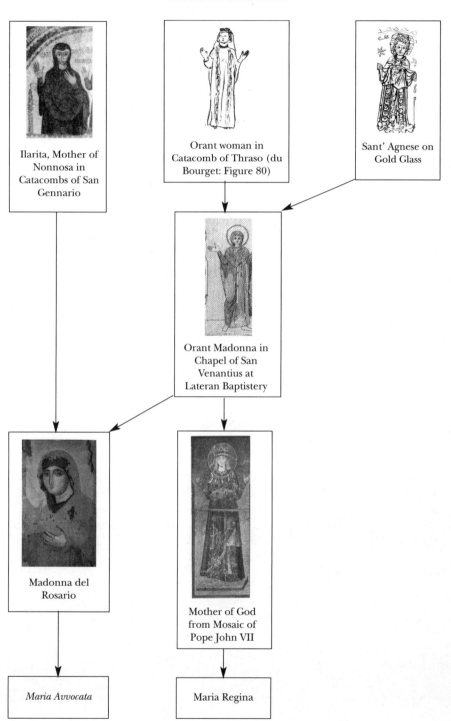

Ilarita, Mother of Nonnosa in Catacombs of San Gennario

Orant woman in Catacomb of Thraso (du Bourget: Figure 80)

Sant' Agnese on Gold Glass

Orant Madonna in Chapel of San Venantius at Lateran Baptistery

Madonna del Rosario

Mother of God from Mosaic of Pope John VII

Maria Avvocata

Maria Regina

183

panels of Christ and Mary with angels at Sant' Apollinare Nuovo and in the 'Turtura' fresco in the Catacombs of Commodilla.[53] The Santa Maria Antiqua and the *Madonna della Clemenza* images are two examples where Christ continues to be presented as a symbol of the incarnation, not as a son reacting with his mother, and so is facing away from Mary and reacting with the viewer. The angelic court develops to include courts of saints and patrons; it is present in both of these images, with a papal patron in the *Clemenza* example. The 'Turtura' icon is clearly a development from this including a less august patron. This type continues into the ninth century in such images as that of Mary in the apse at Santa Maria in Dominica, where Mary is surrounded by a host of angels and the kneeling Pope Paschal I (817–824).[54]

In the *Hodegitria*-type images that develop from this iconography (Figures 9, 10, 11 and possibly 12), Mary is no longer enthroned, but stands with the Christ-child turned towards her, and there is interaction between the two figures. Standing images wearing a *maphorion* clearly echo the orant figures in the catacombs, and probably are also influenced by images of mothers with children, such as the one in the catacombs of Priscilla, and the frequently quoted earliest example of Mary with Christ, that is almost certainly just a nursing mother (see Parlby's chapter in this book).[55] This modification reflects a change of emphasis in meaning, the message no longer being solely salvation through the incarnation of Christ, but including an element of expiation of sins before and after death through the personal intercession of the Mother of God, who now interacts directly with her Son. This version may have arisen in the East and certainly became very popular there as the *Hodegitria* image. In Rome it is exemplified by the *Salus Populi Romani*, Pantheon Madonna and probably the *Madonna di San Luca*.

(b) The Virgin Saint (Table 2b)

The Magi scene at Santa Maria Maggiore (Figures 3 and 4) introduced a different Mary by aligning her with the early imagery of Virgin saints such as Sant' Agnese (Figure 5c), whose cult appears to have enjoyed much greater initial popularity than Mary's in Rome.[56] Like the early Virgin saints, Mary is here dressed in a golden *palla*, with a gemmed collar and gems in her hair. This image also contributes to the Maria Antiqua enthroned Mary which probably was a source for the Sant' Agnese image in the sixth-century apse of her titular church.

(c) The Empress (Table 2c)

The coronation image of Eudoxia and the mosaic of Theodora at Ravenna (possibly also of a coronation) introduce the imperial elements into the *Maria Regina* image, seen without the Christ-child in the Oratory of John VII and then combined with the Christ-child in the *Madonna della Clemenza* in Trastevere.

(d) The Orant woman (Table 2d)

Finally the orant woman (who can be a mother, a virgin or indeed a man in the catacombs) (Figure 15) as the orant mother type produces the orant Mary at St Venantius and in the *Madonna Avvocata* at San Sisto. Combined with the empress image, it forms the orant Empress Mary at John VII's oratory. This group expresses the cult of Mary as an iconography that can exclude the image of the Christ-child.

(e) Discussion

The crowned images of Mary in Rome have the most complex origins, the *Clemenza* image, in particular, drawing elements from three of the four original types. Crowned images of Mary remained a minority form in Rome, after their efflorescence under Pope John VII (who is reported to have decorated many churches with his own image and so may well have distributed many more images of Mary with a crown around Rome in his short pontificate). Apart from the fresco in the atrium at Santa Maria Antiqua mentioned above, later versions survive, for example, in the lower church at San Clemente and at Santa Susanna.[57] The image at Trastevere was copied by Pope Callixtus II (1119–1124) when he decorated the St Nicholas Chapel at the Lateran Palace in the twelfth century.[58] This type was used again in the apse mosaic of Santa Maria in Trastevere in the 'Triumph of Mary' by Innocent II (1130–1143), which was probably copied directly from the *Madonna della Clemenza* icon. There Mary sits on the right hand of an enthroned Christ and the inscription makes it clear she sits with Christ as his bride, not his mother.[59] So here is a further development of her cult, in which she becomes associated with the adult Christ. This association reaches its full efflorescence in the Coronation of the Virgin at Santa Maria Maggiore, commissioned by Pope Nicholas IV (1288–1292), an innovation that links into the later explosion of Coronation of the Virgin imagery in Siena and throughout the Renaissance.[60]

The *Clemenza* image clearly has strong compositional links with the icon of Mary with saints and angels from the sixth century at St Catherine's monastery on Mount Sinai, although, as she invariably does in Eastern imagery, the Mary there lacks a crown.[61] This image underlines the close interrelations between the Eastern and Western imagery in this period, also evidenced in the frequent similarities between early icons and the Fayyum mummy portraits. In Byzantium the development of Marian iconography is more difficult to trace because of iconoclasm and later depredations due to Muslim conquest.

CONSIDERATION OF THE CONTEXT OF THE DEVELOPMENT OF THE CULT OF MARY IN ROME

Having traced the development of the different images of Mary in Rome up to 707, this section will consider some of the social and religious issues that this imagery suggests lay behind the emergence of the cult of Mary.

(a) Attitudes to Death and Images of Mary in the Seventh and Eighth Centuries

John VII was the first pope to dedicate an oratory to Mary at St Peter's for personal use as a burial chamber. Previously popes had simply been buried under the floor either at the south-east end of the basilica or in the adjoining *secretarium*.[62] John's action reflected the changing approach to the afterlife developing in the seventh and eighth centuries as the period between death and the attainment of paradise (assuming one was going to get there eventually) began to be seen as both more important and more negotiable. The change starts with the writings of St Augustine of Hippo (354–430) who described how, after death and before entry into paradise, there would be a period for the expiation of sins.[63] Gregory the Great then expanded on his ideas.[64] Eventually these themes were to develop into the elaborate concept of purgatory of the later Middle Ages.

Before the seventh century and the writings of Gregory the Great, the dead were considered to wait in a *refrigerium interim*, or waiting room, in a shadowy state until the arrival of the last judgement when they would be judged. For those who had been decidedly wicked and sinful there was a further place, the *tormentum*. In contrast, according to Tertullian, those Christians who had been martyred proceeded straight to heaven and paradise.[65] At this time the concept of fighting with demons and temptation was confined to this life; the afterlife was more a pause and period of rest than a period of activity.

Gregory the Great was the first to change the perception of the afterlife, by developing the concept of an intermediate space between the *refrigerium interim* and the *tormentum* which became purgatory. Exactly where this place was was not clear to Gregory or others writing at the time. For example, Engelbet d'Admont, in his *Tractatus de statu defunctorum 12*, wrote: 'Locus purgatorii est sub terra, secundum legem communem; secundum dispensationem specialem est in diversis locis.'[66]

It was in this context that the practice of saying Masses for the souls of the departed developed. Gregory recounts the story of a monk called Justus, from the convent of St Andrew in Rome, who was found to have hidden a large sum of money under his bed when he died and was consequently buried in unconsecrated ground. However, a month later, Gregory relented and asked that 30 Masses be said for his soul. After this the monk appeared to his brother to announce that he had been delivered and Gregory concludes, 'It is clear that our dead brother was freed from travail by the sacrifice of the mass.'[67] It is from this innovation that the habit of saying numerous Masses for the souls of the dead developed.

Augustine took the matter further in his *Enchiridion*, or 'Treatise on Faith, Hope and Love', which states in Chapter 109:

> During the time, moreover, which intervenes between a man's death and the final resurrection, the soul dwells in a hidden retreat where it enjoys rest or suffers affliction just in proportion to the merit it has earned by the life which it led on earth.[68]

Chapter 110 goes on to say:

> Nor can it be denied that the souls of the dead are benefited by the piety of their living friends, who offer the sacrifice of the Mediator, or give alms to the church on their behalf.

Augustine does then go on to qualify the benefits of such interventions so that:

> ... when ... sacrifices either of the altar or of alms are offered on behalf of ... the baptized dead, they are thank-offerings for the very good, they are propitiatory offerings for the not very bad, and in the case of the very bad, even though they do not assist the dead, they are a species of conciliation to the living.[69]

The idea of offering a Mass on behalf of dead Christians, as part of the ritual for expiation of sins after death, had been around since Late Antiquity, but this greater structuring and perceived importance of the concept of the afterlife led to an enormous increase in the offering of Masses, which became seen, notwithstanding what Augustine had written, as the vehicle for speeding the soul into 'the bosom of Abraham' and heaven.[70] Money was left in wills so that family and friends could pay for Masses to be said for the soul of the departed. Concrete evidence amongst the popes for this increase in concern about the fate of their own souls can be found in the increasingly frequent donations made by the seventh-century popes in their wills specifically for such Masses. The pattern starts with Pope Deusdedit (615–618), who left 'an entire stipend to all the clergy'.[71] Three of the next five popes do the same. Following the deposing of Martin I (649–653) and his death in exile in Cherson, mention of this practice in the *Liber Pontificalis* lapses, but in the eighth century it returns with several popes leaving several pounds of gold for the same function. The overall impression is of an increasing concern for one's soul and the need to ensure that the living continued to intercede on one's behalf after death.

At this time, God was seen as stern and difficult to approach, and the idea of accessing him through his Mother, the Virgin Mary, soon developed and must have encouraged the development of her cult. Thus initially the liturgy for the dead focused on appealing to Christ directly. But as this concept of the special intercessionary relationship between the Mother of God and Christ, her Son, developed, she became increasingly identified as the person most likely to be able to sway a stern judge, and so her role increased in prominence. The Liturgy for the Dead, which began to be firmed up in Rome at this time, places her at the head of the saints asked to intercede on behalf of the defunct in the Prayer of the *Communicantes*.[72]

> Having communion with and venerating the memory, first, of the glorious Mary, ever a virgin, mother of Jesus Christ, our God and our Lord: likewise of Thy blessed apostles and martyrs, Peter, and Paul. Andrew, James ... and of all thy saints, for the sake of whose merits and prayers do Thou grant that in all things we may be defended by the help of Thy protection.[73]

It was no doubt this aspect of her cult that encouraged Pope John VII to express so clearly his devotion to her, in the context of his preparations for his death and the subsequent progress of his soul. The presence of his body in the oratory he dedicated to her at St Peter's was no doubt intended to be the focus of Masses said in her presence with the aim of speeding his journey through the afterlife. His epitaph (see page 158 above) makes this quite clear. In this context, depicting her as an orant was clearly appropriate, but why did John also make her an empress?

(b) The Political Situation in Rome at the Time of John VII

The catacomb image of the orant, melded with the imperial image of the empress, created a new iconography portraying Mary as a figure of power, divorced from Christ. This appears singularly out of character with her intercessionary role in the expiation of the sins of the dead. Nothing even remotely similar developed in the East; the *Akathistos* hymn, developing around this period, lauds her praises through a variety of titles, but does not use the title *Maria Regina*. The nearest equivalent is the one occasion when it calls her 'Throne of the Heavens', and here it arguably sees her more as the throne itself than its occupant; in other words, it is echoing the iconography discussed in the Adoration of the Magi scenes.[74] The imperial image of Mary wearing a crown is a peculiarly Roman concept, bearing such a strong resemblance to the image of the Empress Theodora that it is reasonable to seek an explanation through papal relations with the imperial couple. Is it possible that John was paying a subtle compliment to Emperor Justinian II, even perhaps asking his wife, the second Empress Theodora, to intercede for him with the Emperor? Was this mosaic a political statement as well as a religious one, in the same way that the mosaics at Santa Maria Maggiore were possibly part of an expression of a contemporary religio-political struggle in relation to Chalcedon in the fifth century?

As mentioned above, John was indeed having difficulties with Emperor Justinian II (681–695 and 705–711), who had recently regained the throne after being deposed by Leontius, a soldier in his army.[75] The Acts of the Quinisext Council in 691 had been drawn up by a strongly Eastern Council, and some of its Canons attacked ancient customs of worship in Rome.[76] Pope John VII, himself of Greek extraction, may have been naturally sympathetic to the East, but the Roman papacy that he led would not accept these Canons. Justinian was proving to be a violent emperor after having regained the throne. John was undoubtedly mindful of the experience of the martyr Pope Martin I in 649, who, confronted with a similar problem over the *Typus* and *Ecthesis*, texts from Emperor Constans II relating to the Monothelite heresy, had convened his own Council at the Lateran Palace and refuted the emperor's documents. Following this blatant opposition to the imperial will, Martin had been arrested on the orders of Constans, tried in Constantinople and banished to Cherson on the Black Sea. He had died without returning to Rome and the emperor had imposed a new Pope on Rome.[77] When Justinian II asked John VII to convene a Council and identify which of the Acts agreed at the Quinisext Council were acceptable to the West, the Pope must have wondered nervously if history was about to repeat itself.

Is it possible that, by depicting the Mother of God as an Empress in an image clearly based upon that of the wife of the first Justinian, John was trying to make a propitiatory gesture? Justinian II was known to model himself on his famous predecessor, and his recently crowned empress (a Khazar princess and so something of an outsider, like the first Theodora who had been a dancer) had also taken the name of Theodora. She had recently given birth to a son. To use the image of the first Theodora as the model for an image of Mary, the Mother of God and great interceder with God, would be flattering to the imperial couple, equating the second Theodora's devotion to her son and to Christ with that of Mary. Perhaps she might effectively intercede with Justinian and avert his wrath too. If I am right, and the panel at Ravenna was indeed to commemorate the coronation by proxy of the imperial couple in the West, John's mosaic might also have been intended to signal the papacy's recognition of the newly reinstated Justinian II's right to the imperial throne, pleasure in his regaining it, and a reference to the recent coronation of his new empress that had no doubt taken place in Constantinople once she had joined him there after the battle.

This may seem to overstate the power of images, but in the eighth century their greater rarity value meant their influence and importance in both the religious and the political context was considerable. The novelty of such a chapel in St Peter's and the cost of the extensive mosaic panels would have generated widespread publicity, especially since the imagery broke new ground iconographically, as the image of Mary certainly did. Pope Martin had had frescoes of the Church Fathers painted at Santa Maria Antiqua, on the same apse as the palimpsest Madonna had occupied 100 years previously. Each of the Fathers depicted had held a scroll with the texts that the Pope had used to refute Constans II's documents on the Monothelite heresy.[78] This action set a clear precedent for the further use of imagery in churches as conveyors of a political message. There are numerous occasions in the *Liber Pontificalis* when an image evokes great emotions in the people, even up to riots and death. Indeed, the image of Justinian II's successor, Philippicus, was rejected by the Romans and refused a space in the churches because he was seen as heretical.[79] Using an imperial face to represent important figures in the past in images was a common way of paying a compliment. The tenth-century icon of the *Mandylion* of Christ at Sinai, for example, has a portrait of Constantine *Porphyrogenitos* as the face of King Abgar, probably to signify that it was he who had brought the *Mandylion* to Constantinople.[80] Images were both important as messengers and able to evoke powerful emotions at this time.

(c) Other Features of the Emerging Cult of Mary Displayed by these Images

The Santa Maria Maggiore mosaics, the Santa Maria Antiqua fresco and the *Clemenza* icon all include angelic courts, a feature more prominent up to the eighth century than in later medieval periods. Before iconoclasm, angels were themselves frequently the focus of cult worship. Although no major churches dedicated to St Michael have survived in Rome (the only significant reference to an angel being the St Michael on the top of Castel Sant' Angelo who sheathed his sword and so stopped the plague in Rome in the sixth century), there were many churches dedicated to the angels elsewhere in the West at this period.[81] In the seventh century angels were definitely higher in the heavenly hierarchy than Mary, so placing her in a court of angels would have raised her status. Only later, when crowned as *Maria Regina* by Christ, was Mary arguably higher than the angels.

The *Akathistos* hymn, probably composed by Romanos in the seventh century, is a valuable source of the additional titles that she begins to attract. It addresses her as:

> O Virgin, Mother of God, thou art the defence of virgins
> And of all those who turn to thee in prayer . . .
> Hail, gate of salvation . . . [82]

The second part of the hymn is a prayer for the faithful to use to invoke Mary's protection, and ends with a further wider entreaty to Mary to protect the people from adversity before they die:

> O Mother, praised by all, who gave birth to the Word,
> Holiest of all the saints,
> As thou dost accept the present offering,
> Redeem all people from every disaster,
> And redeem from future punishment those who cry:
> 'Hallelujah'![83]

The idea of defending people from disaster is perhaps echoed in the pose of the *Madonna della Clemenza*, for here she is a more military or powerful Mary. She carries a cross in her right hand, no doubt implying that she will conquer in the same way as Constantine did in the fourth century. This militant image also appears in the Grado seal, but it does not develop in the West. It does better as a Marian theme in the East, where Pentcheva has recently proposed there was a widespread belief in the militant and defensive powers of Mary.[84]

CONCLUSIONS

A consideration of the ten works surviving in some shape or form in Rome has permitted the development of a possible path by which the major surviving eighth-century images can be traced back to third- to fifth-century female imagery, most of which was unrelated to Mary. The development of the iconography of Mary in Rome has been shown to be dependent on the merging of her image in the Adoration of the Magi scenes in catacomb art with images of female saints, of orants and of Eastern empresses. The result was a range of types that included depicting her as the 'Mother of God' either presenting the child to the world as a symbol or interacting with him as 'the Way'. She also developed into an advocate for the sinner and especially for the souls of those who had died, able to intercede with a stern God and obtain concessions for the soul because of her special position. Finally she was presented as an empress, wearing an imperial crown. Oddly, even though some of the later images gave her a militant appearance, this aspect does not appear to have developed to any significant extent in the West.

This assessment of the development of images of Mary has confined itself to surviving examples from Rome, or examples that are known about from drawings of the lost originals. It is as well to be aware of the limitations of such a study. The ten images considered do not include a single apse image of Mary from a major Marian church, since none have survived. I have avoided considering 'reconstructions' of major apses in Rome, of which there are a number, because it would have taken more space than was available to me to deal adequately with these speculative images. For the present I will merely point out that, as far as I am aware, there is no pictorial or textual evidence that the main apse was, during this period in Rome, even in a church dedicated to Mary, seen as a necessary site for a prominent image of Mary. Most of the surviving images of Mary are either icons, apse images from funerary or other minor chapels, or images from triumphal arches. Although art not commissioned by the papacy has not been considered in detail, examples of this that survive tend to follow the themes set by papal art. Consider, for example, the fresco commissioned by the son of the widow Turtura (Table 2a).

This study has not considered imagery of Mary from the East, where there are further problems with interpretation due to the severe losses during iconoclasm. Mary's cult probably developed in the East roughly concurrently with that in the West.[85] There it included types of image not found in Rome, such as the image of Christ held by Mary in a *mandorla*. However, here again examples of major apse imagery of Mary before iconoclasm are lacking. The only surviving such image is that from the Basilica at Poreč, where the entire apse focuses on female saints. Mary wears a *maphorion* and is enthroned in the apse with a symbolic Christ-child in her lap and flanked by angels; Christ is above on the triumphal arch, in majesty and surrounded by apostles.[86]

This paper has avoided consideration of whether these images originated in the East or the West, and has avoided consideration of aspects of style, since these issues are extensively discussed elsewhere.[87] Instead it focuses on the information these images provide about the growth of the cult of Mary in Rome. Five of these ten images were seen as 'miraculous icons', or *acheiropytae*. The *Madonna di San Luca*, Pantheon Madonna and even possibly the *Madonna della Clemenza* were plausibly acquired for their church at the time it was dedicated to Mary, probably serving as a substitute for the relics usually required to dedicate an altar in a church. Only the *Madonna della Clemenza* shows unequivocal signs of cultic devotion with its loss of paint around the feet of Mary and the Christ-child. These images may not be typical of the 'ordinary' imagery of Mary in Rome between the fourth and eighth centuries, but they are the images that have survived and the aim in this paper has been to interpret what has survived, not to speculate on what is lost.

What is clear is that by the beginning of the eighth century the cult of Mary was sufficiently strong that a pope could dedicate a chapel in St Peter's to Mary,

191

inscribe it with texts that lauded her praises and choose her as his preferred advocate and personal intercessor before Christ when he died. It is also clear that the range of images of Mary, and the possible meanings that could be attached to them, had broadened by then, from a focus on the incarnation to seeing Mary as an intercessor for sins in this life and the next, as the leader of the court of female virgin saints attaining greater importance as the cult of virginity also developed and, to a limited but significant extent, as a powerful imperial figure. The cult of Mary clearly developed vigorously through the period from 450 to 707 in Rome, enjoying the sanction of the papacy, who dedicated four churches to her during this period as well as obtaining from a variety of sources the varied and meaningful images of her with and without the Christ-child described in this paper.

BIBLIOGRAPHY

Alfarano, T. (1589–1590), *Additione Overo Supplimento all' Libri di Maffeo Vegio e Petro Mallio.* Vatican City: Bibliotheca Apostolico Vaticano Archivio di San Pietro, Cod. G5.

Andaloro, M. (1973), 'La datazione della tavola di S Maria in Trastevere', *Rivista dell' Istituto Nazionale d'Archeologia e Storia dell' Arte, n.s.* 19–20, 139–213.

—— (2004), 'La parete palinsesto: 1900, 2000', in J. Osborne, J. R. Branch and G. Morganti (eds), *Santa Maria Antiqua al Foro Romano Cento Anni Dopo: Atti del Colloquio Internazionale, Roma, 5–6 maggio 2000.* Rome: Campesane Editore, 97–112.

Andreescu-Treadgold, I. and W. Treadgold (1997), 'Procopius and the Imperial Panels of S. Vitale', *The Art Bulletin* (College Art Association of America) 79, 708–23.

Antin, P. (trans.) (1980), *Grégoire le Grand, Dialogues Tome 3, Livre IV* (*Sources Chrétiennes* 265). Notes by A. de Vogüé. Paris: Éditons du Cerf. Also available in O. J. Zimmermann (trans.) (1959), *The Fathers of the Church* 39. New York.

Belting, H. (1996), *Likeness and Presence*, trans. E. Jephcott. Chicago: University of Chicago Press.

Bertelli, C. (1961a), 'La Madonna del Pantheon', *Bollettino d'Arte* 46, 24–32.

—— (1961b), *La Madonna di Sta Maria in Trastevere: storia – iconographia – stile – di un dipinto Romano dell'ottavo secolo.* Rome: Eliograf Press.

—— (1961c), 'L'Immagine del Monasterium Tempuli dopo il restauro', *Archivum Fratrum Praedicatorum* 31, 82–111.

Bosio, A. (1632), *Roma Sotterranea: opera postuma di Antonio Bosio Romano, antiquario ecclesiastico singulare de' suoi tempi. Compits, disposita, et accresciuta dal M. R. P. Giovanni Severani de S. Severino.* Rome: Guglielmo Facciotti Press.

Bovini, G. (1957), *Ravenna Mosaics.* London: Oldbourne Press.

Bulletti, E. (ed.) (1931), *Fra Mariana da Firenze: Itinerarium Urbis Romae (Studi di Artichità Castiana).* Rome: Pontificio Istituto di Archeologia Cristiana.

Calvino, R. (1976), 'Peintures et mosaiques des catacombe napolitaines', *Dossiers d'Archeologie* 19, 22–33.

Carpenter, M. (trans.) (1970–1973), *Kontakia of Romanos: Byzantine Melodist.* 2 volumes. Colombia: University of Missouri Press.

Cecchelli, C. (1956), *I Mosaici della Basilica di S Maria Maggiore.* Torino: Ilte.

Cellini, P. (1950), 'Una Madonna molto antica', *Proporzioni* 3, 1–6, and Figures I–IX.

Cerrati, D. M. (1914), *Tiberii Alpharani de Basilicae Vaticanae Antiquissima et Nova Structura* (*Studi e Testi*, 26). Rome: Bibliotheca Apostolico Vatican.

Cormack, R. (2000), *Byzantine Art.* Oxford: Oxford University Press.

—— (2005), 'Virgin and child', in R. Temple, *Masterpieces of Early Christian Art and Icons.* London: The Temple Gallery, 22–9.

Davis, R. (trans.) (2000), *The Book of Pontiffs (Liber Pontificalis)*. Liverpool: Liverpool University Press.

—— (trans.) (1992), *The Lives of the Eighth Century Popes (Liber Pontificalis)*. Liverpool: Liverpool University Press.

—— (trans.) (1995), *The Lives of the Ninth Century Popes*. Liverpool: Liverpool University Press.

De Boor, C. (ed.) (1880), *Nikephoros: Opuscula Historica or Breviarum*. Leipzig: B. G. Lipsiae in Aedibus Teubneri.

De Fleury, G. Rouhault (1877), *Le Latran au Moyen Age*. Paris: A. Morel.

Dragas, G. D. (trans.) (2004), *Cyril of Alexandria: Against those who are unwilling to confess that the Holy Virgin is Theotokos*. Greek text from *PG* 76.256–92. New Hampshire: Orthodox Research Institute.

Du Bourget, P. (1965), *Early Christian Painting*. New York: Viking Press.

Duchesne, L. (ed.) (1886), *Liber Pontificalis Volumes 1 & 2*. Paris: E. Thorin.

Elsner, J. (1998), *Imperial Rome and Christian Triumph*. Oxford: Oxford University Press.

Gardner, J. (1973), 'Pope Nicholas IV and the decoration of Santa Maria Maggiore', in *Patrons, Painters and Saints, Studies in Medieval Italian Painting*. Aldershot: Variorum Press, article III, 1–50.

Garrucci, P. R. (1876), *Storia della Arte Christiana nei primi Otto Secoli della Chiesa Volume 3*. Prato: Guasti & Giachetti.

Grabar, A. (1954), 'Note sur l'iconographie ancienne de la Vierge', *Les Cahiers Techniques de l'Art* 3, 5–9.

Grierson, P. (1968), *Phocas to Theodosius III, 602–717: Catalogue of Byzantine Coins in the Dumbarton Oaks Collection and in the Whittemore Collection*. Washington: Dumbarton Oaks.

Grierson, P. and M. Mays (1992), *Catalogue of Late Roman Coins in the Dumbarton Oaks Collection and in the Whittemore Collection*. Washington: Dumbarton Oaks.

Grimaldi, G. (1620), *Instrumenta autentica translationum sanctorum corporum et sacrarum reliquiarum e veteri in novam principis apostolorum basilicam* (Barb. Lat. 2733). Vatican: Bibliotheca Apostolica Vaticana. Also available as facsimile: R. Niggl (ed.) (1972), Vatican: Bibliotheca Apostolica Vaticana.

—— (1621), *Instrumenta autentica translationum sanctorum corporus et sacrarus reliquiarum e veteri in novus Templum Sancti Petri sub Paulo V. Pont. Max. cum multis memorijs epitaphijs et inscriptionibus Basilicae eiusdem* (Vat Lat 11988). Vatican: Bibliotheca Apostolica Vaticana.

Gruneisen, W. de (1911), *Ste Marie Antique avec le concourse de C Hulsen, G Giorgis, V Federici and J David*. Rome: Bretschneider.

Hänggi A. and I. Pahl (1968), *Prex eucharistica textus e variis liturgiis antiquioribus selecti (Spicilegium Friburgense* 12). Friburg: Éditions Universaires.

Head, C. (1972), *Justinian II*. Wisconsin: University of Wisconsin Press.

Houston, M. G. (2003), *Ancient Greek, Roman and Byzantine Costume and Decoration*. New York: Dover Publications.

Ihm, C. (1960), *Die Programme der Christlichen Apsismalerei vom vierten Jahrhundert bis zur Mitte des achten Jahrhunderts*. Wiesbaden: Franz Steiner Verlag.

Kinney, D. (1975), *S. Maria in Trastevere from its founding to 1215*. (Unpublished doctoral dissertation, University of New York.)

Koudelka, V. J. (1961), 'Le "monasterium Tempuli" et la fondation Dominicaine de San Sisto', *Archivum Fratrum Praedicatorum* 31, 5–81.

Krautheimer, R., S. Corbett and W. Frankl (1959), *Corpus Basilicarum Christianarum Romanae* 2. Vatican City/New York: Pontificio Istituto di Archeologia Cristiana/Institute of Fine Arts.

Le Goff, J. (1984), *The Birth of Purgatory*, trans. A. Goldhammer. London: Scolar Press.

Levison, W. (1910), 'Aus Englischen Bibliotheken: II', *Neues Archiv der Gesellschaft für ältere deutsche Geschichtskunde* 35, 334–80. *Cambridge University Library Cod KK IV 6*, (2021) is the twelfth-century English manuscript he refers to.

Limberis, V. (1994), *Divine Heiress: The Virgin Mary and the Creation of Christian Constantinople*. London: Routledge.

Lowden, J. (1997), *Early Christian and Byzantine Art*. London: Phaidon.

Mango, C., R. Scott and G. Greatrex (trans.) (1997), *Theophanes: Chronographia*. Oxford: Clarendon Press.

Markus, R. (1997), *Gregory the Great and his World*. Cambridge: Cambridge University Press.

Matthiae, G. (1961), *Mosaici Medioevali delle Chiese di Roma*. 2 volumes. Rome: Instituo Poligrafico dello Stato, Libreria dello Stato.

—— (1987), *Pittura Romana del Medioevo I: Secolo IV–XV*. Rome: Fratelli Palombi.

Migne, J. P. (1857–1866), *Cursus Completus Patrologiae Graecae*. Paris: Éditions Garnier. Referred to in the notes as *PG*.

New Roman Missal in Latin and English (1945). New York: Benziger. A translation is available in F. M. Nichols (trans.) (1889), *Mirabilia Urbis Romae: The Marvels of Rome or a Picture of the Golden City*. London: Ellis & Elvey.

Nicolai V. F., F. Bisconti and D. Mazzoleni (2002), *The Christian Catacombs of Rome: History, Decoration, Inscriptions* (trans. C. C. Stella and L. A. Touchette). Regensburg: Schnell & Steiner.

Nordhagen, P. J. (1962), 'The earliest decorations in Sta Maria Antiqua and their date', *Acta Institutum Romanum Norvegiae* 1, 53–72. Also in P. J. Nordhagen (1990), *Studies in Byzantine and Early Medieval Painting*, Paper VIII. London: Pindar Press.

—— (1965), 'The Mosaics of John VII (705–707): The mosaic fragments and their technique', *Acta Institutum Romanum Norvegiae* 2, 121–66. Also in P. J. Nordhagen (1990), *Studies in Byzantine and Early Medieval Painting*, Paper VI. London: Pindar Press.

—— (1968), 'The Frescoes of John VII (AD 705–7) in S Maria Antiqua in Rome', *Institutum Romanorum Norvegiae: Acta ad archeologiam et atrium historiam pertinentia* 3.

—— (1988), 'Icons for the display of sumptuous votive gifts', *Dumbarton Oaks Papers* 41, 453–60.

—— (1990), *Studies in Byzantine and Early Medieval Painting*. London: Pindar Press.

Ntedika, J. (1971), 'L'évocation de l'au-delà dans la prière pour les morts: Études patristique et de liturgie latines (IVième–VIIIième siècle)', *Recherches Africaines de Théologie* 2. Louvain and Paris: Éditions Nauwelaerts.

Oakeshott, W. (1967), *The Mosaics of Rome*. London: Thames & Hudson.

Osborne, J., J. R. Branch and G. Morganti (eds) (2004), *Santa Maria Antiqua al Foro Romano cento anni dopo: atti del colloquio internazionale Roma, 5–6 maggio 2000*. Rome: Campesano Editore.

Paluzzi, C. G. (1975), *La Basilica di S Pietro* (*Series Roma Cristiana* Volume 17). Bologna: Case Editrice Licinio Cappelli.

Paxton, F. S. (1990), *Christianising Death, the Creation of a Ritual Process in Early Medieval Europe*. London/Ithaca: Cornell University Press.

Peltomaa, L. M. (2001), *The Image of the Virgin Mary in the Akathistos Hymn*. Leiden: E. J. Brill.

Pentcheva, B. (2006), *Icons and Power: The Mother of God in Byzantium*. Philadephia: Pennsylvania University Press.

Percival, H. R. (1997), *The Seven Ecumenical Councils of the Undivided Church*. Edinburgh: T.&T. Clark.

Picard, J.-C. (1969), 'Étude sur l'emplacement des tombes des papae du IIIe au Xe siècle', *Mélanges d'archeologie et d'histoire* 81, 757–62.

Pietrangeli, C. (1988), *Santa Maria Maggiore a Roma*. Rome: Nardini Editore.

Proja, G. B. (1990), *The Lateran Basilica*. Rome: Lateran Palace.

Romanelli, P., and P. J. Nordhagen (1964), *Santa Maria Antiqua*. Rome: Istituto Poligrafico dello Stato.

Rushforth, G. M. (1902), 'The church of S Maria Antiqua', *Papers of the British School at Rome* 1, 1–123.

Russo, E. (1979), 'L'affresco di Turtura nel cimiterio di Commodilla, l'icona di S Maria in Trastevere e le più antiche feste della Madonna a Roma, *Bulletino dell'instituto storico Italiano per il medio evo e Archivio Muratoriano* 88, 35–85.

Schaff, P. (ed.) (1956), *Nicene and Non-Nicene Fathers 3*. Grand Rapids: Michigan.

Spain, S. (1979), 'The Promised Blessing: The Iconography of the Mosaics of S. Maria Maggiore', *Art Bulletin* 61, 518–40.

Storoni, P. B. (1987), 'La chiesa di San Gregorio Nazianzeno', in N. Iotti (ed.), *Santa Maria in Campo Marzio*. Rome: Editalia, 103–48.

Van Dijk, A. K. (1995), *The Oratory of Pope John VII (705–7) in Old St Peter's*. Baltimore: Johns Hopkins University (PhD thesis).

Velmans, T. (1974), 'Un portrait familial de la catacombe de Naples et ses rapports avec la tradition Byzantine', *Bollettino di Storia dell'arte dell'Università degli Studi di Salerno*, 3/4.

Verzone, P. (1967), *From Theodoric to Charlemagne: a History of the Dark Ages in the West*. London: Methuen.

Vogel, C. (1986), 'Deux conséquences de l'eschatologie grégorienne: la multiplication des messes privées et les moines-prêtres', in G. Le Grand and J. Fontaine (eds), *Grégoire le Grand: Colloque Internationaux du Centre National de la Recherches Scientifique, Chantilly, 15–19 September 1982*. Paris: CNRS, 268–76.

Walter, C. (1970), 'Papal political imagery in the medieval Lateran Palace', *Cahiers Archéologiques* 20, 155–76.

Weitzmann, K. (1960), 'The Mandylion and Constantine Porphyrogenitos', *Cahiers Archéologiques* 11, 163–84.

—— (1976), *The Monastery of St Catherine at Mount Sinai: The Icons from the Sixth to Tenth Century*. Cambridge: Harvard University Press.

Wellesz, E. (1956), 'The "Akathistos", a study in Byzantine Hymnography', *Dumbarton Oaks Papers* 9/10, 141–74.

Wilpert, J. (1917), *Die Römische Mosaiken und Malereien der kirchlichen Bauten vom IV. bis XIII. Jahrhundert*. Freiburg: Herder.

Wolf, G. (1990), *Salus Populi Romani*. Weinheim: VCH Acta Humaniorum.

NOTES

A glossary is given on pages 198–9.

1. *Vita* of Pope Sylvester. Duchesne 1886: 1.170–201; Davis 2000: 14–27. A glossary is given on pages 198–9.
2. Alfarano 1589–1590: 16; Paluzzi 1975. The Latin text is given by Cerrati 1914: 106–7 n. 2: 'Dedicatio domus huius Scae Dei Genitricis Die XXI Mensis Martij Ind III'; Alfarano records that it was found: 'Nello pilastro della ditta navi questa cappella é scritto in marmore appresso l'altare verso oriente . . . in una tavola de marmo della incrostatura.' See van Dijk 1995: 108 n. 160 for an analysis of the source.
3. Grimaldi 1620: folios 90v–91r.
4. Translation taken from van Dijk 1995: 115–16. This epitaph appears as an addendum to a twelfth-century manuscript in Cambridge University Library, Codex KK IV, 6 (2021), which Levison 1910: 334–80, esp. 363, determined derives from an eighth-century copy of the *Liber Pontificalis* with interpolations from a contemporary collection of inscriptions that included the epitaph of John VII.
The Latin text is:

> Hic sibi constituit tumulum, iussitque reponi
> Presul Iohannes sub pedibus domine,

Committens animam sanctae sub tegmine matris,
Innuba quae peperit virgo parensque Deum.
Hic decus omne loco, prisco squalore remoto,
Contulit, ut stupeat prodiga posteritas . . .
Non pompa studio . . .
Sed fervore pio pro genitrice Dei.
Non parcens opibus, pretiosum quicquid habebat
In tua distribuit munera, sancta parens . . .

5. These are dealt with in approximately chronological order, but the dating of some of these images is controversial.
6. Cecchelli 1956: 200–1 (Plate 47): 'Sixtus, Bishop of God and of the people'. Note the mosaics use the letters Xystus, but his name is usually spelt Sixtus nowadays.
7. Spain 1979; Cecchelli 1956: 197–236 are two among many interpretations.
8. In Western art the term 'Byzantine' is frequently used to describe costumes decorated with many pearls and gems. But the style was common to the elite in the East and the West and did not imply Eastern origins or influences on either the costume or the art. The term is best avoided whenever possible.
9. *Vita* of Leo I, Duchesne 1886: 1.239–41; Davis 2000: 38–40, esp. 39.
10. Percival 1997: 206. Original text in St Cyril's works in *PG* 77.119.
11. Limberis 1994: 86, quoting Proclus, in *PG* 65.681.
12. Bovini 1957: 35 and Plate 20.
13. Dragas 2004: 11; see also 23.
14. Oakeshott 1967: 148.
15. Rushforth 1902: 4. This 'palimpsest' wall contains at least five layers of fresco superimposed one upon the other. Careful study has enabled the separate layers to be dated and their iconography established: see Nordhagen 1962.
16. For a description of the various layers of clothes worn by elite women at this period, see the Glossary, and Houston 2003: 132–45.
17. Wolf 1990.
18. Cormack 2000: Figure 13.
19. Belting 1996: 75.
20. *Vita* of Sergius I, Duchesne 1886: 1.371–82; Davis 2000: 85–9, esp. 89. *Vita* of Gregory III, Duchesne 1886: 1.418–25, esp. 418; Davis 1992: 19–28, esp. 23–4.
21. Nordhagen 1988: Figures 2–5; Wilpert 1917: Plate 164b.
22. *Vita* of Boniface IV, Duchesne 1886: 1.317–18; Davis 1995: 64.
23. Bertelli 1961a.
24. *Vita* of John VII, Duchesne 1886: 1.385–7; Davis 2000: 90–1.
25. Rushforth 1902: 1–123, esp. 4.
26. Wilpert 1917: Plate 133.
27. Bovini 1957: 34; see Wilpert 1917: Plate 133 for a colour image of the wall as uncovered in 1910.
28. Damage to this section of the mosaic means that the nature of Mary's head-dress in the sixth century is not known for certain.
29. Krautheimer *et al.* 1959: 2.268; Grabar 1954.
30. The Church of Santa Francesca Romana was originally called Santa Maria Nova to indicate that it had replaced Santa Maria Antiqua: see Krautheimer *et al.* 1959: 2.249–68.
31. Belting 1996: 537, Text 35. Original manuscript is BAV Cod Lat 4265, folios 209–16.
32. Cellini 1950.
33. *Ibid.*; Garrucci 1876: 3.1–20, esp. 19; Grabar 1954: 530.
34. *Vita* of Hadrian I, Duchesne 1886: 1.486–523; Davis 1992: 123–72. The *Vita* of Pope

Julius I (337–352) says he built two basilicas, one 'close to the Forum' and the other 'across the Tiber'. These are both subsequently referred to as Basilica Julii.

35. Bertelli 1961b; Kinney 1975; Russo 1979; Andaloro 1973; 2004 have variously suggested dates up to the ninth century.

36. 'Image that made itself'.

37. As with the images on the churches dedicated to Mary, these are in roughly chronological order, insofar as their dates are known.

38. Oakeshott 1967: 150. An alternative identification would be as Ecclesia, but since Mary is frequently equated with Ecclesia this does not really affect the interpretation of the iconography.

39. *Vita* of John IV, Duchesne 1886: 1.330; Davis 2000: 68.

40. Proja 1990: 68, 75; Ihm 1960: 99; Oakeshott 1967: 150–3.

41. Koudelka 1961: 5–81; Bertelli 1961c: 82–111; Belting 1996: 320.

42. Storoni 1987: 116–17 and Plate XIII.

43. Velmans 1974: 3–9; Calvino 1976: 26.

44. The imperial purple has decayed over time to a brown colour in the icon at Sta Maria in Trastevere.

45. Andreescu-Treadgold and Treadgold 1997.

46. Grierson and Mays 1992: 244–5, Plate 34, Coin 870: Licinia Eudoxia.

47. See, for example, the range in Grierson 1968; and Grierson and Mays 1992.

48. Head 1972: 22 and Fig, 1.

49. *Vita* of John VII, Duchesne 1886: 1.385–7; Davis 2000: 90–1.

50. Although I have suggested the term *Maria Augusta* or *Imperatrix* as more appropriate for this form, I retain the term *Maria Regina*, since this is used in Rome in some frescoes (e.g. those by Pope Hadrian (772–795) in the atrium at Santa Maria Antiqua). See Rushforth 1902: 102–3.

51. Du Bourget 1965: Plate 88.

52. Nordhagen 1965: 122 Plate 1.

53. Russo 1979.

54. Oakeshott 1967: 203–5.

55. Nicolai *et al.* 2002: 123 and Figure 140. Geri Parlby discusses the reasons why du Bourget 1965, Figure 67 is probably not a Nativity in Chapter 3 of this book.

56. The establishment of the church of Sant' Agnese Fuori le Mura pre-dates any Marian church in Rome.

57. Matthiae 1987: 176, Figure 148 and Plate 16.

58. Walter 1970: Figure 3.

59. Oakeshott 1967: 250–5.

60. *Ibid.*: 311–18; Gardner 1973.

61. Weitzmann 1976: 18–21.

62. Picard 1969.

63. Paxton 1990: 66. Biblical references in support of the idea include Mt. 12.32; Jn 14.2; 1 Cor. 3.11.15. See Le Goff 1984: 1–127.

64. Gregory I provided 'eyewitness' accounts in Book 4 of his *Dialogues*. See Antin 1980: 265.146–56 on 'purgatory', and 256.84–204 on the use of the Eucharist as expiator; Ntedika 1971: 82–135.

65. Vogel 1986.

66. *Ibid.*: 268. My loose translation would be: 'Purgatory is situated under the earth, according to common belief; in particular situations it is [found] in a variety of places.'

67. *Ibid.*: 270.

68. Augustine, *Enchiridion*, trans. Shaw, in Schaff 1956: 232–76, esp. 272–3.

69. *Ibid.*

70. Antin 1980: 84–204; Paxton 1990: 66.
71. *Vita* Deusdedit, Duchesne 1886: 1.319–20; Davis 2000: 64–5.
72. Van Dijk 1995: 202, 205; Ntedika 1971.
73. Van Dijk 1995: 232–3, quoting from Hänggi and Pahl 1968: 429–31; trans. van Dijk from the *New Roman Missal* (1945: 778):

> Communicantes et memoriam venerantes in primis gloriosae semper virginis Mariae genetricis Dei et Domini nostri Iesu Christi: sed et beatorum Aposto- lorum ac Martyrum tuorum . . . quorum meritis precibusque concedas, ut in omnibus protectionis tuae muniamur auxilio.

74. ὑμνοῦντες ἔλεγον: Wellesz 1956: 149.
75. Nikephoros, de Boor 1880: 38; Theophanes, Mango *et al.* 1997: 368–9.
76. *Vita* of John VII, Duchesne 1886: 1.385–7; Davis 2000: 90–1. For example, the Acts banned the use of the Lamb of God to represent Christ, and also raised the position of the Patriarch of Constantinople relative to the Pope.
77. *Vita* of Martin I, Duchesne 1886: 1.336–40; Davis 2000: 70–2.
78. Rushforth 1902: 1–123.
79. *Vita* of Constantine, Duchesne 1886: 1.389–91; Davis 2000: 91–5.
80. Weitzmann 1960: 183.
81. Belting 1996: 532, Text 32, referring to the translation of the text by Fra Mariana da Firenze (1517), in Bulletti 1931: 2.42–3; 189–90: an example is S Michele in Africisco in Ravenna.
82. Van Dijk 1995: 228; Wellesz 1956; Peltomaa 2001.
83. Carpenter 1970–1973: 2.307. Quoted in van Dijk 1995: 227, 229.
84. Pentcheva 2006.
85. Cormack 2005: 22–9.
86. Lowden 1997: 139–42 and Figures 84 and 85.
87. Belting 1996; Nordhagen 1965; 1968; Cormack 2005.

GLOSSARY

Acheiropyta: A 'miraculous' image of Mary or of Christ 'not made by human hands', usually believed to have been made by either St Luke (who was thought to have been a painter) or by the angels.

Apocrisarius: An ecclesiastical deputy or other official of high rank. The name was usually given to the Pope's representative in Constantinople. Pope Gregory the Great (590–604) was *apocrisarius* in Constantinople for his predecessor, Pope Pelagius II (579–590).

Chlamys: A long rectangular cloak, fastened at the right shoulder by means of a large brooch. It became a symbolic part of court costume in the sixth century, although it had originally been simply a cloak worn by a soldier.

Encaustic: A type of paint produced by mixing the pigments with wax. Used for Fayyum mummy portraits and for many early icons up to the seventh/eighth century. Because of the presence of the wax the images have a characteristic slightly translucent appearance.

Hodegitria: The famous icon of Mary with the Christ-child that was kept at the Hodegion Monastery in Constantinople. It was believed to have been painted by St Luke and so was an *acheiropyta* (q.v. supra).

Maphorion: A shawl that covered a woman's head and arms. It became the traditional attire for the Virgin, usually being blue, though occasionally red. From catacomb and other early imagery it is clear that it was originally just the normal outside garment worn by a matron or mother.

Mappa: A senatorial handkerchief held by the emperor and allowed to fall to indicate that he was ready for the gladiatorial games to start. Sometimes placed in Mary's hand at this period to indicate that, by accepting the incarnation, she had agreed to the beginning of the salvation of the human race from original sin.

Palla: This was the top layer of formal dress, worn over a tunic and a *stola* (sometimes called a *colobium*), and was formed from a long length of material, decorated at one end and then wound around the body and gathered at the waist by a gemmed belt. Underneath the *palla* a tunic was worn with sleeves gathered into (often gemmed) cuffs.

Pallium: The long band or scarf embossed with crosses and worn by archbishops and bishops from at least the seventh century. It was fastened at the shoulders with three pins. For a considerable period during the Middle Ages, archbishops in the West had to travel to Rome to receive their pallium from the Pope after they had been appointed.

Pendulia (sometimes called *prependulia*): Strings of pearls that were suspended from the lower edge of an imperial crown.

Secretarium: Room where the bishops convened before processing into the Basilica.

Stola: The innermost garment of an aristocratic woman's dress. It had long fitted sleeves, sometimes with highly decorated cuffs, as can be seen at Mary's right wrist in the *Salus Populi Romani* image from Sta Maria Maggiore in Figure 9, or the wrists of the orant Mary in the mosaic from John VII's oratory in Figure 17.

Synthronon: A wide throne that is capable of seating two or more people.

Tunic: A simple T-shaped garment with loose sleeves and often with vertical stripes either side of the neck running down to the hem. It could be simple or ornate, and was the usual garment worn by orants (see Nonnosa in Figure 15). It could be belted or unbelted. In court dress it was often worn over a *stola* and under a *palla*, as is the case in the *Madonna della Clemenza* (Figure 13) and the orant Mary from John VII's oratory (Figure 17).

INDEX OF SUBJECTS AND NAMES

INDEX OF BIBLICAL REFERENCES